ACTING ALONE

INNOVATIONS IN THE STUDY OF WORLD POLITICS

This series provides a forum for the publication of original theoretical, empirical, and conceptual studies that seek to chart new frontiers in the field of international relations. The key emphasis is on innovation and change. Books in the series will offer insights on and approaches to a broad range of issues facing the modern world, in an effort to revolutionize how contemporary world politics are studied, taught, and practiced.

Forgetting Ourselves: Secession and the (Im)possibility of Territorial Identity, by Linda S. Bishai

Multiple Paths to Knowledge in International Relations: Methodology in the Study of Conflict Management and Conflict Resolution, edited by Zeev Maoz, Alex Mintz, T. Clifton Morgan, Glenn Palmer, and Richard J. Stoll

New Directions for International Relations: Confronting the Method-of-Analysis Problem, edited by Alex Mintz and Bruce Russett

Cycles of Violence: The Evolution of the Israeli Decision Regime Governing the Use of Limited Military Force, by Ranan D. Kuperman

Economic Interdependence and Conflict in World Politics, by Mark J. C. Crescenzi

Redrawing the Map to Promote Peace: Territorial Dispute Management Via Territorial Changes, by Jaroslav Tir

Existential Threats and Civil-Security Relations, edited by Oren Barak and Gabriel Sheffer

How International Relations Affect Civil Conflict, by Clayton L. Thyne

ACTING ALONE

A Scientific Study of American Hegemony and Unilateral Use-of-Force Decision Making

Bradley F. Podliska, Ph.D.

LEXINGTON BOOKS

A division of
ROWMAN & LITTLEFIELD PUBLISHERS, INC.
Lanham • Boulder • New York • Toronto • Plymouth, UK

Published by Lexington Books
A division of Rowman & Littlefield Publishers, Inc.
A wholly owned subsidiary of The Rowman & Littlefield Publishing Group, Inc.
4501 Forbes Boulevard, Suite 200, Lanham, Maryland 20706
http://www.lexingtonbooks.com

Estover Road, Plymouth PL6 7PY, United Kingdom

British Library Cataloguing in Publication Information Available

Library of Congress Cataloging-in-Publication Data

Podliska, Bradley F.
Acting alone : a scientific study of American hegemony and unilateral use-of-force decision making / Bradley F. Podliska.
p. cm.
Includes bibliographical references and index.
ISBN 978-0-7391-4251-6 (cloth : alk. paper) — ISBN 978-0-7391-4253-0 (electronic)
1. Hegemony—United States. 2. United States—Foreign relations. 3. Presidents—United States. 4. War and emergency powers—United States. 5. Unilateral acts (International law) 6. Intervention (International law) 7. United States—Military policy. I. Title.
JZ1312.P64 2010
327.1'170973—dc22

2009049874

∞™ The paper used in this publication meets the minimum requirements of American National Standard for Information Sciences—Permanence of Paper for Printed Library Materials, ANSI/NISO Z39.48-1992.

Printed in the United States of America

For my parents and Katy

Contents

List of Figures

List of Tables

Acknowledgments

I DEDICATE THIS BOOK TO MY PARENTS. Always patient and never critical, I owe my parents, Richard and Zee Ann Podliska, a debt of gratitude and appreciation that goes beyond the academic nature of this book. I also appreciate the love and support of my brother, Richard, and sisters, Stephanie and Meghan.

I am grateful for the guidance, patience, and friendship of Dr. Christopher Sprecher. I am similarly grateful to Drs. Alex Mintz, Alexander Pacek, and Michael Desch for their time, intellectual assistance, and service. I would also like to thank Drs. Michael Koch, Nehemia Geva, Sarah Fulton, and Shuhei Kurizaki for their service to this project, namely for offering advice at the IR Works-in-Progress seminar, for allowing me to borrow an undergraduate class (or two) for an experiment, and for their informal, but productive, advice at random points throughout the process.

For their friendship, tolerance in listening to countless anecdotes of Reagan and the Cold War, and for agreeing to get "bogged down" as I discuss the particulars of my book, I would like to thank Jose Villalobos, Benjamin Freeman, Laron Williams, Justin Vaughn, Cigdem Sirin, and Doug Kuberski. I also extend this thanks to friends that go back to my Wisconsin and Washington days—Drs. David McDonald and Bernard Finel, Howard Liao, Adam Clampitt, Darren Ice, Jared Wold, Ed Blythe, Lydia Lewis, Brian Riedl, and Kirk Saylor. I would especially like to thank Zeev Maoz for bringing this book to the attention of Lexington and I would like to thank the excellent staff at Lexington Books—Jana Wilson, Joseph Parry, Tawnya Zengierski, and Jehanne Schweitzer. This book would not have been possible without them—I benefited from their professionalism and expertise and enjoyed working with them over the course of many months.

Lastly, and most importantly, I dedicate this book to my wife, Katy, a loving companion of extraordinary patience, kindness, intellect, and with whom I will always depend on for happiness and success. I love her and a cat named Mrs. Grant, for which life is never about data sets, literature reviews, or the completion of an academic project.

1

Introduction

The Puzzle and Research Question

"Well actually, he forgot Poland," retorted President George W. Bush to Senator John Kerry during the first presidential election debate on September 30, 2004. Kerry was criticizing the 2003 Iraq invasion, saying the U.S. had invaded with a "grand coalition" of three countries—the United Kingdom (UK), Australia, and the U.S.[1] The debate exchange signaled the perceived unpopularity of unilateral uses of force.

So, if acting unilaterally is the unpopular position to take in a foreign policy crisis, why do presidents make such an "unwise" decision as using unilateral force in the first place? A president, in deciding to use military force, is making a calculation that can make or break his presidency. His decision affects thousands of lives, costs millions (or even billions) of dollars, enhances or harms U.S. world standing, and perhaps most personally important to a president, his electoral success may depend on a successful outcome.[2]

The decision to act unilaterally is especially surprising given the unparalleled success of the multilateral campaign of the 1991 Gulf War, in which President George H.W. Bush was able to claim the benefits of multilateralism—legitimacy, burden-sharing, and capability aggregation. To many experts, the 1991 Gulf War would not have been fought without a "comprehensive, firm, and united" United Nations (UN) Security Council.[3] The 1991 Gulf War demonstrated that "international support, cooperation, and legitimacy are essential for any effective use of force by the United States."[4]

So, why would any president, whether Republican or Democrat, decide to enter or respond to a crisis with unilateral U.S. military force, when the perceived "right" decision is to approach the crisis multilaterally and use allies?

The answer to the puzzle is based on a simple explanation—hegemonic power. The U.S., as hegemon, possesses the strength to use unilateral military force, and the disparity in military power between the U.S. and other nations serves as a strong incentive for a president to act unilaterally. Unilateralism can also be viewed as a superior choice given the costs of multilateralism—problems of burden-sharing, legitimacy, inaction, collaboration and cooperation, and reciprocity—and the benefits of unilateralism—lower costs, an ambivalent public, and the necessity to respond quickly to severe crises.

In *Acting Alone*, I argue that the president's unilateral decision to use force follows a sequential process. While the first decision, whether or not to use force, has been exhaustively examined, I argue that an expected utility calculation of America's dominance in terms of military revolutions defines the second decision on whether to use unilateral force. I focus this study on presidential decision making and U.S. uses of force from 1937 to 1995, tracing the decision in each instance from the threat stage to the final outcome. I argue that the U.S., as a hegemon, uses its power to provide and maintain the public good of international order and security, and it does so unilaterally a majority of the time.[5]

Problems with Current Research

In studying American unilateral uses of force, a significant problem I encounter is the assumption that military unilateralism is perceived to be the "wrong" decision. Numerous books detail the "soft imperialism" of America and its "unsafe" unilateral power.[6] Policy experts call upon America to reclaim the idealistic "ghost" of its multilateral past, to voluntarily reduce its military power, and to work with international institutions.[7]

The experts' perception is that for most of its history the U.S. favored a unilateral foreign policy designed to protect and promote its own interests. There was one brief moment at the end of World War II in which the U.S. adhered to "congenial" multilateral interests and established a world order based on "a consensus of the community of nations."[8] Ultimately, this multilateral arrangement faded with the start of the Cold War, when Truman (as well as his successors), chose an anti-totalitarian path instead of an anti-imperialism one.[9] The end of the Cold War and the 1991 Gulf War signaled a new, second round of multilateral hope for America. But, this post-Cold War dream of multilateralism also faded, as an American "hyperpower" saw little need for multilateral action.[10] Unilateralism would become especially pronounced in a post-9/11 world.[11]

Academics have been severe in their criticism of this unilateral history.[12] Assuming unilateralism is the wrong choice to make, scholars tend to operate on the condition that presidents, Congress, and the public prefer multilateral action.[13] The literature states that Democratic and even most Republican presidents (with the possible exception of President Reagan) are proponents of the UN and its multilateral actions.[14] As such, research focuses on examining the propensity for multilateralism.[15]

These assumptions are problematic. There have been no ideal periods of multilateralism in U.S. history, and presidents, whether Democrat or Republican, act unilaterally a majority of the time. Table 1.1 is a cursory frequency count of three crisis data sets that demonstrates presidents are unilateralists. Atsushi Tago created a dataset—U.S. Use of Force Approach Dataset (USUFAD)—to code unilateral, full multilateral, and operational multilateral uses of force from 1948 to 1998. Presidents have used force 212 times, but only 45 of these cases were multilateral.[16] Using my own rules to code unilateral/multilateral actions, I coded two data sets, Benjamin Fordham and Christopher Sarver's 2001 U.S. Uses of Force data set and Michael Brecher and Jonathan Wilkenfeld's 2000 International Crisis Behavior (ICB2) data set and find that presidents have faced 158 crises from 1937 to 1995 (U.S. Uses of Force data set) and 64 crises (ICB2 data set) from 1937 to 2002, but acted multilaterally in only 64 and 36 of the cases, respectively.[17]

Broken into time periods, there does not appear to be idealistic periods of American multilateralism.[18] The fact is presidents, whether in 1948 or in 2003, tend to act unilaterally. A frequency count of the data affirms this unilateralist perspective: the U.S. acts unilaterally and when it does act multilaterally, through such organizations as the UN and NATO, those organizations are only effective when the U.S. takes them seriously and leads them.[19]

The assumptions that presidents are multilateralists and that there have been ideal, multilateral periods in American foreign policy are not the only problems plaguing unilateral-multilateral research. The biggest shortcoming of current research may be a failure to scientifically study unilateralism *at all*. Scholars emphasize a unilateral dependent variable, but few, if any studies, have directly addressed the issue of a presidential unilateral decision.[20] Instead, researchers, without regard to any sort of scientific testing, issue contradictory proclamations: some argue that presidents follow public demands and use unilateral force, while others find that presidents lead and act unilaterally in defiance of Americans' preference for multilateral collective security.[21]

A *second* problem with current research is a failure to adequately identify why the U.S. does not act multilaterally. The U.S., both following World War

TABLE 1.1
Frequency Count of Unilateral-Multilateral Uses of Force

	USUFAD[a]		*ICB2*		*U.S. Uses of Force*	
Years	*Unilateralism*	*Multilateralism*	*Unilateralism*	*Multilateralism*	*Unilateralism*	*Multilateralism*
Interwar Period (1937 – 1938)	—	—	1	0	1	0
World War II (1939 – 1945)	—	—	1	2	4	2
Cold War (1946 – 1990)	141	25	22	27	81	55
Post-Cold War (1991 –)	26	20	4	7	6	9
Presidents						
Republican Presidents	82	20	14	15	56	38
Eisenhower (1953 – 1960)					16 of 28 disputes	
Nixon (1969 – 1974)					5 of 9 disputes	
Ford (1974 – 1976)					2 of 5 disputes	
Reagan (1981 – 1988)					27 of 41 disputes	
George H. W. Bush (1989 – 1992)					6 of 10 disputes	
Democratic Presidents	85	25	14	21	36	28
Roosevelt (1937 – 1945)					5 of 6 disputes	
Truman (1945 – 1952)					8 of 14 disputes	
Kennedy (1961 – 1963)					6 of 12 disputes	
Johnson (1963 – 1968)					9 of 16 disputes	
Clinton (1993 – 2000)					4 of 10 disputes	
Total Crises/Uses of Force	167	45	28	36	92	66

[a] No Data Available for 1937–1945

II and now in a post-Cold War world, is so dominant that it has few incentives to burden itself with multilateral rules and institutions.[22] Presidents simply elect to enter into multilateral agreements as they wish. Following World War II, the U.S. was dominant in East Asia yet had little interest in the region. It was able to negotiate a series of bilateral agreements with Japan, South Korea, and other states without forgoing policy autonomy. Europe was a different story, in which the U.S. had to bargain and agree to institutional restraints in order to form a NATO security pact.[23] In a post-Cold War world, the U.S. faces not a European situation, but an East Asian scenario, in which it can set the terms of agreements.[24]

Is this a bad thing? The assumption is that the consensus of as many as 192 countries (UN member countries) or 193 countries (State Department–recognized countries) is better than the action of one country.[25] But, the majority consensus is not always correct. It often represents the product of negotiation, watering down an agreement to the least common denominator; so, that the resulting pronouncement or call to action simply lacks coherence.[26]

Presidents have legitimate reasons to be skeptical of multilateralism. There are problems of legitimacy, reciprocity, burden-sharing, and inaction. As Charles Maynes writes in *Understanding Unilateralism in American Foreign Relations*, "For many, a commitment to multilateralism is only another way to decide not to act. . . ."[27] Mobilizing governments to act in concert on one operational plan is an extremely difficult endeavor. Hegemons bear the burdens of the world, and even when they organize a multilateral effort around a clear goal, they must organize, persuade, lead, and bear responsibility for less powerful allies. The 1991 Gulf War is a prime example. The reason for fighting the 1991 Gulf War—restoring Kuwait's sovereignty—was a universally accepted principle.[28] Yet, it still took President George H.W. Bush months of diplomatic haggling to organize a multilateral effort. Even multilateral security arrangements, such as NATO, that are designed to spread the costs and burdens have been "distinctly nonmultilateral" with the U.S. having most of the decision-making power and responsibility.[29]

A *third* problem is whether American military power explains a president's unilateral decision. A president's decision to engage in war is a political act and not one driven by a military technological advantage.[30] But, power, or the ability to get others to do what they otherwise would not do, defines a realpolitik system, and presidents possess a lot of power.[31] Whether deciding to act alone or lead a multilateral operation, presidents can rely on a military that has overwhelming, unmatched power and is able to win conflicts with minimal costs. It is a military that has superior technology, training, skills, and weapons vis-à-vis any adversary.[32] There have been other military superpowers, but the U.S. possesses a historically rare "total package" of the world's best army in terms of lethality, technological competence, and ability to project force globally.[33]

The power disparity between the U.S. and the rest of the world reduces incentives to act multilaterally.[34] Even when the U.S. does work through multilateral organizations, such as NATO, American technological superiority grants its exclusive power to define operations in its national interest.[35] Minimal casualties and superior military capabilities are both necessary conditions for a president's decision to use force, and with America's embrace of military revolutions, presidents can achieve unilateral military victory in minimal time and at minimal cost with overwhelming strategic and tactical advantages against an adversary.[36] This overwhelming strength in military power may offer a key piece in solving the puzzle of why a president decides to use unilateral force.

As a note, this book does not propose to answer every nuance of the multilateral-unilateral foreign policy debate. This is a debate that covers a broad swath of topics—legal-institutional arrangements, structural-normative perspectives, and offense-defense theory. The specifics of these topics can range from rejection of international conventions (e.g., Kyoto Protocol and Anti-Ballistic Missile (ABM) Treaty) to complex socioeconomic World Trade Organization (WTO) issues and even to payment of UN dues.[37] It does not focus on the "soft power" of the U.S., in which the U.S. projects its power through a cultural and ideological appeal. It does not even address the "hard power" of America's economic might.[38] Instead, this book concentrates on the explanatory factors of a president's decision to use unilateral force.

Contributions of This Study

To resolve the prevailing problems of current research and fully explain a president's unilateral use-of-force decision, I examine three questions pertinent to the study of U.S. unilateral uses of force:

1. Why does a president make a unilateral use-of-force decision?
2. Should a president's unilateral decision be viewed as a separate and distinct decision from his use-of-force decision?
3. Do international factors, such as U.S. military power vis-à-vis an adversary, offer the greatest explanatory power for a unilateral decision?

Acting Alone is unique in that it offers a rare, if not unprecedented, scientific explanation of unilateral use-of-force decision making. In doing so, it overcomes three major problems in the study of conflict and decision making.

First, it expands studies beyond the traditional *use of force* dependent variable to a *type of force used* (unilateral or multilateral) dependent variable. In doing so, it offers a definition of unilateral use of force—the U.S. acting alone without any military ally or international political support.

Second (and related to the first contribution), studies on presidential decision making have exhaustively examined an executive's decision vis-à-vis a domestic audience and vis-à-vis relative military capabilities.[39] However, these standard explanations have failed to model a president's decisions as a sequential process, which is at odds with significant findings in international relations research that explains crisis escalation as a "series of steps" rising from security issues and leading up to war.[40] I theorize the use-of-force decision as a series of steps involving two situations: the first is a decision to use force and the second is a decision on how to use force (either unilaterally or multilaterally).[41] I concentrate on the second decision.

Third, I build on previous findings that the traditional measure of military capability—the Correlates of War (COW) Composite Indicator of National Capabilities (CINC) index—does not necessarily correlate with a unilateral-multilateral action.[42] Instead, I surmise that a Composite Indicator of Military Revolutions (CIMR) index offers a second alternative measure of power capability and explains unilateral uses of force. The CIMR index is based on three measures of military power—preponderance, technology, and force employment—and I argue that the greater the gap in CIMR index score between the U.S. and an opponent, the greater the likelihood of a president deciding to use unilateral force.[43]

Methodological Strategy: Statistical, Experimental, and Case Studies

In order to address these concerns, I use three methods to determine why a president makes a unilateral decision. In particular, I use statistics, an experiment, and case studies to test my theory and my main explanatory factor—military power—and whether this impacts a president's decision making. Quantitative analysis allows generalizability of my theory. I use an experiment for robustness and to better understand how crisis triggers may impact the explanatory factor. The process-tracing method of the case studies reveals that the military power factor has strong explanatory power. In sum, I am guiding the reader from an aggregate long-term view to a more narrow, detailed view of hegemonic behavior.

Sound scientific inquiry requires sound methods, and it is the goal of this book to use these three methods to have a better scientific understanding of why a president makes a unilateral use-of-force decision. My goal is to produce valid inferences about a president's decision and to explain and predict a president's unilateral decision. While each method has its strengths and weaknesses, all of the methods can effectively be used to put forth a new paradigm of understanding why a president's unilateral decision may not be as "unwise" as commonly assumed.[44]

Statistical Tests: Generalizability of President's Unilateral Use-of-Force Decision

If generalizability and parsimony are the goal of social science research, then using the statistical method with its variable control, generalizable findings, and avoidance of overdetermination allows me to reach that goal.[45] In examining a large number of uses of force over a long temporal span, I am able to draw generalizations and avoid any of the possible selection bias problems of relying on a small number of cases.[46] Moreover, I use an expected utility decision strategy with the rules and methods of statistical analysis to establish a causal relationship between a crisis event and a president's decision to act unilaterally.

The quantitative method may have problems of oversimplification, whole-nation bias, and random sampling and validity, and I must control for these shortcomings with my case study and experimental methods. But, it allows me to model a president's decision theoretically and to link it to the empirical world with scientific tests.[47] Moreover, I contribute to a scientific understanding of a president's unilateral decision in offering a new operational definition of unilateralism, a new model of a president's sequential decision, and a new test of military power.

Experiment: Causal Analysis of a President's Unilateral Use-of-Force Decision

While experimentation remains an alternative methodology in political science research, it is a valuable methodological tool in terms of reliability and validity and in reducing the impact of bias.[48] The experiment in this book can be used to explain (i.e., causal analysis) and predict why a president makes a unilateral decision.[49] An experiment with its controls and precise measurement allows me to determine whether I have correctly specified my theoretical model with my statistical tests.[50] While using college students as subjects in my experiment may be an unrepresentative subject pool and calls into question the generalizability of the study, it does add to the robustness of the book results.[51] As one of the three methods used in this book, it fully complements the scientific inquiry of this book.

Historical Cases: Accuracy of President's Unilateral Use-of-Force Decision

A president's decision to use unilateral force involves a complex pattern of factors that may not be adequately captured with quantitative analysis. Quantitative analysis requires generalization (or simplification), in which a president's unilateral decision is modeled sequentially with six explanatory variables. This may not be an accurate reflection of reality. In order to truly understand the president's decision, I must test the main explanatory factor of a president's unilateral decision—military power—with a random assortment of historical cases. While generalizability is sacrificed in this scientific pursuit, accuracy is achieved in understanding a set of "particulars" (e.g., individual crises, historical context, president's decision-making style, etc.) that do not lend themselves easily to generalizations.[52]

Historical cases are interwoven throughout the book and cases on the Bay of Pigs invasion, the Panama invasion, and the 1991 Gulf War are included as a separate chapter to offer a more accurate, nuanced explanation of the other two methods—statistical and experimental. In using case studies, I make this book available to a wider audience, an audience that may not care to understand the world in mathematical terms but rather as a world of unique, to be intensely studied empirical events. Case studies also allow me to complement the book's quantitative aspects in using an evidence-oriented strategy to describe complex social phenomenon.[53]

Plan of the Book

The following section outlines the plan of *Acting Alone.*

Chapter 2

In the second chapter, I state the case for why a president acts unilaterally a majority of the time. I first state the theoretical foundation of the book—America's unrivaled power serves as the main explanation for a unilateral use of force. I detail America's military power, organized along preponderance, technology, and force employment lines, and further conceptualize power using a military revolution paradigm. In employing its military might, the president's use-of-force decision making follows a sequential process. First, the president decides to use force, and I review the domestic factors—political, congressional involvement, and public opinion—and international factors of that first decision.

Next, I lay out the case for why a president, as a separate, second decision, takes unilateral military action. I list the criticisms of multilateralism—problems of burden-sharing, legitimacy, inaction, collaboration and coordination, and reciprocity. I then investigate the unilateral decision and explain why a president makes that decision. In particular, I detail the benefits of unilateralism and make the following arguments: (1) the unilateral decision bears lower costs; (2) the president receives little domestic pressure to act multilaterally, as the public is ambivalent about how force should be used; and (3) presidents are more likely to rely solely on the U.S. military, as the severity of the crisis increases.

In the second half of the chapter, I offer a new model of unilateral use-of-force decision making. I argue that presidents make an expected utility calculation, and I model this calculation as being based on one objective—whether unilateral or multilateral force offers the greatest probability of advancing or protecting U.S. interests. I conclude the chapter with a rational actor explanation for the president's unilateral decision.

Chapter 3

In the third chapter, I conduct the first of my three methods, statistical tests, in order to give an aggregate view of the unilateral decision. Using arguments from Chapter 2, I formulate hypotheses that propose a president will use force unilaterally as a military gap widens vis-à-vis an opponent, if the opponent nation is in the Western hemisphere, and if the crisis is a national security threat. Second, I detail the two main data sets I use to identify the crisis dyads and construct the use-of-force dependent variable. Third, I develop original coding rules to construct the unilateral use-of-force dependent variable. Fourth, I advance the notion that traditional measures of military power may not provide an adequate explanation of how a president measures the strength of the U.S. military vis-à-vis an opponent. So, I construct a CIMR index, based on measures of preponderance, technology, and force employment, and use it to calculate the gap in military revolution between the U.S. and its adversary. Then, I list the remaining situational factors—*Monroe Doctrine, national security, regime change*, and *humanitarian* variables—and control variables.

To operationalize a president's decision as a two-step, sequential process, I use a heckman probit model. In order to ensure this is the correct model, I first test the domestic, target characteristics, and international variables using two separate probit models. Next, I test my unified model and find that a president's decision-making process is sequential: a president first makes the decision to use force and then makes the decision to use unilateral force. The decision to use force does not seem to be correlated with domestic factors, but rather, it is positively correlated with a target being a rival or being in an alliance. The decision to use unilateral force is positively correlated with an opponent not employing its forces based on the appropriate military revolution, lagging behind in terms of military technology, being located in the Western hemisphere, or posing a national security threat.

Chapter 4

In the fourth chapter, I use an experiment method to further add to the robustness of my findings. It offers an explanation (i.e., causal analysis) of why a unilateral decision is made.[54] The experiment tests the crisis triggers to determine if and why the crisis trigger is important to a president's unilateral decision. In opening up the black box of realism, I argue that presidents do not blindly make just a military capability calculation, but also calculate the stakes involved in a crisis. The more severe the crisis, the more likely a president is to make a unilateral decision. Subjects making a unilateral decision seemed to be more confident in their decision, believed the crises less dangerous, and perceived higher public support for unilateral action than the multilateral-choosing subjects. This suggests a president will likely want to take fewer risks with less severe crises and will choose to disseminate the costs through allied partners.

The experiment uses 360 Texas A&M student subjects exposed to one of three international crisis scenarios: (1) humanitarian, (2) regime change, or (3) national security crisis. In each crisis, the difficulty of the military mission and level of public support varied and the participant had to respond and rate support for either an American unilateral or multilateral force option. For each crisis, I explain the results and whether military capabilities and/or domestic factors influenced a unilateral decision. I conclude the chapter with a discussion of why a unilateral decision is made.

Chapter 5

In the fifth chapter, I use case study examinations of the 1991 Gulf War, the 1961 Bay of Pigs invasion, and the 1989 Panama invasion to examine the accuracy of the unilateral use-of-force decision-making theory. The cases are selected based on the extreme values of the dependent variable: (1) the 1991 Gulf War is an ideal multilateral case; (2) the 1961 Bay of Pigs is a "middle ground" unilateral-multilateral case; and (3) the 1989 Panama invasion is an ideal unilateral case. The results highlight the importance of international and situational factors with presidents acting unilaterally or multilaterally based on a cost calculation of military power, the type of crisis, and the location of the crisis.

For each case, I begin with an introduction and summary of the crisis events. I then review the domestic politics aspects, noting how little domestic politics influenced the president's decisions. I next cover the international and situational factors with an explanation of the crisis trigger and a detailed assessment of U.S. and crisis opponent military power as well as any other parties involved in the dispute. Subsequently, I trace the president's decision-making process, including the two decisions—using force and using unilateral or multilateral force. I conclude with an assessment of the case, finding that the theory fares well in terms of accuracy.

Chapter 6

In the concluding chapter, I analyze the results from the three methods to answer the fundamental question of the book: why does a president make a unilateral use-of-force decision? Previous research has addressed different aspects of a president's use of decision (e.g., domestic politics and the use-of-force decision, the influence of military capabilities on the decision, the consequences of the decision to a president's political future, etc.), but it has failed to address the final decision before a president calls on his military commanders to carry out his orders. This is a puzzle in need of an answer, and this book fills that crucial academic- and policy-relevant gap.

Notes

1. A debate transcript is available at http://www.washingtonpost.com/wp-srv/politics/debatereferee/debate_0930.html.

2. Alastair Smith, "International Crises and Domestic Politics," *American Political Science Review* 92, no. 3. (September 1998): 623; H.E. Goemans, "Fighting for Survival: The Fate of Leaders and the Duration of War," *Journal of Conflict Resolution* 44, no. 5 (October 2000): 577; Alex Mintz and Nehemia Geva, "The Poliheuristic Theory of Foreign Policy Decision Making," in *Decision Making on War and Peace: The Cognitive-Rational Debate*, eds. Nehemia Geva and Alex Mintz (Boulder, Colo.: Lynne Reinner Publishers, 1997), 83; Bruce Bueno de Mesquita and David Lalman, *War and Reason* (New Haven, Conn.: Yale University Press, 1992); Bruce Bueno de Mesquita and Randolph M. Siverson, "War and the Survival of Political Leaders: A Comparative Study of Regime Types and Political Accountability," *American Political Science Review* 89, no. 4 (December 1995): 841-55; Anthony Downs, *An Economic Theory of Democracy* (New York: Harper and Brothers, 1957); Bruce Bueno de Mesquita et al., "An Institutional Explanation of the Democratic Peace," *American Political Science Review* 93, no. 4 (December 1999): 791-807; Bruce Bueno de Mesquita et al., "Policy

Failure and Political Survival: The Contribution of Political Institutions," *Journal of Conflict Resolution* 43, no. 2 (April 1999): 147-61; Bruce Bueno de Mesquita et al., "Testing Novel Implications from the Selectorate Theory of War," *World Politics* 56, no. 3 (April 2004): 363-88.

3. John G. Ruggie, "Multilateralism: The Anatomy of an Institution," *International Organization* 46, no. 3 (Summer 1992): 564.

4. Ekaterina Stepanova, "The Unilateral and Multilateral Use of Force by the United States," in *Unilateralism and U.S. Foreign Policy: International Perspectives*, eds. David M. Malone and Yuen Foong Khong (Boulder, Colo.: Lynne Rienner, 2003), 182.

5. See Robert Gilpin, *War and Change in World Politics* (New York: Cambridge University Press, 1981).

6. Clyde Prestowitz, *Rogue Nation: American Unilateralism and the Failure of Good Intentions* (New York: Basic Books, 2003), 6, 272; Peter Beinart, *The Good Fight: Why Liberals–and Only Liberals–Can Win the War on Terror and Make America Great Again* (New York: HarperCollins, 2006); Robert S. McNamara and James G. Blight, *Wilson's Ghost: Reducing the Risk of Conflict, Killing, and Catastrophe in the 21st Century* (New York: PublicAffairs, 2001).

7. Prestowitz, *Rogue Nation*, 283; David B. Rivkin Jr. and Lee A. Casey, "Enfeebling the Presidency: The Executive Branch Is a Co-equal Branch, or so the Framers Said," *National Review* 58, no. 11 (June 2006): 38; Beinart, *The Good Fight.*

8. Prestowitz, *Rogue Nation*, 174.

9. Beinart, *The Good Fight*; Prestowitz, *Rogue Nation.*

10. French Foreign Minister Hubert Vedrine first used the term, "hyperpower," to label America's simultaneous dominance in the military, economic, monetary, technological, and cultural realms: Stewart Patrick, "Multilateralism and Its Discontents: The Causes and Consequences of U.S. Ambivalence," in *Multilateralism and US Foreign Policy: Ambivalent Engagement*, eds. Stewart Patrick and Shepard Forman (Boulder, Colo.: Lynne Rienner, 2002), 14. See John B. Attanasio, "Introduction: Multilateralism, Unilateralism, and Leadership," in *Multilateralism v Unilateralism: Policy Choices in a Global Society*, eds. John B. Attanasio and Joseph J. Norton (London: The British Institute of International and Comparative Law, 2004), 19; James Cockayne and David Malone, "Creeping Unilateralism: How Operation Provide Comfort and the No-Fly Zones in 1991 and 1992 Paved the Way for the Iraq Crisis of 2003," *Security Dialogue* 37, no. 1 (March 2006): 123.

11. G. John Ikenberry, "Is American Multilateralism in Decline?," *Perspectives on Politics* 1, no. 3 (September 2003): 533.

12. See Jose E. Alvarez, "Multilateralism and Its Discontents," *European Journal of International Law* 11, no. 2 (2000): 393-411; Alan Pellet, "Brief Remarks on the Unilateral Use of Force," *European Journal of International Law* 11, no. 2 (2000): 385-92; Ruth Wedgwood, "NATO's Campaign in Yugoslavia," *American Journal of International Law* 93, no. 4 (October 1999): 828-34; Nico Krisch, "Unilateral Enforcement of the Collective Will: Kosovo, Iraq, and the Security Council," *Max Planck Yearbook of United Nations Law* 3 (1999): 59-103; David M. Malone and Yuen Foong Khong, "Unilateralism and U.S. Foreign Policy: International Perspectives," in Malone and

Khong, eds., *Unilateralism*; David M. Malone and Yuen Foong Khong, "Resisting the Unilateral Impulse: Multilateral Engagement and the Future of U.S. Leadership," in Malone and Khong, eds., *Unilateralism*; Stephen G. Brooks and William C. Wohlforth, "International Relations Theory and the Case against Unilateralism," *Perspectives on Politics* 3, no. 3 (September 2005): 509-24.

13. Notably though, Ole R. Holsti, "Public Opinion and U.S. Foreign Policy after the Cold War," in *After the End: Making U.S. Foreign Policy in the Post-Cold War World*, ed. James M. Scott (Durham, N.C.: Duke University Press, 1998), finds that post-Cold War Republicans (Congress members, elites, and party supporters) are more willing to favor the U.S. acting unilaterally. See also Ruggie, "Multilateralism"; John G. Ruggie, *Winning the Peace* (New York: Columbia University Press, 1996); G. John Ikenberry, *After Victory: Institutions, Strategic Restraint, and the Rebuilding of Order after Major Wars* (Princeton, N.J.: Princeton University Press, 2001); Ikenberry, "Is American Multilateralism."

14. Bert A. Rockman, "Reinventing What for Whom?: President and Congress in the Making of Foreign Policy," *Presidential Studies Quarterly* 30, no. 1 (March 2000): 141.

15. Renato Corbetta and William J. Dixon, "Multilateralism, Major Powers, and Militarized Disputes," *Political Research Quarterly* 57, no. 1 (March 2004): 5-14; Atsushi Tago, "Determinants of Multilateralism in US Use of Force: State of Economy, Election Cycle, and Divided Government," *Journal of Peace Research* 42, no. 5 (September 2005): 585-604.

16. Tago, "Determinants of Multilateralism," 585, 599-603.

17. Benjamin O. Fordham and Christopher C. Sarver, "Militarized Interstate Disputes and United States Uses of Force," *International Studies Quarterly* 45, no. 2 (September 2001): 455-66; Michael Brecher and Jonathan Wilkenfeld, *A Study of Crisis* (Ann Arbor: University of Michigan Press, 2000). Coding rules are detailed in Chapter 3.

18. Robert W. Tucker, "Alone or With Others: The Temptations of Post-Cold War Power," *Foreign Affairs* 78, no. 6 (November—December 1999): 16; Steven Holloway, "U.S. Unilateralism at the UN: Why Great Powers Do Not Make Great Multilateralists," *Global Governance* 6, no. 3 (July—September 2000): 361-81.

19. John R. Bolton, "Unilateralism Is Not Isolationism," in *Understanding Unilateralism in American Foreign Relations*, ed. Gwyn Prins (London: Royal Institute of International Affairs, 2000), 66; Charles William Maynes, "Two Blasts Against Unilateralism," in Gwyn Prins, ed., *Understanding Unilateralism*, 31.

20. Bruce W. Jentleson and Rebecca L. Britton, "Still Pretty Prudent: Post-Cold War American Public Opinion on the Use of Military Force," *Journal of Conflict Resolution* 42, no. 4 (August 1998): 395-417; Steven Kull, "What the Public Knows that Washington Doesn't," *Foreign Policy* 101 (Winter 1995-1996): 102-15; Steven Kull, "The FP Interview: Vox Americani," *Foreign Policy* 126 (September—October 2001): 28-38; Tago, "Determinants of Multilateralism."

21. RFD, "Unilateral and Multilateral Options in the Execution of Foreign Policy," *International Organization* 23, no. 3 (Summer 1969): 641-754; Thomas M. Franck and Nigel S. Rodley, "After Bangladesh: The Law of Humanitarian Inter-

vention by Military Force," *American Journal of International Law* 67, no. 2 (April 1973): 275-305; Richard N. Haass, "Military Force: A User's Guide," *Foreign Policy* 96 (Autumn 1994): 21-37; Alvin Richman, "Poll Trends: American Support for International Involvement," *Public Opinion Quarterly* 57, no. 2 (Summer 1993): 264-76; Alvin Richman, "Trends: American Support for International Involvement: General and Specific Components of Post-Cold War Changes," *Public Opinion Quarterly* 60, no. 2 (Summer 1996): 305-21; Kull, "The FP Interview"; Rockman, "Reinventing What."

22. Ikenberry, "Is American Multilateralism," 544; Qingguo Jia, "In Search of Absolute Security: U.S. Nuclear Policy," in Malone and Khong, eds., *Unilateralism*, 204-5.

23. G. John Ikenberry, "Multilateralism and U.S. Grand Strategy," in Stewart Patrick and Shepard Forman, eds., *Multilateralism*, 129-30; Ikenberry, "Is American Multilateralism," 536.

24. Ikenberry, "Multilateralism," 130-31; Ikenberry, "Is American Multilateralism," 539.

25. The one country difference is the Vatican City, an independent but non-UN member country. Both the UN and the U.S. do not recognize arguably the 194th country, the Republic of China or Taiwan. See a list of UN member countries at http://www.un.org/Overview/unmember.html and a list of State Department-recognized countries at http://www.state.gov/s/inr/rls/4250.htm.

26. Daniel Bodansky, "What's So Bad about Unilateral Action to Protect the Environment?," *European Journal of International Law* 11, no. 2 (2000): 345.

27. Maynes, "Two Blasts," 31.

28. Maynes, "Two Blasts," 31.

29. Steve Weber, "Shaping the Postwar Balance of Power: Multilateralism in NATO," *International Organization* 46, no. 3 (Summer 1992): 633; Sophia Clement, "The United States and NATO: A Selective Approach to Multilateralism," in Malone and Khong, eds., *Unilateralism*, 399.

30. Bruce Bueno de Mesquita et al., "Testing Novel," 364; Keir A. Lieber, *War and the Engineers: The Primacy of Politics over Technology* (Ithaca, N.Y.: Cornell University Press, 2005), 152-53.

31. Robert Dahl, *Who Governs? Democracy and Power in an American City* (New Haven, Conn.: Yale University Press, 1961).

32. See President Obama's "Defense Guiding Principles" at http://www.whitehouse.gov/issues/defense/.

33. William R. Thompson, "Systemic Leadership, Evolutionary Processes, and International Relations Theory: The Unipolarity Question," *International Studies Review* 8, no. 1 (March 2006): 14; Prestowitz, *Rogue Nation*, 27; Ikenberry, "Is American Multilateralism," 538; Maynes, "Two Blasts," 36.

34. Ikenberry, "Is American Multilateralism," 537.

35. Clement, "The United States," 399.

36. Edward N. Luttwak, "Toward a Post-Heroic Warfare," *Foreign Affairs* 74, no. 3 (May—June 1995): 121; Lukasz Kamienski, "The RMA and War Powers," *Strategic Insight* (September 2003): 2; Jia, "In Search of Absolute Security," 204.

37. See Wayne S. Smith, "The Trend Towards Unilateralism in US Foreign Policy," in Gwyn Prins, ed., *Understanding Unilateralism.*

38. See Joseph S. Nye Jr., "Redefining the National Interest," *Foreign Affairs* 78, no. 4 (July—August 1999): 22-35.

39. For an executive's decision vis-à-vis a domestic audience, see Brett Ashley Leeds and David R. Davis, "Domestic Political Vulnerability and International Disputes," *Journal of Conflict Resolution* 41, no. 6 (December 1997): 814-34; James D. Fearon, "Domestic Political Audiences and the Escalation of International Disputes," *American Political Science Review* 88, no. 3 (September 1994): 577-92; James D. Fearon, "Signaling Versus the Balance of Power and Interests: An Empirical Test of a Crisis Bargaining Model," *Journal of Conflict Resolution* 38, no. 2 (June 1994): 232-69; Karl R. DeRouen Jr., "The Indirect Link: Politics, the Economy, and the Use of Force," *Journal of Conflict Resolution* 39, no. 4 (December 1995): 671-95; Karl R. DeRouen Jr., "Presidents and the Diversionary Use of Force: A Research Note," *International Studies Quarterly* 44, no. 2 (June 2000): 317-28; Tago, "Determinants of Multilateralism." For an executive's decision vis-à-vis relative military capabilities, see Bruce Bueno de Mesquita, James D. Morrow, and Ethan Zorick, "Capabilities, Perception, and Escalation," *American Political Science Review* 91, no. 1 (March 1997): 15-27; James D. Morrow, "Capabilities, Uncertainty and Resolve: A Limited Information Model of Crisis Bargaining," *American Journal of Political Science* 33, no. 4 (November 1989): 941-72; Jacek Kugler and Douglas Lemke, eds., *Parity and War: Evaluations and Extensions of "The War Ledger"* (Ann Arbor: University of Michigan Press, 1996); Jacek Kugler and Douglas Lemke, "The Power Transition Research Program: Assessing Theoretical and Empirical Advances," in *Handbook of War Studies II*, ed. Manus I. Midlarsky (Ann Arbor: University of Michigan Press, 2000); Zeev Maoz, "Resolve, Capabilities, and the Outcomes of Interstate Disputes, 1816-1976," *Journal of Conflict Resolution* 27, no. 2 (June 1983): 195-229.

40. John A. Vasquez, *The War Puzzle* (Cambridge: Cambridge University Press, 1993); John A. Vasquez, "Reexamining the Steps to War: New Evidence and Theoretical Insights," in Midlarsky, ed., *Handbook*; John A. Vasquez, "The Probability of War, 1816-1992: Presidential Address to the International Studies Association, March 25, 2002, New Orleans," *International Studies Quarterly* 48, no. 1 (March 2004): 1-28; J. David Singer, *The Correlates of War II* (New York: Free Press, 1980); William Reed, "A Unified Model of Conflict Onset and Escalation: Capabilities, Democracy, and Status Quo Evaluations," *American Journal of Political Science* 44, no. 1 (January 2000): 84-93; Ruggie, "Multilateralism."

41. The "series of steps" includes a decision to become involved in a crisis, which precedes the decision to use force. This has been a well-studied step and is not the focus of this book. For further explanation, see footnote 52 in Chapter 3.

42. Corbetta and Dixon, "Multilateralism, Major Powers," 11; Stephen Biddle, *Military Power: Explaining Victory and Defeat in Modern Battle* (Princeton, N.J.: Princeton University Press, 2004), 20-21.

43. I also test the marginal effects of these three measures, as well as the effect of my other explanatory and control variables, to determine how much these factors are impacting a president's use of force and unilateral use of force decisions.

44. Thomas S. Kuhn, *The Structure of Scientific Revolutions*, 2nd ed. (Chicago: The University of Chicago Press, 1970).

45. Adam Przeworski and Henry Teune, *The Logic of Comparative Social Inquiry* (New York: Krieger Publishing Company, 1970), 22-23, 34; Arend Lijphart, "The Comparable-Case Strategy in Comparative Research," *Comparative Political Studies* 8, no. 2 (July 1975): 165, 172.

46. Michael Coppedge, "Thickening Thin Concepts and Theories: Combining Large N and Small in Comparative Politics," *Comparative Politics* 31, no. 4 (July 1999): 465.

47. Lijphart, "The Comparable-Case Strategy," 166-71; John P. Frendreis, "Explanation of Variation and Detection of Covariation: The Purpose and Logic of Comparative Analysis," *Comparative Political Studies* 16, no. 2 (July 1983): 258-59; Charles C. Ragin, "The Distinctiveness of Comparative Social Science," in *The Comparative Method: Moving Beyond Qualitative and Quantitative Strategies*, ed. Charles Ragin (Berkeley: University of California Press, 1987), 16.

48. Rose McDermott, "Experimental Methods in Political Science," *Annual Review in Political Science* 5 (June 2002): 33-35.

49. Rose McDermott, "Experimental Methodology in Political Science," *Political Analysis* 10, no. 4 (Autumn 2002): 326.

50. McDermott, "Experimental Methods," 39-40.

51. Douglas G. Mook, "In Defense of External Invalidity," *American Psychologist* 38, no. 4 (April 1983): 379-87; David O. Sears, "College Sophomores in the Laboratory: Influences of a Narrow Data Base on Social Psychology's View of Human Nature," *Journal of Personality and Social Psychology* 51, no. 3 (1986): 515-30.

52. Przeworski and Teune, *The Logic of Comparative*, 17; Gary King, Robert O. Keohane, and Sidney Verba, *Designing Social Inquiry: Scientific Inference in Qualitative Research* (Princeton, N.J.: Princeton University Press, 1994), 35.

53. John Gerring, "What Is a Case Study and What Is It Good For?," *American Political Science Review* 98, no. 2 (May 2004): 342; Ragin, "The Distinctiveness of Comparative," 53.

54. McDermott, "Experimental Methodology," 326.

2

Unilateral Use-of-Force Decision Making

Introduction

IN THIS CHAPTER, I BUILD A NEW CONCEPTUAL FRAMEWORK of why a president uses unilateral force, based on a realist paradigm. In doing so, I overcome the three significant problems affecting the unilateral-multilateral debate that I outlined in Chapter 1. I do not place a normative value on whether unilateralism is right or wrong, but I do argue that all presidents act unilaterally a majority of the time, given the obligation to maintain the order of the international system and to protect American interests. I identify the specific reasons why a president acts unilaterally: presidents, facing a crisis, have the freedom to rely on American military power to resolve the crisis unilaterally, if necessary. After all, America is the world's greatest military power and its embrace of military revolutions allows a president the freedom to act unilaterally.

I first review hegemonic theory and emphasize how the U.S. ensures the stability of its governance of the system through unilateral military action. Next, I model a president's crisis decision making as a sequential process. I use prior studies as a building block to argue that a president's first decision, whether or not to use force, is based on a mixture of domestic and international factors.[1] I then review and analyze unilateral-multilateral research to argue that a president's second decision, whether or not to use unilateral force, is based on the proposition that unilateralism is a more efficient, lower cost option than multilateralism. The multilateral option bears heavy costs: problems of burden-sharing, legitimacy, inaction, collaboration and coordination, and reciprocity. Whereas, unilateralism has a multitude of benefits: it is a lower cost option brought about by an ambivalent public and a president wanting to rely solely on the U.S. military, as the severity of a crisis increases.

American Hegemonic Behavior

America is a hegemonic power, and as such, its behavior can be generalized to theories of hegemony.[2] Theories of hegemony refer to a paradigm of dominant powers, challengers and general wars confirming a new distribution of power in the system.[3] The theories do have different assumptions and propositions ranging from definition of hegemony to the consequences of general war, but the focus of this book is on one aspect common to all of the theories—a hegemon's (i.e., U.S.) willingness to use its power, specifically its military power, to maintain the status quo.[4]

The U.S., as a hegemon, has the power to act alone, and when it acts alone, its action can be defined as unilateralism. This is a conclusion that stems from realism, and this book assumes an inherent bond between realism and unilateralism. As such, a realist-based international and power explanation should explain American unilateralism.

Realism and Hegemonic Theory

To realists, anarchy defines the international system.[5] Given this, states must guarantee their own sovereignty and security and increase their power relative to other states.[6] The nation-state is the key actor in a world in which there is no "government over governments."[7] Competition and the quest for self-preservation define international behavior among states.[8]

In a realist world, power is either balanced or distributed unequally. When power is distributed unevenly, it is often the result of hegemony, defined as a situation in which "a single powerful state controls or dominates the lesser states in the system."[9] Political hegemony is "being able to dominate the world militarily."[10] Systemic theories, notably the theory of long cycles, define hegemony as a concentration of economic and military power. Realist theories, notably hegemonic stability, power transition, Doran's cycle, and neorealism, define hegemony by a state's relative power to other states in the international system.[11] No matter which definition is used—America governs the international system politically, economically, and militarily.

American Hegemony

America is a hegemonic power, but its hegemony is different from that of its historical predecessors—Greece, Rome, the Ottoman Empire, and Great

Britain. Hegemonic states are *alike* in their goal of articulating and enforcing the rules of the international system, but as John Ruggie argues using counterfactuals, it should *not* be assumed that all hegemonies are indistinguishable from one another.[12] Nazi Germany would have had different rules from the Soviet Union, if either one would have been the dominant power following World War II. If Britain had maintained its hegemony, colonialism would have lasted longer and the international monetary system would have been based on sterling.[13]

Ruggie credits *American* hegemony and not American *hegemony* for the establishment of the post-World War II institutions.[14] Using the New Deal regulatory state as a model, Presidents Roosevelt and Truman simply institutionalized America's economic and social order at the international level.[15] The U.S. took responsibility for the welfare of the world and designed international institutions based on its regulatory agencies.[16]

According to realists, the U.S. took these measures in order to protect and advance its own interests. Robert Cox writes of how the UK from 1845 to 1875 and the U.S. from 1945 to 1967 obtained consensus on a generalized set of principles that ensure the supremacy of the hegemon.[17] The U.S. established the UN, the Bretton Woods system, the International Monetary Fund (IMF), and the General Agreement on Tariffs and Trade (GATT), as well as the universality of democratic norms because it makes its hegemony legitimate in the eyes of other nations, and as such, other states are behaving as the U.S. prefers.[18]

Hegemonic Governance

The U.S. international institutionalization of its principles was a method of hegemonic governance, in which a dominant state brings "order and stability to the system."[19] The hegemon uses its material resources to order the system in a manner that satisfies its political and economic interests. The hegemon expands it spheres of influence and redistributes territory in order to gain resources.[20] In setting the rules that shape international interactions, the dominant state manages to minimize conflict and maximize cooperation.[21] The necessary condition for international economic order is a stable politico-military framework.[22]

Hegemonic governance is based on three factors. First, the distribution of power determines who governs the system and which state is able to promote its interests.[23] Second, governance is based on a hierarchy of prestige. Prestige is closely linked to power and is defined as the probability that a command will be obeyed. A state's prestige is based on its economic and military power.[24] Robert Gilpin writes, "Prestige is the reputation for power, and military power in particular."[25] Third, governance sets out rights and rules that govern or influence the system. The rights and rules are based primarily on the dominant state's interests.[26]

Many authors agree with this last point: the U.S. designed the UN and international system to reflect its interests.[27] Gilpin, in particular, agrees with this assessment and cites several multilateral treaties throughout history as being designed to assert the rights of the dominant state.[28] He writes, "In the modern era, what we call international law was imposed on the world by Western civilization, and it reflects the values and interests of Western civilization."[29] Western civilization is based on the UK and U.S. hegemonies dating back to the industrial revolution. In its present form, the U.S. enforces Western values and ensures its dominant position through a mixture of unilateral military action, financing of allies, and foreign aid.[30]

Hegemonic Military Power

A state must be militarily dominant to be a hegemon. To Gilpin, a hegemon must possess both superior economic capabilities and "corresponding political-military strength." An economically strong but militarily weak state is not a hegemon. The state is a hegemon based on two factors: the ability to enforce its will on other states and the ability to provide public goods of security. Hegemons use their military unilaterally to ensure a world economy that is profitable to them.[31]

This ability to enforce its will and the fact global governance is based on prestige explains why the U.S. must be willing to use force unilaterally. If negotiations fail or a UN coalition cannot be established, an adversary must believe that the U.S. is willing to act alone. Maintaining a "hierarchy of prestige" and lessening ambiguity about its potential action are necessary for the U.S. to maintain a stable system organized around its interests.[32] Prestige is achieved through successful uses of force.[33]

A decline in power relative to other states makes it less likely that the hegemon will be able to "impose its will on others" (i.e., act unilaterally).[34] The British hegemony, from 1815 to 1914, and its subsequent decline during the interwar period, from 1918 to 1939 serves as a good example of the negative correlation between relative military power and unilateralism.[35] Table 2.1 is a cursory frequency count of UK unilateral actions from 1825 to 2001.[36] I find that the UK acted unilaterally in 48 of 89 disputes during its hegemonic period (1825 to 1914), but in only 15 of 40 disputes during its decline (1915 to 1939). Its CINC score dropped from 0.3312 in 1825 to 0.1428 in 1918. By 1938, the UK CINC score was 0.0778.

Given this overriding concern of relative gains, each dominant power fears a significant military technology breakthrough by another dominant power.[37]

TABLE 2.1
Frequency Count of British Unilateral-Multilateral Uses of Force

	COW MID Data Set	
Years	*Unilateralism*	*Multilateralism*
Hegemonic Period (1825–1914)	48	41
Interwar Period (1915–1939)	15	25
American Hegemonic Period (1940–2001)	52	35
Total	115	101

But, if one nation (i.e., the U.S.) has preponderant capabilities, then there is systemic stability. Military innovation, defined as superior armament or technique, is positively correlated with system dominance.[38] The U.S., which is at the leading edge of military revolutions, can supply public goods of security and economic order, resulting in stability and the absence of major conflict.[39] The cost to a state wishing to challenge U.S. hegemony would require advancing past the U.S. in terms of military innovation, a cost that no state has been able or willing to bear.

American Military Power

Realist theories, at their core, are about power in a realpolitik system, a system in which states "take care of [themselves]" and "no one can take care of the system."[40] As such, America's unrivaled power should serve as the main explanation for a unilateral use of force. International norms and rules require enforcement, and America is the only country able to militarily enforce the norms and rules.[41]

Measures of Military Power

To understand U.S. military enforcement of the norms and rules, it is best to first understand how capability can be measured using three benchmarks of military power: (1) preponderance, (2) technology, and (3) force employment.[42] I explain these three categories and argue in the following section that military revolutions encapsulates the aggregate of these categories.

Preponderance

The prevailing measure of military capability is numerical preponderance. States with the largest military, military expenditures, population, economy, and so forth, are expected to win conflicts.[43] Realism and hegemonic theory, in particular, use preponderance to define power and explain the nature of international relations.[44] A state seeks to gain a numerical advantage or increase its relative capability to another state (or states).

The study of capabilities and its influence on conflict initiation and outcome has been well examined but with mixed results. Zeev Maoz and other scholars examine a nation's military capabilities and conclude that allocating more resources to the military does not equate to outcome success.[45] Unilateral military buildups are also not related to conflict initiation.[46] In fact, the side with weaker military capabilities achieves success more often, and the most accurate estimators of success are industrial and urban capabilities.[47] Moreover, a supreme advantage in military capability, such as possessing nuclear weapons, does not deter a challenger from initiating militarized disputes.[48]

Specific military capabilities may not matter, but in general, democracies, which "possess greater national wealth, and devote greater absolute resources to national security," usually win their wars, at least in the short run.[49] Stuart Bremer reinforces this point, as he suggests the strength of a great military power may matter as the absence of "overwhelming preponderance" often characterizes a war-prone dyad.[50]

America is certainly a great military power, and as illustrated in table 2.2, the U.S. is willing to spend a significant portion of its budget to maintain its military advantage. The U.S. has superior military technology, training, skills, and weapons vis-à-vis any adversary.[51] This is an especially poignant point in a post-Cold War unipolar world in which the U.S. possesses a historically rare "total package" of the world's best army in terms of lethality, technological competence, and ability to project force globally.[52]

Clyde Prestowitz and John Ikenberry write about the totality of the package the U.S. military can bring to bear in projecting power.[53] The U.S. has 12 carrier battle groups (no other country has even one battle group). One forward deployed carrier with more than 50 strike aircraft can deliver more than 150 strikes a day, if called upon to do so. The U.S. has more than 250,000 troops at more than 700 U.S. installations in 40 countries. It has a 40 percent share of the total defense spending of all countries in the world, spending as much as the next 14 countries combined. It accounts for 80 percent of world military research and development. Prestowitz writes, "In terms of sheer military dominance the world has never seen anything like this."[54]

This type of power disparity between the U.S. and other world powers, as illustrated in table 2.3, reduces incentives to act multilaterally.[55] Multilateralism may even impugn a nation's deterrence capability, if an adversary can block any international effort against it. Ruth Wedgwood cites the credibility costs

TABLE 2.2
U.S. Defense Spending, 1940 to 2008

Years	*Percentage of Budget Outlays*	*Percentage of GDP*
1940	17.5	1.7
1941	47.1	5.6
1942	73.0	17.8
1943	84.9	37.0
1944	86.7	37.8
1945	89.5	37.5
1946	77.3	19.2
1947	37.1	5.5
1948	30.6	3.6
1949	33.9	4.9
1950	32.2	5.0
1951	51.8	7.4
1952	68.1	13.2
1953	69.4	14.2
1954	69.5	13.1
1955	62.4	10.8
1956	60.2	10.0
1957	59.3	10.1
1958	56.8	10.2
1959	53.2	10.0
1960	52.2	9.3
1961	50.8	9.3
1962	49.0	9.2
1963	48.0	8.9
1964	46.2	8.6
1965	42.8	7.4
1966	43.2	7.7
1967	45.4	8.8
1968	46.0	9.5
1969	44.9	8.7
1970	41.8	8.1
1971	37.5	7.3
1972	34.3	6.7
1973	31.2	5.9
1974	29.5	5.5
1975	26.0	5.5
1976	24.1	5.2
1977	23.8	4.9
1978	22.8	4.7
1979	23.1	4.7
1980	22.7	4.9
1981	23.2	5.2
1982	24.8	5.7
1983	26.0	6.1

(*continued*)

TABLE 2.2
(continued)

Years	Percentage of Budget Outlays	Percentage of GDP
1984	26.7	5.9
1985	26.7	6.1
1986	27.6	6.2
1987	28.1	6.1
1988	27.3	5.8
1989	26.5	5.6
1990	23.9	5.2
1991	20.6	4.6
1992	21.6	4.8
1993	20.7	4.4
1994	19.3	4.0
1995	17.9	3.7
1996	17.0	3.5
1997	16.9	3.3
1998	16.2	3.1
1999	16.1	3.0
2000	16.5	3.0
2001	16.4	3.0
2002	17.3	3.4
2003	18.7	3.7
2004	19.9	4.0
2005	20.0	4.0
2006	19.7	4.0
2007	20.5	4.2
2008	20.9	4.2

Source: Information from "Table 3.1: Outlays by Superfunction and Function: 1940-2012" of *Historical Tables, Budget of the United States Government, Fiscal Year 2008*, http://www.whitehouse.gov/omb/budget/fy2008/pdf/hist.pdf.

of multilateralism if adversaries can block the "mechanisms of multilateral machinery."[56] This may result in more international conflict, thus it is wise for the U.S. to maintain a reputation of a willingness to act alone and avoid the time-consuming, cumbersome process of establishing a multilateral coalition.

Technology

A second measure of military capability is technology, which can be organized into one of two categories: systemic and dyadic. Systemic technology holds that technology affects the international system and not particular states. Offense-defense theory is a prime example in which technology either favors the attacker or defender.[57] Relative capability between states matters

TABLE 2.3
UN Security Council Individual Member Expenditure[a], 1988 to 2008

	Countries				
Years	*U.S.*	*UK*	*China[b]*	*France*	*Russia[c]*
1988	483,987	62,982	—	56,868	218,402
1989	479,053	62,028	12,276	57,565	202,512
1990	457,641	60,696	13,147	57,310	171,322
1991	401,943	62,348	13,691	57,683	—
1992	424,699	58,560	16,534	55,869	42,521
1993	402,369	56,393	15,331	55,250	37,563
1994	377,861	54,579	14,607	55,534	36,608
1995	357,376	50,818	14,987	52,785	21,680
1996	337,941	50,554	16,606	51,518	19,145
1997	336,179	48,276	16,799	51,695	21,242
1998	328,605	47,691	19,263	50,344	13,555
1999	329,416	47,542	21,626	50,787	14,042
2000	342,167	47,778	23,767	50,205	19,138
2001	344,927	49,417	28,515	50,036	21,242
2002	387,297	52,423	33,436	51,063	23,601
2003	440,806	55,347	36,405	52,615	25,107
2004	480,444	55,112	40,631	54,059	26,120
2005	503,353	55,152	44,911	52,917	28,488
2006	511,171	55,043	52,199	53,198	31,176
2007	524,591	55,746	57,861	53,403	33,821
2008	548,531	57,392	63,643	52,565	38,238

Source: Information from the Stockholm International Peace Research Institute (SIPRI), http://www.sipri.org/databases/milex.
[a] Millions of U.S. Dollars at Constant (2005) Prices
[b] No Data Available for 1988
[c] No Data Available for 1991

little; the systemic technological advantage of being the attacker or defender is what determines conflict outcomes. For example, the invention of the machine gun and utilization of trenches favored all defenders regardless of nationality. Dyadic technology specifies that individual states can gain an advantage over an opponent by incorporating the latest technology. The U.S. military and policy communities follow this relative technological capability concept. The U.S. can use technology to outpace potential opponents and to minimize casualties in the event of conflict.

Even when the U.S. does work through multilateral organizations, such as NATO, American technological superiority grants its unilateral power to define operations in its national interest.[58] For example, the U.S. military capability for the 2001 Afghanistan campaign so far exceeded NATO's capabilities that NATO's capabilities "proved irrelevant."[59] Max Boot writes about the temptation of such overwhelming strength, "Power breeds unilateralism. It is as simple as that."[60] The unipolarity of the international order is what explains American unilateralism. Ikenberry dismisses domestic factors, "It matters little who is president and what political party runs the government."[61]

Force Employment

In *Military Power*, Stephen Biddle argues that force employment is a significant, yet overlooked, third measure of military power. Force employment involves intangible factors, such as tactics, doctrine, leadership, and morale. Preponderance and technology do not adequately explain or predict conflict outcome; the inclusion of force employment is necessary.[62] Force employment, when used, is often held as a constant, causing problems when interacted with tangible factors.[63] Realists, in particular, largely ignore force employment based on the assumption that force is employed optimally.[64]

The modern system of force employment has been in place since 1918, in which trench warfare was replaced with "reducing exposure to hostile fire and enabling friendly movement while slowing the enemy's."[65] The tactics involve coordinating infantry and artillery efforts. A brief artillery barrage suppresses defenders, as small tactical infantry units use covering terrain to attack and exploit the defender's weak points. The limited artillery barrage and the small, independent attack units do not allow a defender the time or ability to decipher the place of attack and mass reserve troops at the breakthrough point.[66] To successfully defend against an attack, a modern defensive system requires depth, reserves, and counterattack.[67] States win or lose conflicts based on mastery of this modern force employment system.

Military Revolutions

As discussed, military capability can be measured as preponderance, technology, and force employment. Traditionally, power has been defined as preponderance or the possession of certain resources. These resources include population, territory, natural resources, economic size, political stability as well as traditional measures of military capabilities (e.g., military expenditures and size of the armed forces).[68] These traditional measures of military capabilities play a role in a president's decision, but, as Biddle and others find, there is more to it.[69]

The Correlates of War project defines a major power as having tangible assets, such as military capabilities, and intangible assets, such as reputation and global (and regional) interests and domination.[70] Gilpin, while not explicit about what military capabilities are necessary for a hegemon, does cite the importance of significant military revolutions and how it affects the relative gains argument.[71] He writes, "The introduction of a novel military weapon or technique into an international system may give a particular type of society a significant advantage over others."[72] As an example of military technological breakthroughs, he cites nuclear weapons and the Strategic Defense Initiative.[73] For this reason, it is necessary to include an under-examined measure of military power—military revolutions.[74]

Fordham writes of how tangible assets affect a president's calculation, "Improvements in American military technology are at least partly offset by improvements in the capabilities of potential adversaries."[75] Presidents certainly need to account for an opponent's improved capabilities, but what about a factor that bridges the tangible-intangible gap? This factor is military revolutions. How does the president calculate for the fact that an opponent is operating on an outdated military paradigm?

The U.S., dating back to the Civil War, has embraced military revolutions, and the fact that the U.S. is often at the front of them, may be the determining factor in whether a president chooses unilateral force.[76] After all, military revolutions are like "earthquakes," and states that embrace these revolutions and transform their militaries find themselves at an advantage in projecting power and winning conflicts.[77] Military revolutions are comprised of technological change, systems development, operational innovation, and organizational adaptation that "fundamentally alters the character and conduct of conflict."[78] Presidents may use military revolutions as a significant, yet simplified measure to calculate potential success in deciding to act alone.

Employing American Military Power: A Two-Step Decision Process

American military power, whether measured in terms of preponderance, technology or force employment, is unrivalled. So, in a crisis, how does a president make the decision to employ this power?

In order to answer this puzzle—why does a president make a unilateral use-of-force decision?—research findings modeling international crises as a series of steps can be utilized. For instance, John Vasquez details the steps that states go through with each step involving increasing hostility, resulting in violence, and perhaps in full-scale war.[79] The steps are a sequential process with de-escalation becoming increasingly difficult with each step toward war taken. Ruggie also concludes that conflict can be modeled sequentially. He models multilateral collective security as a community of states responding to potential or actual aggression. The states first respond through diplomatic means, second through economic sanctions, and finally by collective force.[80] U.S. action in the 1991 Gulf War followed this model, and NATO offers a truncated version of the model.[81] Finally, Renato Corbetta and William Dixon agree with a sequential model based on their conclusion that third-parties may join ongoing conflicts gradually, following a "steps of war" process. The progressive involvement of third-parties may even be included as an additional step to war.[82]

Notable findings from the Correlates of War project also explain crisis escalation as a "series of steps" rising from security issues and leading up to war.[83] Dispute onset and escalation are "interconnected but distinct" processes with contextual (e.g., democratic peace and power transition) variables playing a significant role in onset and the interdependent relationship between states probably playing a significant role in escalation.[84]

A leader's decision comports to this "interconnected but distinct" process.[85] As a first step, presidents contemplate using force in order to gain "stakes" that they have not yet been able to attain.[86] As a next step, leaders use threats and coercion in a test of their willingness to use their capabilities (either unilaterally or multilaterally) vis-à-vis an opponent's willingness to use their capabilities.[87] Throughout the process, a leader, in facing a crisis, has both a domestic and international audience that compels him to take escalatory actions.[88]

As shown in figure 2.1, a president's use-of-force decision can be modeled using this series of steps conceptual framework. In a crisis, a president has the option to employ American military power, and as such, he must choose whether or not to employ that power. After he decides to use force, he must decide how to employ American military power—either unilaterally or multilaterally. This decision process can be modeled as two steps, the decision to use force and the decision on how to force. The literature has thoroughly examined the first decision but largely ignored the second decision, and as such, this book focuses on the second decision while controlling for the first decision.

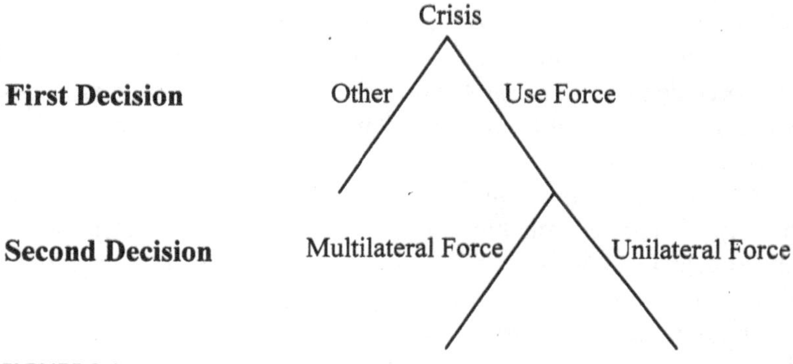

FIGURE 2.1.
Two-Step Decision Process

The First Decision: Why a President Makes a Use-of-Force Decision

A president's first decision to use force is based on a mixture of domestic and international factors. This has been a well-researched area with both levels needing to be understood in order to draw reliable conclusions about the second unilateral decision. Princeton Lyman reinforces this point, writing of the "increasingly blurred" dividing line between domestic and international explanations for a president's use-of-force decision.[89]

Domestic Factors

So, to begin, it is best to review domestic factors affecting a use-of-force decision.[90] In particular, this section covers the domestic environment, specifically politics, congressional involvement, and public opinion.

Political Use of Force[91]

Recent efforts have focused on a political-based explanation of a president's decision to use force as a challenge to the realist view that the international environment shapes this decision. Richard Betts writes that nations go to war for political reasons, and domestic political factors often explain a leader's crisis decisions (e.g., domestic politics reinforced Israel's reluctance to mobilize in September–October 1973 despite Arab threats).[92] These efforts have bore significant results, and now domestic political forces are commonly associated with being the impetus for a president's decision to use force.[93] In fact, these domestic factors are found to be "more consequential" in the president's political decision to use force than international factors.[94]

Most significantly, absolute and relative levels of popular support are "the most important influence" on a political use-of-force decision.[95] Presidents can translate these high levels of support in to successful uses of force in order to secure U.S. interests or to stabilize a deteriorating situation until a more suitable policy can be orchestrated.[96] They can also synchronize "low-cost military actions" with elections or use a weak economy as the impetus for using force abroad to divert attention from domestic problems.[97]

Congress and the Use of Force[98]

Presidents want congressional support for their use-of-force decision.[99] Congress has the exclusive power to authorize war, a power that can muddy the Constitutional waters of placing U.S. troops at the behest of a collective security organization.[100] So, a president would be wise to consult with Congress and have its approval for military action. Congressional approval convinces Americans that the action was decided upon multilaterally.[101] The intention is to diffuse the cost in the case of military defeat. But, Congress can be a fair-weather supporter and its members can be influenced by a vocal minority.[102]

Public Opinion and the Use of Force

John Mueller and several others use polls as a proxy measure, to cite the importance of the public's opinion to a president's crisis decisions.[103] Mueller claims polls "can suggest patterns of popular response that seem to have considerable generality."[104] Democratic leaders are dependent on public consent, and the greater the level of public participation in choosing leaders, the less likely a state is to initiate a dispute.[105]

After all, presidents view domestic politics as "the essence of decision" (i.e., a noncompensatory decision) and use force as the public desires in order to ensure their political survival.[106] The domestic audience (i.e., constituents) serves as a constraint on the president's decision to use force, but it can also empower a president to use force.[107] Presidents, in using force may receive an initial "hawkish" boost of public support, but their electoral success often depends on a successful outcome.[108] Moreover, the public becomes disillusioned with wars that become prolonged, especially as casualties increase.[109]

Americans are "pretty prudent" in how American military force should be used. When they want force to be used, they issue "marching orders," telling the president to reject "non-force" alternatives.[110] The American public is supportive of using force for "restraining" governments or resisting aggression but not for fostering regime change.[111] Americans are also "highly selective" of the countries they want the U.S. military to defend, and their support for defending these countries depends "strongly on the nature of the threat."[112]

The American public also recognizes the costs and problems associated with using force, and in general, they "almost always" prefer non-force options to using force.[113] Americans understand that military humanitarian operations are difficult and long-term responsibilities with U.S. soldiers often becoming the target of military opposition forces (e.g., Somalia).[114] They also tend not to support committing U.S. military forces outside the Western hemisphere and do not support intervention in countries located in the "less strategic area of the global economy."[115]

International Factors

There are notable international level assessments of regime type, rivalry, and military power that should influence a president's decision. For regime type, democratic peace theory, in which democracies rarely, if at all, fight each other, has become a lawlike theory in international relations and should matter to a president's decision.[116] In particular, scholars find that democracies are more willing to negotiate with one another, rather than fight given the potential high costs.[117] Also, whether the adversary is a rival should matter, based on the work of Gary Goertz and Paul Diehl and the finding that the U.S. and an enduring rival have historically used military action to deal with issues.[118]

Realists assume the state is a unitary actor, and the president uses the military to advance U.S. interests. Uses of force are a result of a combination of U.S. interests and capabilities.[119] The crisis trigger and location of the crisis are less an influence on a president's decision to use force, than the international distribution of power. Charles Gochman and Maoz studied over 160 years of military conflicts and concluded that the "objectives, motives, and methods of states remain the same."[120] James Meernik and Peter Waterman also studied domestic political factors, specifically the diversionary theory, and conclude that presidents use force when national security is at stake, when compelled to do so as a hegemon, and depending on the "peculiarities" of the crisis.[121]

Presidents should marginalize public opinion and act in the national interest. Favorable public opinion allows more freedom of action, but national security is objective and adherence to sound realist policies creates a favorable public.[122] In fact, Bradley Lian and John Oneal find a president's approval rating increase is close to zero following a use of force, and Giacomo Chiozza and H.E. Goemans find that a president's tenure in office is not affected either positively or negatively with a win or a loss in conflict.[123]

The Second Decision: Why a President Makes a Unilateral Use-of-Force Decision

In addition to understanding the influence of American military power, a theoretical foundation as to why a president chooses the unilateral, as opposed to multilateral, option is needed for a fully developed scientific explanation. What are the justifications for acting unilaterally? Researching the policy implications of both multilateralism and unilateralism leads one to conclude that the arguments for multilateralism are often the same arguments used against unilateralism and vice versa. Proponents state the burden-sharing and legitimacy aspects as a benefit if multilateralism is used and a cost if unilateralism is used. For example, Ikenberry reinforces the advantages of multilateralism—reciprocity and burden-sharing—stating the U.S. locks other states' cooperative policies in at the price of lost policy autonomy.[124] But, the advantages of multilateralism tend to be a myth rather than a reality, as burden-sharing, legitimacy, inaction, reciprocity, and lack of collaboration plague multilateralism.

These myths of multilateralism are mostly captured with international explanations, thus adding more evidence to a realist-based unilateral decision. First, I detail the significant international-level problems for a president wanting to exercise a multilateral option. Next, I list the reasons for a unilateral decision, which are positively enhanced by international factors.

Criticisms of Multilateralism

Multilateralism is criticized on five main counts: problems of burden-sharing, inaction, collaboration and cooperation, reciprocity, and legitimacy. These problems represent an international-based explanation for why a president should act unilaterally.[125]

A Problem of Burden-sharing

Multilateralism makes burden-sharing difficult. It minimizes U.S. coercive power and makes it difficult to extract payment from free riders. From a choice-theoretic perspective, multilateralism does not seem a "convincing bargain."[126] Multilateral arrangements include transaction costs, which is defined as all exchange costs, including "the costs of acquiring information, bargaining, and enforcement, as well as the opportunity cost of the time allocated to these activities."[127] Transaction costs "almost certainly" increase as the number of actors involved increases.[128]

These institutionalized inefficiencies are why neoliberals argue that multilateralism will fail, especially as obstacles are raised with increasing membership.[129] Mancur Olson specifies three reasons to explain an inverse relationship between increasing group size and likelihood of providing a collective good: (1) the group benefit fraction received by an individual declines as group size increases; (2) larger groups are less likely to engage in small-group strategic interaction; and (3) organization costs increase with a group size increase.[130]

Rather, bilateral arrangements, such as the ones the U.S. negotiated in East Asia, represent a better deal to minimize opportunistic behavior and free riding.[131] While South Korea and Japan receive a U.S. military presence for "cheap," the U.S. wins as well. South Korea, Japan, and its other Asian allies provide the U.S. with forward-basing options, intelligence on adversaries, and military support.[132] As a result, the U.S. is better positioned to counter China (and North Korea), which follows the Pentagon's strategy of countering emerging capabilities rather than intentions.[133]

Realists argue that multilateralism fails because hegemonic powers, such as the U.S., can exploit their power advantage in a bilateral bargain without the scrutiny of other nations.[134] In a bilateral arrangement, both sides agree to fund defense, and the U.S. does so without forgoing autonomy.[135] Establishing nuclear deterrence bilateral deals is the cheapest form of extending security, as the U.S. can extend the nuclear umbrella with little or no cost and without detracting from the security of others.[136]

Steve Weber argues that one of the major goals with regard to NATO was to create a multipolar world with Europe bearing the costs of its own defense.[137] This effort failed as the U.S. decided preventing Soviet victory was better than avoiding European dependency, and as illustrated in table 2.4, Europe has continued to lag behind the U.S. in terms of military resources and means.[138] This lack of burden-sharing continues in a post-9/11 world, as the U.S. continues to provide financial incentive payments to coalition partners (e.g., Coalition Solidarity Fund).[139]

TABLE 2.4
U.S./Europe Military Expenditures[a], 1988 to 2008

Years	*U.S.*	*Europe[b]*
1988	483,987	514,000
1989	479,053	498,000
1990	457,641	468,000
1991	401,943	—
1992	424,699	326,000
1993	402,369	314,000
1994	377,861	308,000
1995	357,376	283,000
1996	337,941	282,000
1997	336,179	283,000
1998	328,605	276,000
1999	329,416	280,000
2000	342,167	287,000
2001	344,927	288,000
2002	387,297	295,000
2003	440,806	302,000
2004	480,444	306,000
2005	503,353	306,000
2006	511,171	311,000
2007	524,591	319,000
2008	548,531	320,000

Source: Information from SIPRI, http://www.sipri.org/databases/milex.
[a] Millions of U.S. Dollars at Constant (2005) Prices
[b] No Data Available for 1991

A Problem of Inaction

While unilateralism is blindly criticized as illegitimate and a violation of a state's right to act as a sovereign, some international lawyers and leaders have raised questions about unilateralism being a better choice than doing nothing at all.[140] Multilateralism often means inaction.[141] Enter the "good Samaritan" of unilateralism, in which actors capable of responding to a crisis will act and will not be stymied by the antiquated process of obtaining UN approval.[142]

Originally, the UN was expected to have a permanent international military force established under Article 43 in order to respond quickly to international threats. But, a military force was never established, and the founders did not envision a competing U.S.-Soviet bipolar world in which the veto power of the permanent Security Council members would stymie most international responses to humanitarian crises.[143] Whether intentional or not, the UN for the past several decades has played a "peripheral" role in international relations.[144] Not only has the UN failed to respond rapidly to crises (e.g., Kosovo and Rwanda), but it also has largely failed to respond *at all* to vital crises (e.g., Vietnam and the Middle East peace process).[145]

Fear of abuse (i.e., citing humanitarian intervention as a camouflage for illegal intervention) is used as an argument against unilateralism.[146] Even a seemingly clear-cut humanitarian case, such as Kosovo, draws criticism. Before being arrested on April 1, 2001, Serbian (and later Yugoslav) President Slobodan Milosevic had overseen the unilateral killing of hundreds of thousands of people and turning approximately 1.6 million more into refugees as part of a 10-year reign of violence.[147] In doing so, he had violated a formal 1991 European foreign ministers condemnation, a 1992 UN peace plan, the 1995 Dayton Accords, a 1998 NATO ultimatum, as well as Security Council Resolutions 713 (1991), 1160 (1998), 1199 (1998) and 1203 (1998).[148] Gwyn Prins writes of the collective failure, "Milosevic was told formally [on November 9, 1991], with all of Europe's assembled will, to cease and desist from the bombardment of the ancient city [Dubrovnik], or else; and he did not; and we did nothing."[149]

But, at least NATO eventually took action in Kosovo. There was no Australia, New Zealand, United States Security Treaty (ANZUS) response to the humanitarian crisis in East Timor in 1999. One thousand people were killed before Australian peacekeepers arrived to restore order.[150] The actions of General Manuel Noriega in Panama in 1989 are another example of inaction. With the international community (including OAS) condemning U.S. actions, President George H.W. Bush invoked Article 51 of the UN Charter and Article 21 of the OAS charter and invaded Panama on December 20, 1989, in order to restore democracy, protect Americans living in Panama, and bring Noriega to justice on drug trafficking charges.[151]

The inaction problem can be traced to the UN's relative lack of power, given the paralysis of the Security Council.[152] Collective action requires power, and power is often a zero-sum exchange: increases in UN influence reduce state-based influence.[153] But, a post-Cold War UN, specifically its Security Council, is only willing to take multilateral action in cases of sovereignty violations (e.g., Iraq's invasion of Kuwait). The Security Council becomes paralyzed by vetoes in matters of intra-state problems (e.g., human rights violations in Kosovo).[154]

Rudolf Dolzer even goes so far as to describe the Council member voting system as a form of unilateralism.[155] Each member of the five permanent member Council has the right to block an international military action, and thus prevent a multinational-based military solution from being labeled multilateralism. Russia and China's blocking of a UN response to the genocide in Kosovo is a prime example.

A Problem of Collaboration and Cooperation

The U.S. does have the power to overcome collaboration and cooperation problems, but it requires a significant amount of effort by the U.S. and other involved states. In order for collaboration to work, the U.S. and another state must engage in a joint effort and mutually adjust their policies, move away from their suboptimal equilibrium, and reject their dominant strategy. As illustrated in figure 2.2, the well-cited Prisoner's Dilemma collaboration game exemplifies the collective action problem.[156]

The collaboration problem can be overcome with proper strategy, extensive exchange of information between states, extending the shadow of the future to ensure immediate costs are offset by long-term benefits, and relying on a centralized mechanism (i.e., an international organization).

However, the multilateral norms of diffuse reciprocity and indivisibility exasperate attempts to collaborate.[157] As such, the best solution for a collaboration problem is to minimize the number of actors responding to the crisis: the

		Country B 0	Country B 1
U.S.	0	3, 3	1, 4
	1	4, 1	2, 2

FIGURE 2.2.
Prisoner's Dilemma Game

		Country B	
		0	1
U.S.	0	4, 3	1, 2
	1	2, 1	3, 4

FIGURE 2.3.
Battle of the Sexes Game

smaller the number of actors, the lower the transaction costs, and the quicker and more decisive the response.[158]

Cooperation is also another significant problem with multilateralism. Cooperation requires two states with divergent interests to choose one equilibrium outcome over the other. Once an equilibrium is established, there is no incentive to defect. As illustrated in figure 2.3, the Battle of the Sexes game demonstrates the coordination problem.[159]

Establishing a military interoperability standard amongst military allies is an example of a coordination problem. Standards are often set at the domestic level, but coordination is required at the international level. NATO suffered from an interoperability problem with its Kosovo campaign.[160] The increasing gap between American military technology and the technology of its allies exasperates this problem.

A Problem of Reciprocity

Article 1 of the UN Charter specifies the organization's three constitutive pillars: (1) maintain peace and security, (2) develop friendly relations among nations, and (3) achieve international cooperation. This last principle, cooperation, is interpreted to mean that no state can unilaterally impose its will on another state (i.e., violate Article 2(1)—the principle of sovereign equality of states). Instead, states must make good faith efforts to find a solution through dialogue.[161] Cooperation, also, implicitly requires reciprocity, or as Pierre-Marie Dupuy points out, an aggrieved state may resort to "unilateral countermeasures."[162]

Multilateralism requires a diffuse reciprocity arrangement between states.[163] Reciprocity is defined as the exchange of "roughly equivalent values in which the actions of party are contingent on the prior actions of the others in such a way that good is returned for good, and bad for bad."[164] Diffuse reciprocity, while not establishing a quid pro quo exchange as in specific reciprocity, does require that a state benefit over the long term from a relationship with other states.[165] This long-term benefit is often lacking in multilateral situations given the incentives to free ride.[166] The "rough equivalence" requirement is also lacking in terms of U.S. military capabilities vis-à-vis its allies, as such the U.S. cannot expect reciprocity in terms of military actions with its allies.[167]

The prime example of the failure of reciprocity is NATO's response to military operations in Afghanistan following the September 11th attacks. The U.S. practically rejected NATO assistance in Afghanistan, instead relying heavily on the Russians for their experience in the area. The high-tech American military has interoperability problems with NATO members (a significant issue also in Kosovo), and the interoperability gap continues to increase as the U.S. defense budget increases relative to European defense budgets.[168]

Unilateralism may even spur reciprocal arrangements. The act of the bully, a state imposing its policy without regard to the interests of others, is often criticized.[169] But it can induce a positive international response. Though addressing environmental problems, Daniel Bodansky cites several examples of how unilateral action prompted international standards.[170] In the 1970s, the U.S. threatened to unilaterally enforce a double-hull standard on all oil tankers entering U.S. ports. The international community responded by adopting the double-hull standard with the 1973 MARPOL Convention and its 1978 Protocol.[171]

A Problem of Legitimacy

The problem of legitimacy represents, as Lyman writes, the "increasingly blurred" dividing line between domestic and international explanations.[172] Presidents seek international support, but this often fails due to Russia and China vetoes on the Security Council. Failing a lack of UN support, presidents will "shop around" for legitimacy, but as Edward Luck finds, international legitimacy matters little for domestic audiences and whether or not they support a use-of-force action.[173]

Presidents want international legitimacy when they decide to use force.[174] Nico Krisch and others cite the 1998 airstrikes on Iraq as an example of an attempt to justify unilateral military actions based on UN Security Council legitimacy.[175] With the 1998 airstrikes, Iraq began prohibiting UNSCOM (UN Special Commission) from visiting strategic sites associated with disarmament obligations in January 1998. After a series of Iraqi provocations, the U.S. and UK attacked Iraq from December 16th to 20th to force compliance with disarmament obligations.[176] In attacking Iraq, the U.S. and the UK claimed a multilateral basis, specifically Iraq's violations of Security Council Resolutions 678 (1990), 687 (1991), 1154 (1998), and 1205 (1998). Western nations mainly supported the airstrikes, while opposing nations, such as Russia and China, cited legal arguments against it.[177]

Krisch cites the enforcement of the no-fly zones as a second example of presidents claiming unilateral military actions are based on UN consensus.[178] In enforcing the no-fly zones, the U.S., UK, and France (up until 1998) attacked Iraqi aircraft and sites in January 1993, September 1996, and December 1998.[179] In doing so, the allies justified their actions by referring to Security Council Resolution 688 (1991).[180] Russia and China opposed the actions, citing the lack of UN Security Council authorization.[181]

These are examples of action taken in the context of UN Security Council resolutions, but in general, the veto powers of UN Security Council members make approval difficult and raises the costs for presidents seeking multilateral approval.[182] So, if UN Security Council support is not possible, presidents can resort to regional organizations for legitimacy. Presidents have often relied on the OAS to convey legitimacy for essentially unilateral action in the Western hemisphere.[183] But, legitimacy cannot be conveyed, if no region-wide organization exists to convey it, as is the case in Asia, Europe, and the Middle East. For example, the Arab League is limited due to the fact Israel is not a member. In Europe, there is NATO, the EU, and the Council of Europe, but none of these organizations include all European countries.[184]

If no institution exists to convey legitimacy, presidents can adapt or create an entity willing to endorse their action. For example, President Clinton was forced to improvise, selecting an option of "narrow multilateralism," in dealing with the former Yugoslavia.[185] President Clinton and his European allies initially sought EU legitimacy, then UN legitimacy, and then they created a group to include NATO allies and Russia. Eventually, a group of 19 democratic countries endorsed the war against Serbia.[186]

A more prominent example is the "coalition of the willing" for the 2003 Iraq invasion.[187] The U.S. from 1990 to 2002 followed a multilateral path through the UN, overseeing 16 resolutions passed against Saddam Hussein. It even scored a diplomatic victory with Resolution 1441 passing (15-0 vote) on November 8, 2002, but as Peter Dombrowski and Rodger Payne describe, the process for authorizing UN force became "bogged down" as some states began pleading for more time.[188] President Bush's response to a mid-March 2003 final, failed new UN resolution is well known. He organized a 46-state coalition, representing 20 percent of the total world population and invaded Iraq. In this coalition, the UK and Australia were the only countries to provide a substantial number of troops (though it should be noted that Poland did contribute troops).[189]

But, most importantly, presidents do not need international legitimacy to increase domestic support for a use of force. Luck cites the 1991 Gulf War, invasions of Grenada, Panama, and Haiti, as evidence of the modest influence of legitimacy on domestic support.[190] President George H.W. Bush has acknowledged that he would have acted without a UN mandate, probably by putting together a multinational coalition to invade Iraq.[191] President Reagan tried to win UN and OAS approval but ended up being internationally condemned for the Grenada invasion. The footage of the jubilant returning students and their testimony of the danger on the island was all that was needed to convince the American public that it was a legitimate operation. President Bush invaded Panama without consulting the UN and OAS, and as in the case of Grenada, the invasion was internationally condemned. But, the American public viewed the unilateral invasion as legitimate based on national interests, the values at stake, the high probability of success, and the modest military commitment.[192]

President Clinton, unlike Reagan with Grenada and Bush with Panama, did win UN approval for invading Haiti. But, international legitimacy did not compensate for a doubting public and Congress that did not see U.S. national interests at stake. The operation was carried out successfully and President Clinton received a modest boost in approval ratings but not the significant boost that Reagan and Bush received for Grenada and Panama, respectively.[193] In short, a president is less concerned with the rules and procedures of legitimacy than making a unilateral-multilateral decision based on benefit-cost calculations.[194]

So, presidents, wanting legitimacy in a U.S.-dominated system, have many options, and as realists, they will bypass an inept international organization, whether it is the UN or another organization, in finding a military solution that serves U.S. interests. They can turn to regional organizations (e.g., OAS) or existing alliances (e.g., NATO) if individual Security Council members (e.g., Russia and China) stymie a UN response. A UN response may not even be an "ideal" multilateral response. Often, the U.S. and UN nations are involved in a quid pro quo deal; the U.S. leads a UN response and furthers its interest in exchange for legitimacy.[195]

For example, Charles Krauthammer describes the Council authorization to use force in the 1991 Gulf War as "pseudo-multilateralism."[196] Samuel Huntington writes of the legitimacy-leadership tradeoff:

> Decisions made at the U.N. Security Council . . . that reflect the interests of the West are presented to the world as reflecting the desires of the international community. The very phrase "world community" has become the euphemistic collective noun (replacing the "Free World") to give global legitimacy to actions reflecting the interests of the United States and other Western powers.[197]

Even under the strictest operationalization of multilateralism—UN Security Council approval—a country still has to militarily lead the operation. The

UN does not possess command elements; so, this task often falls to the U.S.[198] A fact recognized by the UN Secretary-General when asked about Iraqi compliance with UN inspections in February 1998, "You can do a lot with diplomacy, but with diplomacy backed up by force you can get a lot more done."[199]

The UN Security Council passes a resolution (or two), and the U.S. enforces the resolution with military force.[200] Krisch labels this process the "unilateral enforcement of the collective will," Jules Lobel and Michael Ratner term it "contracting out," and Yutaka Kawashima calls it "giving the green light."[201] Security Council authorization leaves the U.S. with wide discretion to initiate, conduct, and terminate conflicts based on ambiguous resolutions. Security Council resolutions are implicit, not explicit authorizations.[202]

All of this suggests that even in UN-authorized multilateral actions, there are problems of legitimacy. A president may simply be using the UN as cover for an operation that serves U.S. interests.

The Reasons for a Unilateral Decision

In this section, I detail the benefits of unilateralism and make the following arguments: (1) the unilateral decision bears lower costs; (2) the president receives little domestic pressure to act multilaterally, as the public is ambivalent about how force should be used; and (3) presidents are more likely to rely solely on the U.S. military, as the severity of the crisis increases.

Benefits of Unilateralism

Based on the work of Corbetta and Dixon, Stewart Patrick, and Luck, a list of international-based reasons a president may act unilaterally can be deduced.[203] These reasons are summarized in table 2.5. First, the U.S. and a potential, less powerful ally may simply have conflicting interests. Second, the

TABLE 2.5
Reasons for Unilateralism

1. Conflicting interests: the U.S. and its potential, less powerful state may have conflicting interests.
2. Loss of power and prestige: the U.S. may fear the erosion of its power and status in a coalition.
3. Lack of burden-sharing: less powerful states may contribute insignificant political or military support and may even be a hindrance on U.S. military commanders.
4. Problems of inaction: the U.S. has the military capability to act quickly and win a conflict, so garnering political and military ally support may simply cause unnecessary, even costly, delays.

U.S. may fear erosion of its power and status, if it agrees to join a coalition. Third, less powerful allies may not share the burden. They may offer insignificant political or military support and may even be a hindrance to U.S. military commanders. Fourth, multilateralism suffers from free riders and inaction. The U.S. has the military capability to act quickly and win conflict; so, garnering political and military support may cause unnecessary, even costly, delays.

Unilateralism: The Lower Cost Option

Examining the international-level costs assumed to be associated with unilateralism, Stephen Brooks and William Wohlforth conclude that unilateralism does not necessarily have high costs.[204] Rather, it makes sense for a president to act multilaterally based on the substance of a given issue/crisis, rather than blindly as part of a process.[205] They examine the key cost arguments of unilateralism: (1) U.S. power will be checked by the formation of a counterbalancing coalition (balance-of-power theory); (2) reduced efficiency and lost opportunities realized through institutional cooperation (institutionalism) and (3) the legitimacy of the U.S.-led international order will be undermined (constructivism).[206]

For the first argument against unilateralism—U.S military power, Brooks and Wohlforth identify three causal factors that make counterbalancing against the U.S. "improbable."[207] The first is geography. The U.S. is isolated from Eurasia, and historically, counterbalancing coalitions have occurred against centrally located land powers. The second is material capabilities. The gap between the U.S. and all other states is larger than any other gap in the history of the modern system. The U.S. is dominant militarily and economically, other leading states have been dominant militarily or economically but not both simultaneously. Moreover, the U.S. maintains its military dominance with devoting only a small proportion of its economy to national defense (about 4 percent of GDP in 2008), and the U.S. leads the way in terms of technology and shifting to new military revolution paradigms. The third factor is American primacy. Historically, counterbalancing coalitions were established to check a rising power from reaching hegemony, but the U.S. is clearly the hegemonic power. Also, potential counterbalancers seem unwilling to pay the costs to overthrow American hegemony, given the problems of coalitional collective action and free rider problems.[208]

For the second argument against unilateralism—reduced efficiency gains from institutionalized cooperation, Brooks and Wohlforth believe that the costs of unilateralism may apply to economic matters but not to military matters.[209] The U.S. has asymmetric bargaining power and absorbs little cost if it fails to establish multilateral cooperation.[210] Institutionalists claim a loss of reputation if the U.S. squanders its multilateral reputation, but Brooks and Wohlforth specify George Downs and Michael Jones's 2002 rational choice model, in which states have multiple reputations with each reputation specific to an agreement or issue area.[211] So, the U.S. failure to act multilaterally in terms of the military will probably not impact its efforts to gain cooperation on an economic issue.[212]

For the third argument against unilateralism—undermining legitimacy of the American-led international order, Brooks and Wohlforth argue that the fear of American policy makers creating a cognitive and social mind-set in other actors that American hegemony offers unilateral military action without legitimate authority is underspecified.[213] They argue that some unilateral actions threaten legitimacy more than others, compensating strategies may mitigate the costs of unilateralism, and unilateralism can produce legitimacy benefits. For this latter point, they cite the U.S. response to the 9/11 attacks and the U.S. pushing through new rules based on an expanded definition of self-defense as potentially leading other states to see the American action as the new standard of legitimacy.[214]

Unilateralism: An Ambivalent Public

The president receives little domestic pressure to act multilaterally, as the public is ambivalent, and even contradictory, in terms of whether force should be used unilaterally or multilaterally. Americans prefer unilateralism the larger the U.S. stakes in a crisis, and they are disinclined to believe in the effectiveness of collective security.[215] The inherent nature of collective security organizations, such as the UN, is that reliance is placed on a collection of nations not chosen by the U.S. It is difficult, if not impossible, to convince the average American that such countries as Pakistan, Malaysia, or Montenegro are going to be able to, much less want to, protect America. Conceding American decision-making authority to the Security Council or any other entity is simply unacceptable to the average American.[216]

But, as Alvin Richman, Steven Kull, and Lyman argue, Americans, in general, have an internationalist attitude and want a multilateral approach to foreign policy.[217] A German Marshall Fund and Chicago Council on Foreign Relations study supports the public's multilateral bent. Seventy-one percent of Americans said the U.S. should act to solve problems together with other countries, and 61 percent said the U.S. should not act alone in responding to an international crisis.[218] A 1995 Program on International Policy Attitudes (PIPA) poll found that 89 percent of Americans believe that the U.S. should work through the UN when using military force, and only 29 percent favor acting alone, even when the U.S. would be more successful on its own. A 2000

PIPA poll found that 79 percent of Americans favored using allies, regardless of the lack of confidence in allies effectively protecting shared interests.[219]

This preference for multilateralism carries over to "helping hand" military operations (i.e., humanitarian or human rights).[220] If the U.S. acts alone, it leads to the perception of the U.S. acting as a bully.[221] But more importantly, Americans want to minimize the costs, especially in terms of casualties. They are reluctant to accept casualties in cases in which the singular goal is unreciprocated humanitarian interests. One humanitarian disaster (e.g., Somalia) can even result in Americans being unwilling to assist in more serious humanitarian crises (e.g., Rwanda).[222]

Moreover, intervention in the name of human rights often means violating the sovereignty of another state. Fifty-nine percent of Americans are willing to support a multilateral intervention in the internal affairs of other countries, while only 39 percent support unilateral intervention.[223] NATO's intervention in Kosovo is a prime example of public support for multilateralism. President Clinton, as well as other NATO leaders, presented the intervention as an international police action with an international mandate. The fact, however, was that the U.S. largely conducted the air war with the UK, France, and Germany conducting less than 10 percent of the airstrikes. President Clinton, understanding the fragility of public support, sought to minimize the costs (e.g., ruling out using ground force and keeping bombers at an altitude above the range of Serb ground fire) while trumpeting the burden-sharing components.[224]

Unilateralism: The Crisis Matters

Corbetta and Dixon in their multivariate analysis of the positive correlation between major power status and multilateral dispute participation argue that controls are necessary for state level and situational factors, as they may possibly mediate the effect of major power status on multilateral proneness.[225] They find that situational factors do have an effect in that major powers tend to act multilaterally in disputes that escalate to war, that are of long duration, and have multiple opponents. Interestingly, they find that multilateralism is negatively correlated with a major power opponent.[226]

Ekaterina Stepanova, though confining her analysis to the 1990s, believes that U.S. unilateral military operations were based on a series of situational factors (tactical in nature): (1) conventional operations limited in scope, intensity, and duration; (2) highly selective and used against "semi-isolated backlash states or statelets" (Iraq, North Korea, Bosnian Serbs); and (3) based on vague military goals.[227] Kanti Bajpai focuses on strategic threats and finds that the U.S. is more likely to act unilaterally when national security is at stake.[228]

So, it seems that a crisis, involving a minor power, of limited duration and scope, and when national security is threatened, strongly influences a president to act unilaterally.

A New Model of Unilateral Use-of Force Decision Making

American hegemonic military power shapes a president's decision (whether Republican or Democrat) and answers the research question: why does a president make a unilateral use-of-force decision? Hegemonic theories use expected utility as a basis for explaining how states determine their foreign policy.[229] As such, I also argue that a president makes an expected utility calculation in determining whether to use unilateral or multilateral force.

A relative military power gap vis-à-vis an adversary is positively correlated with a president deciding to use unilateral force. However, all use-of-force decisions are not alike, and the crisis trigger (i.e., situational factor) may play a significant role in a president's calculation. For example, a president is likely to respond differently to a national security threat as opposed to a humanitarian crisis. Other determinants (Western hemisphere and military revolution gap) also make the president more likely to act unilaterally, given the problems of multilateralism.

A president decides to use unilateral force in a sequential manner. As I argued earlier in this chapter, a president first decides to use force, based on traditional domestic explanations for uses of force: presidential decision making, political uses of force, congressional involvement, and public opinion as well as some traditional international- and target-level explanations: rivalry, regime type, and power. The president then makes a second expected utility calculation on how to use force. For this second decision, I advocate two types of explanatory factors—military revolutions and situational factors—that make it more likely a president will make a unilateral decision.

Modeling Presidential Decision Strategy

Hegemonic theories, in particular hegemonic stability theory, can be applied to a presidential decision strategy. Gilpin argues that states "have no interests" and foreign policies are determined by "dominant members or ruling coalitions."[230] Gilpin uses an indifference analysis, in which decision makers do not maximize based on a hierarchy of goals, but they make tradeoffs in seeking to find an optimum position.[231] The relative cost of objectives and the capacity of the state to achieve the objective largely influences a president's decision.[232]

Hegemonic power can take the form of economic, political, diplomatic, or military might, but in this book, I am modeling a president's decision *after* he has already decided to use force. This negates the necessity of focusing on other state powers and allows me to model a president's military calculation with a rational choice approach. The president's tradeoff decision in this book is whether to enforce the rules of U.S. governance alone or with allies, and this tradeoff decision is based primarily on an international factor of relative military power.

I argue that a president's unilateral-multilateral decision is calculated based on one objective—whether unilateral or multilateral force offers the greatest probability of advancing or protecting U.S. interests. As I detailed earlier in this chapter, Americans, in general, are ambivalent about how force should be used, and this level of ambiguity affords a president the "freedom" to make an expected utility calculation for his unilateral-multilateral decision.

Expected Utility Decision Strategy

The lack of domestic pressure to act multilaterally and the abundance of international factors to act unilaterally must be modeled as a presidential decision strategy. Expected utility is a natural fit for how a hegemonic leader should make his decisions.[233] Gilpin writes, "Statesmen try to make rational or cost/benefit calculations concerning their efforts to achieve national objectives."[234] Subordinate states make a calculation and if the expected benefits outweigh the expected costs, they challenge a dominant power. This calculation is made based on a relative power difference between the subordinate and dominant state.[235] The greater the disparity in power between a dominant and subordinate state, the less likely a challenge will occur. A hegemon's self-interest in maintaining the status quo compounds a subordinate's calculation.[236]

As part of the rational school of decision making, expected utility theory focuses on predicting decision outcomes and relies on a basic premise: actors are assumed to be utility maximizers, make holistic and compensatory decisions, and "do what they believe is in their best interest at the time they must choose."[237] Using a game theory approach of strategic interaction, actors in a game consider the other actor's motivations and choice sets before making their own choice.[238] This basic assumption of utility maximization and strategic interaction belies the predictive capability of expected utility, a president's decision to use force can be modeled based on choices available and costs and benefits information.[239]

In *The War Trap*, Bruce Bueno de Mesquita puts forth a formal model of an expected utility of war strategy.[240] Decision makers, assumed to be single actors and rational expected utility maximizers, calculate going to war as the sum of the utilities of the possible outcomes (i.e., winning or losing) times their probabilities. When expected utility is estimated to be negative, maximization rules out use of force, but when it is positive, the option to negotiate is ruled out.[241] Each leader is assumed to be a rational actor, but each leader has his own inclination for risk and uncertainty.[242] Risk-acceptant leaders attach some added utility to taking a gamble and are less constrained in making war decisions than risk-adverse leaders.[243] Both the expected utility model and the risk attitude have been supported with formal and empirical tests.[244]

Presidents base their expected utility calculation on military capabilities and can estimate the following with relatively little uncertainty: (1) the marginal advantage (or disadvantage) in war capabilities of his nation vis-à-vis a potential opponent; (2) how much he values the policies of his own nation vis-à-vis a potential opponent's value of his policies; and (3) the capabilities of other nations that might become involved in the war.[245] A fourth item, the relative value or utilities that other countries may contribute to him vis-à-vis the value they may contribute to his potential opponent, is more difficult to calculate.[246]

There is usually not a great amount of uncertainty with the first three issues. The first two points address the initiator's capabilities and motivation and his knowledge of his opponent's capabilities, and the third point concerns the capabilities of third parties. Given that national capabilities change slowly, these first three points should not involve a lot of uncertainty. However, national interests and commitments from third parties change quickly, and these changes may increase or decrease uncertainty.[247] Also, the theory assumes that a nation's power to wage war decreases as the location of the war increases in distance from the nation's territory.[248]

A Rational Actor Unilateral-Multilateral Calculation

As discussed in the "Employing American Military Power" section and as shown in figure 2.4, presidential decision making follows a sequential process with the president making an expected utility calculation as a second decision *after* he has already decided to use force. In general, democracies win wars they start, suffer fewer casualties, and they do so by choosing military strategies that "promise" short, low-cost victories.[249] Major powers, engaging in collective security initiatives or multilaterally, lower the costs and are also more victorious.[250] So, the president is likely to win the conflict regardless of choosing a unilateral or multilateral option, but he must still calculate the utility of acting alone or with allies.

Domestic politics may compel presidents to use force and influence how they use force, but the president himself, must answer the question of utility

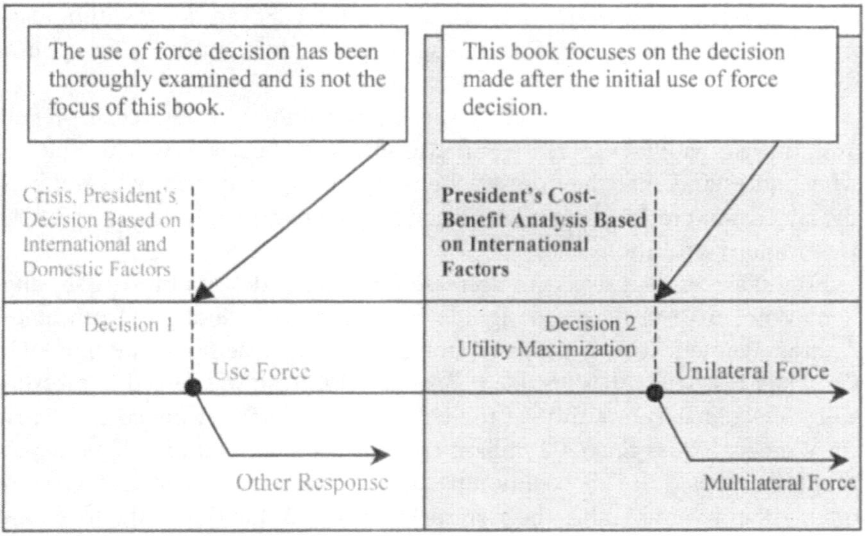

FIGURE 2.4.
Sequential Expected Utility Model of Use-of-Force Decision Making

in terms of how best to project American military power.[251] For this, a president may make an expected utility calculation, in which he calculates how easily victory can be obtained with and without ally military support.[252] This is a tradeoff decision: maximize cooperation but minimize ineffectual action.[253] More specifically, for how to use force decisions, a president can either increase the "benefit" side of the calculation by acting quickly, albeit alone, to defeat an opponent before that opponent has time to increase its capabilities or recruit additional allies. Or, the president can decrease the "cost" side with the addition of allies.[254]

A president may choose a multilateral track if the benefits flowing from policy coordination outweigh the costs of lost policy autonomy.[255] President Clinton made this calculation during the 1990s civil war in Bosnia and the 1999 Kosovo crisis and decided that the loss in the U.S. preferred course was not greater than the delays and diplomatic bargaining used to convince other NATO countries to carry out airstrikes.[256]

Multilateral force can be just as an important goal to Europeans as the end result, but U.S. presidents make multilateral decisions on whether or not they advance U.S. interests.[257] Multilateralism slows down the process of using force.[258] Multilateralism also means entangling rules and institutions.[259] The U.S. has little incentive to burden itself with rules or to bargain away its interests. All nations want to shed entanglements, rules, and institutions, if they can, but only powerful nations, such as the U.S. can do so without significant cost.[260] This is why Robert Kagan calls multilateralism a "weapon of the weak."[261]

This also explains why presidents are more willing to use force, especially as military capabilities increase.[262] It also solves the puzzle of why presidents, who understand that they must achieve victory quickly and with minimal casualties, want to forgo multilateral actions that may simply delay or hamper U.S. military operations.[263]

Even if a president selects to decrease the "cost" side with burden-sharing, it may not necessarily mean significant military contributions from allies. Andrew Bennett, Joseph Lepgold, and Danny Unger demonstrate in a 1991 Gulf War case study that President George H.W. Bush was forced to pressure allies for contributions and yet the U.S. still bore most of the cost.[264] Patricia Weitsman cites the $200 million cost (in 2005 dollars) to U.S. taxpayers that is being paid to U.S. coalition partners in Afghanistan and Iraq.[265] More often, other nations realize the asymmetric power of the U.S. and understand the U.S. is willing to act unilaterally without international approval; so, they offer tacit UN Security Council political support of a U.S. draft resolution in exchange for putting some conditions on the proposed action.[266] These instances of nominal international political and military support may appease the public's preference for multilateral action, but presidents are still faced with—what is for all practical matters—a decision to act alone.

Perhaps the best evidence that a president's unilateral-multilateral decision is a cost calculation is the 2001 military campaign against Al-Qaida and the Taliban. The campaign was a procedural and operational multilateral effort, but President Bush relied on a "hub-and-spoke" strategy. The U.S. alone made the key decisions and drew on its coalitional partners individually as needed for military or diplomatic purposes.[267]

As illustrated in table 2.6, Brooks and Wohlforth summarize the benefits and costs of acting multilaterally and the specific military factors a president must weigh when making a unilateral-multilateral decision.[268]

TABLE 2.6
Benefits and Costs of Multilateralism

Benefits	*Costs*
1. Common war plans	1. Slow decision making
2. Economies of scale	2. Loss of secrecy
3. Sharing of burdens and risks	3. Circumscribed freedom of action
4. Specialization of military tasks	4. Cumbersome systems of command and control
5. Common equipment and interchangeable parts	

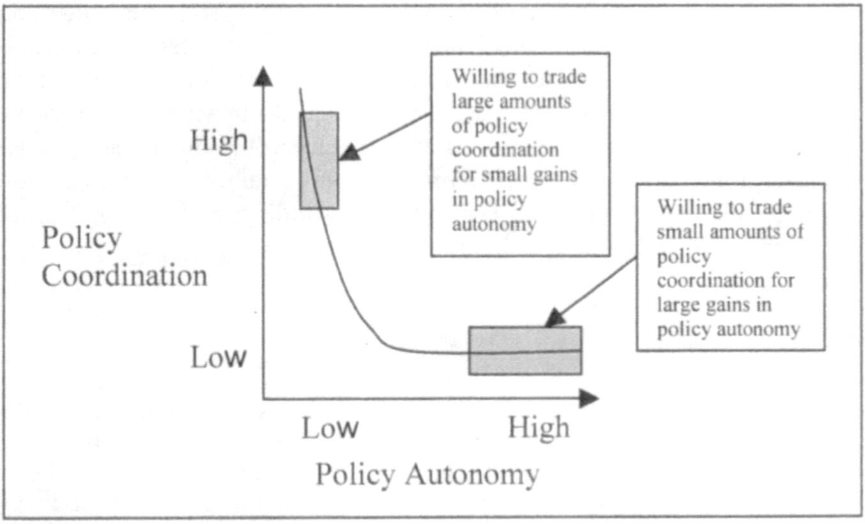

FIGURE 2.5.
The Policy Coordination-Policy Autonomy Calculation

A president weighs these military factors in making a rational choice calculation of whether to act unilaterally. Per figure 2.5, these factors are weighed in the context of a policy coordination-policy autonomy trade-off which is difficult to calculate in advance. Nonetheless, a president must attempt to estimate the trade-off in determining how best to use force.[269]

Conclusion

In this chapter, I critiqued the domestic and international explanations for a use-of-force decision and how hegemonic theory can be used to conceptualize a president's unilateral decision. I modeled a president's crisis decision as a sequential process. After deciding to use force, presidents weigh the significance of international factors and act unilaterally based on a cost-benefit calculation. In this unilateral decision stage, domestic political factors are marginalized. Instead, the president chooses the best strategy to maintain the status quo of the international system. The best strategy and the best decision is to act unilaterally, given the dominant capabilities of the U.S. military, the costs of multilateralism, and the benefits of unilateralism.

In Chapter 3, I conduct the first of my scientific tests in answering the question of why a president decides to use unilateral force. First, I formulate hypotheses, detail my selection of two prominent data sets, and offer coding rules and sources for my dependent, explanatory, and control variables. I then use a heckman probit model to test a president's use-of-force decision and his unilateral use-of-force decision as a sequential process. I use a maximum likelihood procedure to test the two decisions, and I offer models of the two decisions. For my results, I detail the marginal impact of each variable on separate probit models (the decision to use force and the decision to use unilateral force) and on the unified model of unilateral use-of-force decision making. I then focus on the unilateral decision findings and the significance of the military revolution and situational explanations.

Notes

1. See Brett Ashley Leeds and David R. Davis, "Domestic Political Vulnerability and International Disputes," *Journal of Conflict Resolution* 41, no. 6 (December 1997): 814-34; James D. Fearon, "Domestic Political Audiences and the Escalation of International Disputes," *American Political Science Review* 88, no. 3 (September 1994): 577-92; James D. Fearon, "Signaling Versus the Balance of Power and Interests: An Empirical Test of a Crisis Bargaining Model," *Journal of Conflict Resolution* 38, no. 2 (June 1994): 232-69; Karl R. DeRouen, Jr., "The Indirect Link: Politics, the Economy, and the Use of Force," *Journal of Conflict Resolution* 39, no. 4 (December 1995): 671-95; Karl R. DeRouen, Jr., "Presidents and the Diversionary Use of Force: A Research Note," *International Studies Quarterly* 44, no. 2 (June 2000): 317-28; Atsushi Tago, "Determinants of Multilateralism in US Use of Force: State of Economy, Election Cycle, and Divided Government," *Journal of Peace Research* 42, no. 5 (September 2005): 585-604; Bruce Bueno de Mesquita, James D. Morrow, and Ethan Zorick, "Capabilities, Perception, and Escalation," *American Political Science Review* 91, no. 1 (March 1997): 15-27; James D. Morrow, "Capabilities, Uncertainty and Resolve: A Limited Information Model of Crisis Bargaining," *American Journal of Political Science* 33, no. 4 (November 1989): 941-72; Jacek Kugler and Douglas Lemke, eds., *Parity and War: Evaluations and Extensions of "The War Ledger"* (Ann Arbor: University of Michigan Press, 1996); Jacek Kugler and Douglas Lemke, "The Power Transition Research Program: Assessing Theoretical and Empirical Advances," in *Handbook of War Studies II*, ed. Manus I. Midlarsky (Ann Arbor: University of Michigan Press, 2000); Zeev Maoz, "Resolve, Capabilities, and the Outcomes of Interstate Disputes, 1816-1976," *Journal of Conflict Resolution* 27, no. 2 (June 1983): 195-229.

2. While American hegemonic behavior can be generalized to theories of hegemony, the particulars of American hegemony are unique as discussed in the "American Hegemony" section.

3. I am referring to the theories of long cycles, hegemonic stability, power transition, and Doran's cycle.

4. Jack S. Levy, "Theories of General War," *World Politics* 37, no. 3 (April 1985): 356.

5. Richard Ned Lebow, "The Long Peace, the End of the Cold War, and the Failure of Realism," *International Organization* 48, no. 2 (Spring 1994): 250; Kenneth N. Waltz, *Theory of International Politics* (Boston: McGraw-Hill, 1979), 111.

6. Hans J. Morgenthau, *Politics Among Nations: The Struggle for Power and Peace*, 5th ed. (New York: Knopf, 1973); Waltz, *Theory of International*; Lebow, "The Long Peace"; Kugler and Lemke, "The Power Transition."

7. Inis L. Claude, Jr., *Swords into Plowshares: The Problems and Progress of International Organization*, 4th ed. (New York: Random House, 1971), 14; Morgenthau, *Politics Among Nations*, 12; John A. Vasquez, "The Realist Paradigm and Degenerative versus Progressive Research Programs: An Appraisal of Neotraditional Research on Waltz's Balancing Proposition," *American Political Science Review* 91, no. 4 (December 1997): 899.

8. Morgenthau, *Politics Among Nations*, 5; Waltz, *Theory of International*, 109.

9. Robert Gilpin, *War and Change in World Politics* (New York: Cambridge University Press, 1981), 29.

10. Joshua S. Goldstein, *Long Cycles: Prosperity and War in the Modern Age* (New Haven, Conn.: Yale University Press, 1988), 281.

11. These theories explain five centuries of the modern system.

12. John G. Ruggie, "Multilateralism: The Anatomy of an Institution," *International Organization* 46, no. 3 (Summer 1992): 585.

13. Ruggie, "Multilateralism," 585.

14. Ruggie, "Multilateralism," 568, 585-93.

15. Ruggie, "Multilateralism," 593; Anne-Marie Burley, "Regulating the World: Multilateralism, International Law, and the Projection of the New Deal Regulatory State," in *Multilateralism Matters: The Theory and Praxis of an Institutional Form*, ed. John Gerard Ruggie (New York: Columbia University Press, 1993), 131, 133.

16. Burley, "Regulating the World," 131, 133. Unfortunately, these international institutions suffer from democratic deficits. Institution decisions affect states and their citizens without national legislatures having a voice in the process: Stewart Patrick, "Multilateralism and Its Discontents: The Causes and Consequences of U.S. Ambivalence," in *Multilateralism and US Foreign Policy: Ambivalent Engagement*, eds. Stewart Patrick and Shepard Forman (Boulder, Colo.: Lynne Rienner, 2002), 17. On the other hand, America's domestic institutions have been so successful at ensuring a consensus-based decision-making approach that some argue international multilateralism is simply an extension of American domestic values. Arguably, the president's unilateral action may be multilateral, given the checks and balances of the American political system: Burley, "Regulating the World"; Peter F. Cowhey, "Elect Locally–Order Globally: Domestic Politics and Multilateral Cooperation," in John G. Ruggie, ed., *Multilateralism Matters*. America's domestic institutions are designed to make war decision making a "difficult and cumbersome" process: Zeev Maoz and Bruce M. Russett, "Normative and Structural Causes of the Democratic Peace," *American Political Science Review* 87, no. 3 (September 1993): 626. Presidents, wanting to wage war, must first mobilize public opinion and successfully navigate the proposal through the legislature, bureaucracies, and interest groups: Maoz and Russett, "Normative." They must convince the American people (and the international community) that they are following an "international legal process," in which due process is carried out in an objective and orderly fashion: W. Michael Reisman, "Unilateral Action and the Transformations of the World Constitutive Process: The Special Problem of Humanitarian

Intervention," *European Journal of International Law* 11, no. 1 (2000): 16-17. In short, the checks and balances of the American government system serve as a powerful barrier against an overzealous president using force arbitrarily: Rudolf Dolzer, "Unilateralism and Current Transatlantic Relations," in *Multilateralism v Unilateralism: Policy Choices in a Global Society*, eds. John B. Attanasio and Joseph J. Norton (London: The British Institute of International and Comparative Law, 2004), 70.

17. Robert W. Cox, *Production, Power, and World Order* (New York: Columbia University Press, 1987).

18. Joseph S. Nye, Jr., "The Changing Nature of World Power," *Political Science Quarterly* 105, no. 2 (Summer 1990): 182.

19. Gilpin, *War and Change*, 42.

20. Gilpin, *War and Change*, 37. Territorial distribution is still a fundamental feature of the governance of the international system, but domestic consolidation and economic expansion complement and partially replace territorial expansion in the modern era: Gilpin, *War and Change*, 146.

21. Gilpin, *War and Change*, 34.

22. Gilpin, *War and Change*, 133.

23. Gilpin, *War and Change*, 28-29.

24. Gilpin, *War and Change*, 30.

25. Gilpin, *War and Change*, 31.

26. Gilpin, *War and Change*, 34-35.

27. Burley, "Regulating the World"; Cowhey, "Elect Locally"; W. Michael Reisman and Scott Shuchart, "Unilateral Action in an Imperfect World Order," in Attanasio and Norton, eds., *Multilateralism v Unilateralism*; Helmut Freudenschuss, "Between Unilateralism and Collective Security: Authorizations of the Use of Force by the UN Security Council," *European Journal of International Law* 5, no. 1 (1994): 492-531; Samuel P. Huntington, "The Clash of Civilizations?," *Foreign Affairs* 72, no. 3 (Summer 1993): 22-49; Nico Krisch, "Unilateral Enforcement of the Collective Will: Kosovo, Iraq, and the Security Council," *Max Planck Yearbook of United Nations Law* 3 (1999): 59-103; Ramesh Thakur, "UN Peace Operations and U.S. Unilateralism and Multilateralism," in *Unilateralism and U.S. Foreign Policy: International Perspectives*, eds. David M. Malone and Yuen Foong Khong (Boulder, Colo.: Lynne Rienner, 2003); Ruggie, "Multilateralism."

28. Gilpin, *War and Change*, 36.

29. Gilpin, *War and Change*, 36.

30. Gilpin, *War and Change*, 156.

31. Gilpin, *War and Change*, 34, 129, 139, 145.

32. Gilpin, *War and Change*, 31.

33. Gilpin, *War and Change*, 32.

34. Gilpin, *War and Change*, 33.

35. Richard T. Cupitt, Rodney L. Whitlock, and Lynn Williams Whitlock, "British Hegemony and Militarized Interstate Disputes, 1815-1939," *Conflict Management and Peace Science* 12, no. 2 (Spring 1993): 41-64; Patrick Karl O'Brien and Armand Clesse, *Two Hegemonies: Britain 1846-1914 and the United States 1941-2001* (Aldershot, UK: Ashgate, 2002); Gilpin, *War and Change*.

36. Using the Correlates of War Militarized Interstate Dispute (COW MID) data set (Daniel Jones, Stuart A. Bremer, and J. David Singer, "Militarized Interstate Disputes, 1816-1992: Rationale, Coding Rules, and Empirical Patterns," *Conflict Management and Peace Science* 15, no. 2 (Fall 1996): 163-213; D. Scott Bennett and Allan C. Stam, III, "*EUGene*: A Conceptual Manual," *International Interactions* 26, no. 2 (2000): 179-204), I coded a one for unilateral use of force when the UK had a COW MID dispute level (hostlev) of 2 or higher (2 = threat to use force, 3 = display of force, 4 = use of force, 5 = war) and joined with one or more countries in a militarized dispute. These coding rules are not as comprehensive as the US unilateral use-of-force coding rules detailed in Chapter 3.

37. Robert Gilpin, "The Theory of Hegemonic War," *Journal of Interdisciplinary History* 18, no. 4 (Spring 1988): 612.

38. Gilpin, *War and Change*, 60.

39. Gilpin, *War and Change*, 145.

40. Waltz, *Theory of International*, 109.

41. Edward Luck, "The United States, International Organization, and the Quest for Legitimacy," in Patrick and Forman, eds., *Multilateralism*, 54.

42. Stephen Biddle, *Military Power: Explaining Victory and Defeat in Modern Battle* (Princeton, N.J.: Princeton University Press, 2004).

43. The CINC score is the ideal example of how preponderance can be quantified.

44. Morgenthau, *Politics Among Nations*; Gilpin, *War and Change*; Joseph M. Grieco, *Cooperation among Nations: Europe, America, and Non-Tariff Barriers to Trade* (Ithaca, N.Y.: Cornell University Press, 1990).

45. Maoz, "Resolve, Capabilities," 195, 207; Frank W. Wayman, J. David Singer, and Gary Goertz, "Capabilities, Allocations, and Success in Militarized Disputes and Wars, 1816-1976," *International Studies Quarterly* 27, no. 4 (December 1983): 497-515.

46. Paul F. Diehl and Jean Kingston, "Messenger or Message?: Military Buildups and the Initiation of Conflict," *Journal of Politics* 49, no. 3 (August 1987): 801.

47. Wayman, Singer, and Goertz, "Capabilities, Allocations," 497, 510.

48. Paul D. Huth, Scott Bennett, and Christopher Gelpi, "System Uncertainty, Risk Propensity, and International Conflict among the Great Powers," *Journal of Conflict Resolution* 36, no. 3 (September 1992): 513.

49. David A. Lake, "Powerful Pacifists: Democratic States and War," *American Political Science Review* 86, no. 1 (March 1992): 24, 32; D. Scott Bennett and Allan C. Stam, III, "The Declining Advantages of Democracy: A Combined Model of War Outcome and Duration," *Journal of Conflict Resolution* 42, no. 3 (June 1998): 344. Gilpin argues that American governance of the international system is in decline; he cites America's military spending, exemplified as the "increasing costs of dominance," as a "nonproductive expenditure" and a "drain on the economy": Gilpin, *War and Change*, 169. But, as illustrated in table 2.2, defense spending as a percentage of GDP has remained at a relatively low 3 to 4.8 percent since the end of the Cold War. Defense spending reached a high of 37.8 percent in 1944, was at 9.5 in 1968, hit a low of 3 percent in 2001, and even in financing two wars remained at a low 4.2 percent in 2008. Gilpin, himself, also concludes that the U.S. "continues to be the dominant and most prestigious state in the system": Gilpin, *War and Change*, 232.

50. Stuart A. Bremer, "Dangerous Dyads: Conditions Affecting the Likelihood of Interstate War, 1816-1965," *Journal of Conflict Resolution* 36, no. 2 (June 1992): 322, 338.

51. See President Obama's "Defense Guiding Principles" at http://www.whitehouse.gov/issues/defense/.

52. William R. Thompson, "Systemic Leadership, Evolutionary Processes, and International Relations Theory: The Unipolarity Question," *International Studies Review* 8, no. 1 (March 2006): 14; Clyde Prestowitz, *Rogue Nation: American Unilateralism and the Failure of Good Intentions* (New York: Basic Books, 2003), 27; G. John Ikenberry, "Is American Multilateralism in Decline?," *Perspectives on Politics* 1, no. 3 (September 2003): 538; Charles William Maynes, "Two Blasts Against Unilateralism," in *Understanding Unilateralism in American Foreign Relations*, ed. Gwyn Prins (London: Royal Institute of International Affairs, 2000), 36.

53. Prestowitz, *Rogue Nation*; Ikenberry, "Is American Multilateralism."

54. Prestowitz, *Rogue Nation*, 26.

55. Ikenberry, "Is American Multilateralism," 537.

56. Ruth Wedgwood, "Unilateral Action in a Multilateral World," in Patrick and Forman, eds., *Multilateralism*, 186.

57. See Robert Jervis, "Cooperation under the Security Dilemma," *World Politics* 30, no. 2 (January 1978): 167-214; Stephen Van Evera, *Causes of War* (Ithaca, N.Y.: Cornell University Press, 1999); Keir A. Lieber, *War and the Engineers: The Primacy of Politics over Technology* (Ithaca, N.Y.: Cornell University Press, 2005).

58. Sophia Clement, "The United States and NATO: A Selective Approach to Multilateralism," in Malone and Khong, eds., *Unilateralism*, 399.

59. David M. Malone, "A Decade of U.S. Unilateralism?," in Malone and Khong, eds., *Unilateralism*, 34.

60. Max Boot, "Doctrine of the 'Big Enchilada'," *Washington Post*, 14 October 2002, A29.

61. Ikenberry, "Is American Multilateralism," 537-38.

62. Biddle, *Military Power*, 20, 23, 52, 190, 196.

63. Biddle, *Military Power*, 18.

64. Biddle, *Military Power*, 18.

65. Biddle, *Military Power*, 28.

66. Biddle, *Military Power*, 33.

67. Biddle, *Military Power*, 46.

68. Nye, "The Changing Nature," 178.

69. Biddle, *Military Power*; Renato Corbetta and William J. Dixon, "Multilateralism, Major Powers, and Militarized Disputes," *Political Research Quarterly* 57, no. 1 (March 2004): 5-14.

70. J. David Singer, "Reconstructing the Correlates of War Data Set on Material Capabilities of States, 1816-1985," *International Interactions* 14, no. 2 (May 1987): 121; Randolph M. Siverson and Harvey Starr, *The Diffusion of War: A Study of Opportunity and Willingness* (Ann Arbor: University of Michigan Press, 1991), 61-62; Corbetta and Dixon, "Multilateralism, Major Powers," 7.

71. Gilpin, *War and Change*, 62; Gilpin, "The Theory," 611.

72. Gilpin, *War and Change*, 63.

73. Gilpin, "The Theory," 612.

74. The term "military revolutions" has been used for many periods in history, even dating back to the Chou dynasty in the 8th century BC. It is prominently used to describe the West's global empires between 1500 and 1750, which included the introduction of firearms, larger armies, complex strategies, and war's larger impact on society: see Geoffrey Parker, *The Military Revolution: Military Innovation and the Rise of the West, 1500-1800* (Cambridge: Cambridge University Press, 1996). However, for this book, military revolutions is defined and coded using the seminal article: Andrew F. Krepinevich, "Cavalry to Computer: The Pattern of Military Revolutions," *National Interest* 37 (Fall 1994): 30-42.

75. Benjamin O. Fordham, "A Very Sharp Sword: The Influence of Military Capabilities on American Decisions to Use Force," *Journal of Conflict Resolution* 48, no. 5 (October 2004): 641.

76. Krepinevich, "Cavalry to Computer"; Richard O. Hundley, *Past Revolutions, Future Transformations: What can the history of revolutions in military affairs tell us about transforming the U.S. military?* (Santa Monica, Calif.: Rand, 1999).

77. Williamson Murray and MacGregor Knox, "Thinking about Revolutions in Warfare," in *The Dynamics of Military Revolution: 1300-2050*, eds. MacGregor Knox and Williamson Murray (Cambridge: Cambridge University Press, 2001), 6-7.

78. Krepinevich, "Cavalry to Computer," 30.

79. John A. Vasquez, *The War Puzzle* (Cambridge: Cambridge University Press, 1993); John A. Vasquez, "Reexamining the Steps to War: New Evidence and Theoretical Insights," in Midlarsky, ed., *Handbook*; John A. Vasquez, "The Probability of War, 1816-1992: Presidential Address to the International Studies Association, March 25, 2002, New Orleans," *International Studies Quarterly* 48, no. 1 (March 2004): 1-28. It should be noted that going through each step is not a necessary condition, as steps can be skipped. Also, states that have gone through some of the steps do not always go to war.

80. Ruggie, "Multilateralism," 569.

81. Ruggie, "Multilateralism," 570.

82. Renato Corbetta and William J. Dixon, "Danger beyond Dyads: Third-Party Participants in Militarized Interstate Disputes," *Conflict Management and Peace Science* 22, no. 1 (March 2005): 42.

83. John A. Vasquez, "The Steps to War: Toward a Scientific Explanation of Correlates of War Findings," in *The Scientific Study of Peace and War*, eds. John Vasquez and Marie Henehan (New York: Lexington Books, 1992); J. David Singer, *The Correlates of War II* (New York: Free Press, 1980); William Reed, "A Unified Model of Conflict Onset and Escalation: Capabilities, Democracy, and Status Quo Evaluations," *American Journal of Political Science* 44, no. 1 (January 2000): 84-93.

84. Reed, "A Unified Model," 92.

85. Reed, "A Unified Model," 92.

86. J. David Singer, "Confrontational Behavior and Escalation to War 1816-1980: A Research Plan," *Journal of Peace Research* 19, no. 1 (1982): 40.

87. Vasquez, "The Steps," 346; Maoz, "Resolve, Capabilities"; Russell J. Leng, "Influence Strategies and Interstate Conflict," in *The Correlates of War II*, ed. J. David

Singer (New York: Free Press, 1980); Russell J. Leng, "When Will They Ever Learn? Coercive Bargaining in Recurrent Crises," *Journal of Conflict Resolution* 27, no. 3 (September 1983): 379-419.

88. J. David Singer, ed., *The Correlates of War I* (New York: Free Press, 1979), 72-78; Singer, "Confrontational Behavior," 40.

89. Princeton N. Lyman, "The Growing Influence of Domestic Factors," in Patrick and Forman, eds., *Multilateralism*, 75.

90. See Charles W. Ostrom, Jr. and Brian L. Job, "The President and the Political Use of Force," *American Political Science Review* 80, no. 2 (June 1986): 541-66; Richard K. Betts, "Why Surprise Succeeds, II: The Fog of Peace," in *Surprise Attack: Lessons for Defense Planning*, ed. Richard Betts (Washington, D.C.: The Brookings Institution, 1982); Patrick James and John R. Oneal, "The Influence of Domestic and International Politics on the President's Use of Force," *Journal of Conflict Resolution* 35, no. 2 (June 1991): 307-32; DeRouen, "The Indirect Link"; DeRouen, "Presidents"; David Brule and Alex Mintz, "Blank Checks or Marching Order? Public Opinion and Presidential Use of Force in the United States," in *Crossing Boundaries*, ed. Harvey Starr (New York: Palgrave Macmillan, 2006).

91. In terms of political uses of force and unilateralism, there is little empirical work. Steven Holloway, "U.S. Unilateralism at the UN: Why Great Powers Do Not Make Great Multilateralists," *Global Governance* 6, no. 3 (July—September 2000): 361-81, tests whether or not partisanship determines nonaccommodating or nonmultilateral (i.e., unilateral) U.S. voting in the UN General Assembly from 1968 to 1993. He finds that the U.S. votes unilaterally (having a negative or "rejectionist" vote) as a general trend regardless of whether a Democrat or Republican is president. In terms of administration changes, he finds more unilateral voting with the Reagan and Ford administrations than with the Carter administration, but there was little variation in voting between the George H.W. Bush and Clinton administrations. In fact, unilateral voting increased as a proportion of total votes from 1968 to 1993. Ekaterina Stepanova, "The Unilateral and Multilateral Use of Force by the United States," in Malone and Khong, eds., *Unilateralism*, 186-87, believes that U.S. unilateral uses of force during the 1990s and early 2000s can be tied to domestic politics. As examples, she cites President Clinton's decision to strike Iraq on the eve of the impeachment vote in December 1998 and ties President Bush's February 2001 strikes against Iraq to a worsening Israeli-Arab crisis.

92. Betts, "Why Surprise," 138-41.

93. Tago, "Determinants of Multilateralism," 588.

94. James and Oneal, "The Influence of Domestic," 307.

95. Ostrom and Job, "The President," 559.

96. Barry M. Blechman and Stephen S. Kaplan, *Force Without War: U.S. Armed Forces as a Political Instrument* (Washington, D.C.: The Brookings Institution, 1978), 532; John E. Mueller, "A Review: American Public Opinion and the Gulf War: Some Polling Issues," *Public Opinion Quarterly* 57, no. 1 (Spring 1993): 85.

97. DeRouen, "The Indirect Link," 671, 686-87; DeRouen, "Presidents," 323, 326; Benjamin O. Fordham, "Partisanship, Macroeconomic Policy, and U.S. Uses of Force, 1949-1994," *Journal of Conflict Resolution* 42, no. 4 (August 1998): 436.

Notably though, the diversionary hypothesis has little direct empirical support: Jack S. Levy, "The Diversionary Theory of War: A Critique," in *Handbook of War Studies*, ed. Manus I. Midlarsky (Boston: Unwin Hyman, 1989); Dennis M. Foster and Glenn Palmer, "Presidents, Public Opinion, and Diversionary Behavior: The Role of Partisan Support Reconsidered," *Foreign Policy Analysis* 2, no. 3 (July 2006): 269-88.

98. As cited here, congressional involvement has been traditionally associated with the use-of-force decision. But, the Tago, "Determinants of Multilateralism," finding that a divided government is correlated with multilateralism is controlled for with the statistical tests. In short, I use a *divided government* variable as a control for the unilateral decision.

99. The Richard E. Neustadt, *Presidential Power and the Modern Presidents: The Politics of Leadership from Roosevelt to Reagan* (New York: Free Press, 1990) case study on Truman's Marshall Plan and the John P. Burke and Fred I. Greenstein, *How Presidents Test Reality: Decisions on Vietnam, 1954 and 1965* (New York: Russell Sage Foundation, 1989) case study on Eisenhower's Dien Bien Phu demonstrate how Congress plays an instrumental role in American foreign policy.

100. Arthur M. Schlesinger, Jr., "Unilateralism in Historical Perspective," in Gwyn Prins, ed., *Understanding Unilateralism*, 21.

101. Though Steven Kull, "Public Attitudes Toward Multilateralism," in Patrick and Forman, eds., *Multilateralism*, blames Congress for wrongly interpreting a public sentiment toward unilateralism.

102. Robert B. Zoellick, "Congress and the Making of US Foreign Policy," *Survival* 41, no. 4 (January 1999): 34; James M. Lindsay, "Congress and the Use of Force in the Post-Cold War Era," in *The United States and the Use of Force in the Post-Cold War Era* (Washington, D.C.: The Aspen Institute, 1995), 88; Lyman, "The Growing Influence," 84-85.

103. John E. Mueller, "Trends in Popular Support for the Wars in Korea and Vietnam," *American Political Science Review* 65, no. 2 (June 1971): 358-75; John E. Mueller, *War, Presidents and Public Opinion* (New York: John Wiley, 1973); Scott Sigmund Gartner and Gary M. Segura, "War, Casualties, and Public Opinion," *Journal of Conflict Resolution* 42, no. 3 (June 1998): 278-300; Brule and Mintz, "Blank Checks."

104. Mueller, *War, Presidents*, 268.

105. Dan Reiter and Erik R. Tillman, "Public, Legislative, and Executive Constraints on the Democratic Initiation of Conflict," *Journal of Politics* 64, no. 3 (August 2002): 824.

106. Alex Mintz and Nehemia Geva, "The Poliheuristic Theory of Foreign Policy Decision Making," in *Decision Making on War and Peace: The Cognitive-Rational Debate*, eds. Nehemia Geva and Alex Mintz (Boulder, Colo.: Lynne Rienner Publishers, 1997), 83; Alex Mintz, "The Decision to Attack Iraq: A Noncompensatory Theory of Decision Making," *Journal of Conflict Resolution* 37, no. 4 (December 1993): 595-618; Brule and Mintz, "Blank Checks."

107. See Douglas Foyle, *Counting the Public In: Presidents, Public Opinion, and Foreign Policy* (New York: Columbia University Press, 1999); Richard Sobel, *The Impact of Public Opinion on Foreign Policy* (New York: Oxford University Press, 2001); Reiter and Tillman, "Public, Legislative"; Brule and Mintz, "Blank Checks."

108. Mueller, "A Review," 85; Bruce Bueno de Mesquita and David Lalman, *War and Reason* (New Haven, Conn.: Yale University Press, 1992); H.E. Goemans, "Fighting for Survival: The Fate of Leaders and the Duration of War," *Journal of Conflict Resolution* 44, no. 5 (October 2000): 555-79.

109. Mueller, "Trends in Popular," 371; Gartner and Segura, "War, Casualties," 296.

110. Brule and Mintz, "Blank Checks."

111. See Bruce W. Jentleson, "The Pretty Prudent Public: Post Post-Vietnam American Opinion on the Use of Military Force," *International Studies Quarterly* 36, no. 1 (March 1992): 49-73; Bruce W. Jentleson and Rebecca L. Britton, "Still Pretty Prudent: Post-Cold War American Public Opinion on the Use of Military Force," *Journal of Conflict Resolution* 42, no. 4 (August 1998): 395-417; John R. Oneal, Brad Lian, and James H. Joyner, Jr., "Are the American People 'Pretty Prudent'? Public Responses to U.S. Uses of Force, 1950-1988," *International Studies Quarterly* 40, no. 2 (June 1996): 261-79.

112. Bruce M. Russett and Miroslav Nincic, "American Opinion on the Use of Military Force Abroad," *Political Science Quarterly* 91, no. 3 (Autumn 1976): 429-30.

113. Jentleson and Britton, "Still Pretty Prudent," 415.

114. Alex de Waal and Rakiya Omaar, "Can Military Intervention Be 'Humanitarian?'," *Middle East Report* 187/188 (March—June 1994): 3; Mark Duffield and John Prendergast, "Sovereignty and Intervention after the Cold War: Lessons from the Emergency Relief Desk," *Middle East Report* 187/188 (March—June 1994): 9-10; Richard N. Haass, "Military Force: A User's Guide," *Foreign Policy* 96 (Autumn 1994): 36.

115. Russett and Nincic, "American Opinion," 430; Mark Duffield and Joe Stork, "Bosnia Is the Classic Case of Using Humanitarian Aid as a Smokescreen to Hide Political Failure," *Middle East Report* 187/188 (March—June 1994): 20.

116. Bruce M. Russett and Harvey Starr, "From Democratic Peace to Kantian Peace: Democracy and Conflict in the International System," in Midlarsky, ed., *Handbook*; Nils P. Gleditsch and H. Hegre, "Peace and Democracy—Three Levels of Analysis," *Journal of Conflict Resolution* 41, no. 2 (April 1997): 283-310; Maoz and Russett, "Normative and Structural."

117. David L. Rousseau et al., "Assessing the Dyadic Nature of the Democratic Peace, 1918-88," *American Political Science Review* 90, no. 3 (September 1996): 512-33; Bruce Bueno de Mesquita et al., "An Institutional Explanation of the Democratic Peace," *American Political Science Review* 93, no. 4 (December 1999): 791-807.

118. Gary Goertz and Paul F. Diehl, "Enduring Rivalries: Theoretical Constructs and Empirical Patterns," *International Studies Quarterly* 37, no. 2 (June 1993): 147-71; Gary Goertz and Paul F. Diehl, "(Enduring) Rivalries," in Midlarsky, ed., *Handbook*.

119. Blechman and Kaplan, *Force Without War*; Philip Zelikow, "The U.S. and the Use of Force: A Historical Summary," in *Democracy, Strategy and Vietnam: Implications for American Policymaking*, eds. George K. Osborn, Asa A. Clark IV, Daniel J. Kaufman, and Douglas E. Lute (Lexington, Mass.: Lexington Books, 1987), 44.

120. Charles S. Gochman and Zeev Maoz, "Militarized Interstate Disputes, 1816-1976," *Journal of Conflict Resolution* 28, no. 4 (December 1984): 585-616.

121. James Meernik and Peter Waterman, "The Myth of the Diversionary Use of Force by American Presidents," *Political Research Quarterly* 49, no. 3 (September 1996): 587.

122. James and Oneal, "The Influence of Domestic," 310.

123. Bradley Lian and John R. Oneal, "Presidents, the Use of Military Force, and Public Opinion," *Journal of Conflict Resolution* 37, no. 2 (June 1993): 277-300; Giacomo Chiozza and H.E. Goemans, "International Conflict and the Tenure of Leaders: Is War Still 'Ex Post' Inefficient," *American Journal of Political Science* 48, no. 3 (July 2004): 604-19.

124. G. John Ikenberry, "Multilateralism and U.S. Grand Strategy," in Patrick and Forman, eds., *Multilateralism*, 122-23.

125. Legitimacy represents both a domestic- and international-based explanation. See the "A Problem of Legitimacy" section.

126. Steve Weber, "Shaping the Postwar Balance of Power: Multilateralism in NATO," *International Organization* 46, no. 3 (Summer 1992): 637.

127. Douglass C. North, "Transaction Costs, Institutions, and Economic History," *Journal of Institutional and Theoretical Economics* 140, no. 1 (1984): 7-17; James A. Caporaso, "International Relations Theory and Multilateralism: The Search for Foundations," *International Organization* 46, no. 3 (Summer 1992): 609.

128. Caporaso, "International Relations," 609.

129. Miles Kahler, "Multilateralism with Small and Large Numbers," *International Organization* 46, no. 3 (Summer 1992): 682.

130. Mancur Olson, *The Logic of Collective Action* (New York: Schocken, 1968), 48.

131. Caporaso, "International Relations," 611. In fact, the Association of Southeast Asian Nations (ASEAN) Regional Forum is the only officially multilateral security organization in the Asia-Pacific region: Andrew Mack, "The United States and the Asia-Pacific Bilateralism Plus 'Multilateralism a' la Carte," in Malone and Khong, eds., *Unilateralism*, 375.

132. Mack, "The United States," 382.

133. Mack, "The United States," 379-80.

134. Kahler, "Multilateralism," 682.

135. Ikenberry, "Is American Multilateralism," 536.

136. Weber, "Shaping the Postwar," 638.

137. Weber, "Shaping the Postwar," 634, 643.

138. Weber, "Shaping the Postwar," 648, 650.

139. Patricia Weitsman, "The High Price of Friendship," *New York Times*, 31 August 2006.

140. Martha Brenfors and Malene Maxe Petersen, "The Legality of Unilateral Humanitarian Intervention—A Defence," *Nordic Journal of International Law* 69, no. 4 (2000): 449-99.

141. Daniel Bodansky, "What's So Bad about Unilateral Action to Protect the Environment?," *European Journal of International Law* 11, no. 2 (2000): 339-47; Gwyn Prins, "US Unilateralism and European Initiatives on Defence and Security," in Prins, ed., *Understanding*.

142. See Christine Chinkin, "The State That Acts Alone: Bully, Good Samaritan or Iconoclast?," *European Journal of International Law* 11, no. 1 (2000): 31-41; Reisman and Shuchart, "Unilateral Action."

143. Brenfors and Petersen, "The Legality of Unilateral," 474.

144. Kishore Mahbubani, "The United Nations and the United States: An Indispensable Partnership," in Malone and Khong, eds., *Unilateralism*, 143.

145. Chinkin, "The State That Acts," 34; Brenfors and Petersen, "The Legality of Unilateral," 474; Mahbubani, "The United Nations," 143.

146. Brenfors and Petersen, "The Legality of Unilateral," 481; James Cockayne and David Malone, "Creeping Unilateralism: How Operation Provide Comfort and the No-Fly Zones in 1991 and 1992 Paved the Way for the Iraq Crisis of 2003," *Security Dialogue* 37, no. 1 (March 2006): 123.

147. A copy of the indictments can be found at http://www.icty.org/.

148. Chinkin, "The State That Acts"; Krisch, "Unilateral Enforcement."

149. Prins, "US Unilateralism," 91.

150. Chinkin, "The State That Acts," 36-37.

151. Ved P. Nanda, "The Validity of United States Intervention in Panama under International Law," *American Journal of International Law* 84, no. 2 (April 1990): 502.

152. See Pierre-Marie Dupuy, "The Place and Role of Unilateralism in Contemporary International Law," *European Journal of International Law* 11, no. 1 (2000): 19-29.

153. Reisman, "Unilateral Action," 13.

154. Reisman, "Unilateral Action," 14-15.

155. Dolzer, "Unilateralism."

156. See Lisa L. Martin, "The Rational State Choice of Multilateralism," in Ruggie, ed., *Multilateralism Matters.*

157. Martin, "The Rational State," 95-98. See the "A Problem of Reciprocity" section.

158. Martin, "The Rational State," 99.

159. See Martin, "The Rational State."

160. Stephen G. Brooks and William C. Wohlforth, "International Relations Theory and the Case against Unilateralism," *Perspectives on Politics* 3, no. 3 (September 2005): 514.

161. Dupuy, "The Place and Role," 22-24.

162. Dupuy, "The Place and Role," 25.

163. Weber, "Shaping the Postwar"; Caporaso, "International Relations"; Robert O. Keohane, "Reciprocity in International Relations," *International Organization* 40, no. 1 (Winter 1986): 1-27.

164. Keohane, "Reciprocity," 8.

165. Caporaso, "International Relations," 602; Keohane, "Reciprocity," 4.

166. Keohane, "Reciprocity," 12.

167. Keohane, "Reciprocity," 8.

168. Alexander Konovalov, "Multilateralism and Unilateralism in a New Security Environment," in Attanasio and Norton, eds., *Multilateralism v Unilateralism*, 219-20; Brooks and Wohlforth, "International Relations," 514.

169. See Chinkin, "The State That Acts."
170. Bodansky, "What's So Bad."
171. Bodansky, "What's So Bad," 344.
172. Lyman, "The Growing Influence," 75.
173. Luck, "The United States." See also Dupuy, "The Place and Role"; Patrick, "Multilateralism and Its Discontents."
174. Luck, "The United States," 58.
175. Krisch, "Unilateral Enforcement"; Cockayne and Malone, "Creeping Unilateralism."
176. Krisch, "Unilateral Enforcement," 64-65.
177. Krisch, "Unilateral Enforcement," 67, 69-73.
178. Krisch, "Unilateral Enforcement."
179. Krisch, "Unilateral Enforcement," 73-74.
180. Krisch, "Unilateral Enforcement," 74-76; Cockayne and Malone, "Creeping Unilateralism," 134.
181. Krisch, "Unilateral Enforcement," 77.
182. Kahler, "Multilateralism," 704; Brenfors and Petersen, "The Legality of Unilateral," 474, 499.
183. Maynes, "Two Blasts," 33.
184. Maynes, "Two Blasts," 34-35. The Organization for Security and Cooperation in Europe includes all of the countries of Europe, but it's an institution in transition.
185. Stepanova, "The Unilateral and Multilateral," 192.
186. Maynes, "Two Blasts," 35-36.
187. Brooks and Wohlforth, "International Relations."
188. Peter Dombrowski and Rodger A. Payne, "Global Debate and the Limits of the Bush Doctrine," *International Studies Perspective* 4, no. 4 (November 2003): 402.
189. Dombrowski and Payne, "Global Debate," 398, 400, 403. The coalition included six unarmed countries: Costa Rica, Iceland, Marshall Islands, Micronesia, Palau, and Solomon Islands.
190. Luck, "The United States."
191. George H.W. Bush and Brent Scowcroft, *A World Transformed* (New York: Alfred A. Knopf, 1998), 356.
192. Luck, "The United States," 64.
193. Luck, "The United States," 66.
194. Luck, "The United States," 62.
195. Reisman and Shuchart, "Unilateral Action"; Freudenschuss, "Between Unilateralism," 1994.
196. Charles Krauthammer, "The Unipolar Moment," *Foreign Affairs* 70, no. 1 (1990-1991): 25.
197. Huntington, "The Clash," 39.
198. Krisch, "Unilateral Enforcement," 61-62; Cockayne and Malone, "Creeping Unilateralism," 136.
199. Krisch, "Unilateral Enforcement," 72.
200. Thakur, "UN Peace Operations," 154.

201. Krisch, "Unilateral Enforcement"; Jules Lobel and Michael Ratner, "Bypassing the Security Council: Ambiguous Authorizations to Use Force, Cease-Fires and the Iraqi Inspection Regime," *American Journal of International Law* 93, no. 1 (January 1999): 124-54; Yutaka Kawashima, "Multilateralism versus U.S. Unilateralism: The Role of the UN Security Council as the Authorizing Body for the United States' Use of Force," in Attanasio and Norton, eds., *Multilateralism v Unilateralism*, 146.

202. Lobel and Ratner, "Bypassing the Security," 125.

203. Corbetta and Dixon, "Multilateralism, Major Powers"; Patrick, "Multilateralism and Its Discontents"; Luck, "The United States."

204. Brooks and Wohlforth, "International Relations," 509.

205. Brooks and Wohlforth, "International Relations," 510.

206. Brooks and Wohlforth, "International Relations," 510.

207. Brooks and Wohlforth, "International Relations."

208. Brooks and Wohlforth, "International Relations," 511.

209. Brooks and Wohlforth, "International Relations," 514.

210. Brooks and Wohlforth, "International Relations," 515.

211. Brooks and Wohlforth, "International Relations"; George W. Downs and Michael Jones, "Reputation, Compliance, and International Law," *Journal of Legal Studies* 31, no. S1 (January 2002): S95-S114.

212. Brooks and Wohlforth, "International Relations," 516.

213. Brooks and Wohlforth, "International Relations," 517.

214. Brooks and Wohlforth, "International Relations," 518.

215. RFD, "Unilateral and Multilateral Options in the Execution of Foreign Policy," *International Organization* 23, no. 3 (Summer 1969): 743; Haass, "Military Force," 35; Schlesinger, "Unilateralism," 20-21; John R. Bolton, "Unilateralism Is Not Isolationism," in Prins, ed., *Understanding Unilateralism*, 64.

216. Bolton, "Unilateralism," 74.

217. Alvin Richman, "Poll Trends: American Support for International Involvement," *Public Opinion Quarterly* 57, no. 2 (Summer 1993): 264; Steven Kull, "What the Public Knows that Washington Doesn't," *Foreign Policy* 101 (Winter 1995-1996): 104; Kull, "Public Attitudes," 99; Lyman, "The Growing Influence," 93.

218. Ikenberry, "Is American Multilateralism," 543-44.

219. Kull, "Public Attitudes," 105.

220. Kull, "Public Attitudes," 107.

221. Steven Kull, "The FP Interview: Vox Americani," *Foreign Policy* 126 (September—October 2001): 30.

222. Joseph S. Nye, Jr., "Redefining the National Interest," *Foreign Affairs* 78, no. 4 (July—August 1999): 32.

223. Kull, "Public Attitudes," 108.

224. Jeremy Rabkin, "When Can America Be Bound by International Law?," in Prins, ed., *Understanding Unilateralism*, 120-21.

225. Corbetta and Dixon, "Multilateralism, Major Powers," 9.

226. Corbetta and Dixon, "Multilateralism, Major Powers," 12.

227. Stepanova, "The Unilateral and Multilateral," 184.

228. Kanti Bajpai, "U.S. Nonproliferation Policy After the Cold War," in Malone and Khong, eds., *Unilateralism*, 217.

229. Gilpin, *War and Change*, 50.

230. Gilpin, *War and Change*, 18-19.

231. Gilpin, *War and Change*, 20.

232. Gilpin, *War and Change*, 23.

233. Gilpin, "The Theory," 605-6; K. Edward Spiezio, "British Hegemony and Major Power War, 1815-1939: An Empirical Test of Gilpin's Model of Hegemonic Governance," *International Studies Quarterly* 34, no. 2 (June 1990): 169.

234. Gilpin, "The Theory," 612.

235. Gilpin, *War and Change*, 187.

236. Gilpin, *War and Change*, 145.

237. James D. Morrow, "A Rational Choice Approach to International Choice," in Geva and Mintz, eds., *Decision Making*, 12; Bueno de Mesquita and Lalman, *War and Reason*.

238. Morrow, "A Rational Choice," 11, 17; Alastair Smith, "Testing Theories of Strategic Choice: The Example of Crisis Escalation," *American Journal of Political Science* 43, no. 4 (October 1999): 1255.

239. Janice Gross Stein and David A. Welch, "Rational and Psychological Approaches to the Study of International Conflict: Comparative Strengths and Weaknesses," in Geva and Mintz, eds., *Decision Making*, 52.

240. Bruce Bueno de Mesquita, *The War Trap* (New Haven, Conn.: Yale University Press, 1981).

241. David Lalman, "Conflict Resolution and Peace," *American Journal of Political Science* 32, no. 3 (August 1988): 596.

242. Bueno de Mesquita, *The War Trap*, 44-45.

243. Bueno de Mesquita, *The War Trap*, 34-35.

244. See Alastair Smith, "International Crises and Domestic Politics," *American Political Science Review* 92, no. 3 (September 1998): 623-38; Huth, Bennett, and Gelpi, "System Uncertainty"; Kevin H. Wang, "Presidential Responses to Foreign Policy Crises: Rational Choice and Domestic Politics," *Journal of Conflict Resolution* 40, no. 1 (March 1996): 68-97.

245. Bueno de Mesquita, *The War Trap*, 36.

246. Bueno de Mesquita, *The War Trap*, 36-37.

247. Bueno de Mesquita, *The War Trap*, 38.

248. Bueno de Mesquita, *The War Trap*, 45.

249. Reiter and Tillman, "Public, Legislative," 824; Dan Reiter and Curtis Meek, "Determinants of Military Strategy, 1903-1994: A Quantitative Empirical Test," *International Studies Quarterly* 43, no. 2 (June 1999): 363-87; Bueno de Mesquita et al., "An Institutional Explanation"; Bueno de Mesquita et al., "Policy Failure and Political Survival: The Contribution of Political Institutions," *Journal of Conflict Resolution* 43, no. 2 (April 1999): 147-61; Bueno de Mesquita et al., "Testing Novel Implications from the Selectorate Theory of War," *World Politics* 56, no. 3 (April 2004): 363-88.

250. Richard J. Stoll, "Nice States Finish . . . Pretty Well: Collective Security Behavior in Militarized Interstate Disputes, 1816-1992," *International Interactions* 24, no. 3 (September 1998): 287-313.

251. The presidential decision-making literature takes two approaches in explaining the interaction between a president and domestic political factors. One approach suggests the president is a strong leader with considerable freedom to conduct foreign affairs as he sees fit: see John F. Kennedy, *Profiles in Courage* (New York: HarperCollins, 1956); Bert A. Rockman, "Reinventing What for Whom?: President and Congress in the Making of Foreign Policy," *Presidential Studies Quarterly* 30, no. 1 (March 2000): 133-54; Zoellick, "Congress"; Prestowitz, *Rogue Nation*; Patrick, "Multilateralism and Its Discontents"; Louis Fisher, *Constitutional Conflicts between Congress and the President*, 3rd ed. (Lawrence: University Press of Kansas, 1991); Louis Fisher, "War Powers: The Need for Collective Judgment," in *Divided Democracy: Cooperation and Conflict between the President and Congress*, ed. James A. Thurber (Washington, D.C.: CQ Press, 1991). A second approach suggests the president is a weak leader and is held to the whims of Congress and the public: see George C. Edwards, III, *At the Margins: Presidential Leadership of Congress* (New Haven, Conn.: Yale University Press, 1989); George C. Edwards, III, "Aligning Tests with Theory: Presidential Approval as a Source of Influence in Congress," *Congress and the Presidency* 24, no. 2 (Autumn 1997): 113-30; Neustadt, *Presidential Power*; Foyle, *Counting the Public In*; Sobel, *The Impact*; Melvin R. Laird, "Iraq: Learning the Lessons of Vietnam," *Foreign Affairs* 84, no. 6 (November—December 2005): 22-43; Rockman, "Reinventing"; Zoellick, "Congress"; Charles M. Cameron, *Veto Bargaining: Presidents and the Politics of Negative Power* (Cambridge: Cambridge University Press, 2000); Sarah A. Binder, "The Dynamics of Legislative Gridlock, 1947-96," *American Political Science Review* 93, no. 3 (September 1999): 519-33; Richard S. Conley, *The Presidency, Congress and Divided Government* (College Station: Texas A&M University Press, 2003); Gary C. Jacobson, "Partisan Polarization in Presidential Support: The Electoral Connection," *Congress and the Presidency* 30, no. 1 (Spring 2003): 1-36; Gary C. Jacobson, "The Bush Presidency and the American Electorate," *Presidential Studies Quarterly* 33 no. 4 (December 2003): 701-29; Burke and Greenstein, *How Presidents.*

252. Bueno de Mesquita, *The War Trap*, 36.

253. John B. Attanasio, "Introduction: Multilateralism, Unilateralism, and Leadership," in Attanasio and Norton, eds., *Multilateralism v Unilateralism*, 19.

254. Bueno de Mesquita, *The War Trap*; Bruce Bueno de Mesquita, "The Contribution of Expected Utility Theory to the Study of International Conflict," in Midlarsky, ed., *Handbook*; Lalman, "Conflict Resolution."

255. Ikenberry, "Is American Multilateralism," 535.

256. Corbetta and Dixon, "Multilateralism, Major Powers," 8; Philip H. Gordon and Jeremy Shapiro, *Allies at War: America, Europe, and the Crisis Over Iraq* (New York: McGraw-Hill, 2004), 33-36.

257. Malone, "A Decade," 21.

258. Stepanova, "The Unilateral and Multilateral," 190.

259. Maynes, "Two Blasts," 36.

260. Ikenberry, "Is American Multilateralism," 538.

261. Robert Kagan, "Power and Weakness," *Policy Review* 113 (June 2002): 4.

262. Benjamin A. Most and Harvey Starr, *Inquiry, Logic and International Politics* (Columbia: University of South Carolina Press, 1989), 43; Fordham, "A Very Sharp Sword," 652.

263. Lukasz Kamienski, "The RMA and War Powers," *Strategic Insight* (September 2003): 2-3; Edward N. Luttwak, "Toward a Post-Heroic Warfare," *Foreign Affairs* 74, no. 3 (May—June 1995): 121; Mueller, "A Review," 85; Konovalov, "Multilateralism," 216.

264. Andrew Bennett, Joseph Lepgold, and Danny Unger, "Burden-Sharing in the Persian Gulf War," *International Organization* 48, no. 1 (Winter 1994): 41, 74.

265. Weitsman, "The High Price."

266. Erik Voeten, "Outside Options and the Logic of Security Council Actions," *American Political Science Review* 95, no. 4 (December 2001): 856.

267. Malone, "A Decade," 33; Clement, "The United States," 403-6.

268. Brooks and Wohlforth, "International Relations," 514.

269. Ikenberry, "Multilateralism," 136.

3

Statistical Tests

U.S. Unilateral Uses of Force since 1937

Introduction

IN THIS CHAPTER, I DETAIL THE HYPOTHESES, data sets, crisis dyad, and dependent, explanatory, and control variables of my research design. In testing my hypotheses, I examine all dispute dyads from 1937 to 1995 using a two-stage bivariate model.[1]

I first continue the arguments from Chapter 2 and use that evidence to formulate my hypotheses. I argue that presidents, making an expected utility calculation, are likely to use force unilaterally given a revolutionized military vis-à-vis an opponent lacking in economic power (i.e., preponderance), military spending (i.e., technology), or not employing or not able to employ its forces consistent with the appropriate military revolution (i.e., force employment). I also believe that presidents are more likely to act unilaterally, when enforcing the Monroe Doctrine or facing a national security crisis.

Second, I review the data sets—Fordham and Sarver's 2001 U.S. Uses of Force data set and the COW Militarized Interstate Dispute (MID) data set—that I use to identify and code the U.S. unilateral use-of-force dyads.[2] These two data sets allow me to identify the crisis dyad and code the use of force, but no data set exists for coding the second decision, the decision to use unilateral force. So, I offer a significant contribution—a decision matrix that allows researchers to code uses of force as unilateral or multilateral to obtain a universally valid unilateral use-of-force definition. The decision matrix allows a historian, social researcher, or novice to consistently define unilateralism as a U.S. use-of-force action without any military ally or political international support.

I next move to my other significant contribution and construct a Composite Indicator of Military Revolutions (CIMR) index as an alternative measure of military power. Both Biddle and Corbetta and Dixon conclude that the traditional CINC score is not an adequate predictor of conflict success.[3] I build on their findings and construct a CIMR index, using accepted measures of military power—preponderance, technology, and force employment. I then list the remaining situational factor and control variables.

For the statistical tests, I detail the assumptions of a maximum likelihood probit model and the models I will be testing in the chapter. I then test and provide estimates from the two separate probit models of the decision process: the decision to use force and the decision to use unilateral force. Next, I detail how a heckman probit model combines the two probit models into a unified model of unilateral decision making. I then discuss the positive results associated with using this sequential model. Finally, to determine the robustness of my unified model, I test an alternative model, using a traditional CINC measure, as well as two control models.

From these empirical results, I discuss their significance and how each of the independent variables fare. In discussing the first decision model, whether or not to use force, I determine that a domestic explanation has little empirical support. But, most importantly, I focus on the unilateral decision and the significant findings of the CIMR index variables, the Americas region variable, and the national security and humanitarian crises variables. In sum, I discuss whether a large-N statistical test reveals that the president is making an expected utility, power-based decision to act unilaterally.

Hypotheses

Using the evidence presented in Chapter 2, I propose an inexorable link between power and unilateral action, based on American hegemony and America's military revolution enabling advantage. The president, using an expected utility calculation, chooses a unilateral force option.[4] Presidents tend to be realists and will rely exclusively on the U.S. military, if a victory can be assured quickly and with minimal costs and as it is necessary to maintain America's governance of the international system.[5] The most significant explanatory factor in a unilateral use-of-force decision should be superior U.S. military power, more specifically a revolutionized military vis-à-vis an opponent.[6]

Military Power

As discussed in Chapter 2, the most appropriate manner to operationalize military revolution, as an alternative measure of military power, is to use its three traditional components—preponderance, technology, and force employment—in a CIMR index. In doing so, I make two assumptions: (1) the president wants to maintain the U.S. position of military dominance and (2) presidents make a unilateral calculation with the goal of "winning" a crisis.

Preponderance

Hegemonic governance is based on power and prestige. The hegemon governs the system in establishing rules that allow it to profit.[7] This is a causal arrow that goes in two directions: a hegemon maintains the stability of the system to reap economic profit and economic profit allows a hegemon to increase its reign over the system.[8] A hegemon must possess both superior economic and military capabilities, and it must be willing to use its military to defeat an opponent that challenges the status quo of the economic system.[9] Based on a "hierarchy of prestige," the hegemon must be willing to use force to defend its economic system and reputation, especially as the gap in material resources widens between it and a challenger. Weak nations cannot be allowed to defy the hegemon's political-economic order.[10]

Hypothesis 1: *A president's decision to use unilateral force will correlate positively with an increasing gap in preponderance between the U.S. and an opponent.*

Technology

Military innovation or technological advancement is associated with hegemonic stability. It is also associated with system dominance, and with the U.S. being at the forefront of technological breakthroughs since the Civil War, it can supply the public good of security unilaterally.[11] As the U.S. fears the relative gains of a technological breakthrough by a challenger, it can also take advantage of a challenger's lack of technological advancement.[12] The greater the technological gap between the U.S. and an opposing nation, the less the opposing nation is able to competently challenge the U.S. Technologically less advanced nations have engaged in conflict with the U.S. (e.g., North Vietnam in 1964 and the Taliban in 2001), and in fact, a military capability advantage may not correlate with victory.[13] But, a president, for better or worse, can still estimate the war capabilities of an opponent with little uncertainty and is likely to choose unilateralism as the gap widens in technologies between the U.S. and the opponent.[14]

Hypothesis 2: *A president's decision to use unilateral force will correlate positively with an increasing gap in technology between the U.S. and an opponent.*

Force Employment

A president calculating how to use force is likely to view an opponent with a military operating on an outdated military paradigm as an easier target for unilateral force. As with a technology gap, the U.S., as a dominant military power, should use innovative military tactics, and if an opponent isn't using innovative tactics, the president should be more willing to act alone and avoid the costs of adding allies.[15]

Hypothesis 3: *Presidents are more likely to use unilateral force, if an opponent is not employing its forces consistent with the appropriate military revolution.*

Situational Factors

Following the Corbetta and Dixon findings and Stepanova presumption detailed in Chapter 2, I also believe situational factors may intervene to affect a president's unilateral decision.[16] Specifically, the U.S. will use unilateral force in enforcing the Monroe Doctrine and when facing a severe crisis (i.e., a national security threat).

Monroe Doctrine

The fundamental goal of rising powers and hegemons is to increase their spheres of influence and territories.[17] In fact, hegemons are likely to defend their spheres of influence at great cost and against great powers, if necessary.[18] To the U.S., the Western hemisphere has been considered its sphere of influence, and presidents may be tempted to act unilaterally against opponents located in the Western hemisphere in order to maintain the status quo.[19] This sphere of influence involves enforcement of the Monroe Doctrine.

The Monroe Doctrine of 1823 informs other nations that the Western hemisphere is to be free from non-U.S. influence, and the U.S. views any violation "as dangerous to [its] peace and safety."[20] The U.S., in turn, vowed to remain neutral in wars between European powers and between European powers and their colonies, unless those colonies were located in the Americas. The Doctrine, while derived independently, succeeded for 100 years because it met British interests and was enforced by the Royal Navy.[21] The UK wanted to prevent France and Spain from colonizing the Americas. So in a sense, for a century, America's right to unilateralism in the Western hemisphere was made possible through the "free security" of the Royal Navy.[22]

But as Joseph Nye writes, the rise of American hegemony and the surpassing of British economic and naval power at the turn of the century resulted in uncontested U.S. leadership of the Western hemisphere. This transition from

British to U.S. power was evident with the U.S. backing Venezuela in its 1895 boundary dispute with British Guiana and the UK appeasing America.[23]

Soon thereafter, the UK formally ceded its naval supremacy in the Caribbean, and the U.S. took additional steps to maintain its hegemony.[24] President Theodore Roosevelt added a Corollary to the Monroe Doctrine, in which the U.S. maintained the right to act as an "international police power" and intervene in Western hemisphere countries. The U.S. would spend the first three decades of the twentieth century sending its troops to the Dominican Republic, Nicaragua, Haiti, and Panama to quell civil disorder and to protect Americans and American interests.[25]

By the 1930s, the U.S. was working to promote more of a multilateral, collective security image. It even agreed to a no forcible intervention agreement with the governments of South American states.[26] But, despite U.S. participation in these Pan American conferences, U.S. agreements were more about advancing its security and less about collective security.[27] The symbolism of a multilateral effort ended with the start of World War II, when the U.S. assumed responsibly for the defense of the hemisphere in a September 1940 "destroyers-for-bases" deal with the UK. In exchange for 50 of its warships, the U.S. gained control of naval stations and airfields in eight British territories that extended a "shield" of American sovereignty from Newfoundland to British Guiana.[28]

After World War II, fear of communism replaced fear of European intervention, and the U.S. aggressively defended the Monroe Doctrine with unilateral force.[29] The Cuban Revolution of 1959, in particular, proved to be a particularly vexing problem for the U.S. The U.S. first sought to overthrow dictator Fidel Castro and then it sought to isolate Cuba and use it as an example to demonstrate the high costs of defying the U.S. to other Western hemisphere countries.[30]

Based on this historical record and given that one of the fundamental goals of a hegemon is to increase its spheres of influence and territories, it can be assumed that a president whether in 1908 or in 2008, will demonstrate the willingness of enforcing the doctrine with unilateral force.[31] This unilateralism should be especially pronounced given the numerous declarations that the U.S. will use unilateral force in the Western hemisphere.[32] In fact, a frequency count illustrates that the U.S. since 1946 has used force unilaterally 24 out of 33 times or 73 percent of the time in the Western hemisphere.

Hypothesis 4: *In accordance with the Monroe Doctrine, presidents are more likely to use unilateral force in the Western hemisphere.*

Crisis Trigger

U.S. unilateral uses of force will correlate positively with severe crisis triggers (i.e., national security threats) and correlate negatively with less severe triggers (i.e., humanitarian interventions). One of the fundamental assumptions of this paper is that presidents are realists, are less concerned about motive, and will use the military to advance and protect U.S. interests.[33] Presidents should act instinctively to national security threats and use the path of least resistance to defend America (i.e., act unilaterally). They should be more calculating for crises (i.e., humanitarian) not vital to national security.

Using unilateral force, when facing a national security threat, should be a necessary condition of being a hegemonic power, and in fact, the U.S. is more likely to act unilaterally than multilaterally when facing a national security threat.[34] Meernik and Waterman find that presidents use force when national security is at stake, and presidents can use military force in national security incidents with little or no negative political effect.[35]

The most significant explanation for a correlation between national security threats and unilateralism may stem from American exceptionalism. Americans, like presidents, are reluctant to rely on international assistance in guaranteeing national security.[36]

Americans have legitimate reasons to be skeptical of allied assistance. From a military perspective, the U.S. military learned from its multilateral Kosovo campaign, lessons which included political constraints, complicated decision making, and marginal allied military capabilities. It then decided to incorporate unilateralism in its strategic doctrine.[37] U.S. strategic doctrine relies on the unmatched military power of the U.S., and its ability to use its intelligence, precision-guided munitions, well-trained armed forces, and global reach capabilities to respond quickly to a threat (i.e., use its RMA advantage). The U.S. military is reluctant to share its strategic and tactical warfare plans with an underwhelming ally for fear collective action will diminish its response capability.[38]

The 9/11 attacks provide an ideal example of the unilateral proclivity of the president, Congress, and the public. After the 9/11 attacks, NATO invoked Article 5 of the NATO Treaty, which regarded the attacks as an attack on all of its members. However, NATO military support was mostly symbolic, as the U.S. military decided to react unilaterally to the asymmetrical attack per its strategic doctrine.[39]

Hypothesis 5a: *Presidents are more likely to use unilateral force when facing a national security crisis.*

As suggested in the "Public Opinion and the Use of Force" subsection in Chapter 2, nations, including the U.S., are reluctant to intervene in humanitarian crises, crises that often involve territorial disputes, ethnic conflicts, civil wars, and the collapse of government authority.[40] Intervention seems to occur only when one of the situations exists as follows: (1) the mission is relatively cheap, (2) against a militarily weak nation, (3) in an accessible and strategic location, (4) supported by public emotion, and (5) does not interfere with other political and economic priorities.[41] Americans, in particular, do not want to use the U.S. military for interventions in less than developed countries and outside the Western hemisphere.[42] They do not want long-term or risky operations (e.g., operations with potentially high casualties).[43]

Bureaucratic obstacles and international criticism also plague both U.S. and UN humanitarian interventions.[44] Humanitarian interventions, often involve violating the sovereignty of another state, and as such, interventions can be criticized as precursors for other strategic interests. James Cockayne and David Malone trace the "creeping unilateralism" of U.S. actions in Iraq from 1991 to 2003.[45] The U.S. initially intervened for humanitarian purposes with its Operation Provide Comfort in 1991, in which the U.S. with ambiguous UN support (Resolution 688) protected the Kurdish refugees in northern Iraq. Operation Provide Comfort led to establishment and enforcement of the no-fly zones in 1991 and 1992, which was tolerated by the Security Council. But, all forms of multilateral legitimacy were shattered in 1998 with Operation Desert Fox and certainly in 2003 with the invasion of Iraq.[46] As such, presidents should be more likely to use multilateral force in a humanitarian crisis to lower the costs and risks.

Hypothesis 5b: *Presidents are less likely to use unilateral force when facing a humanitarian crisis.*

The Data Sets

The U.S. use-of-force dyads are derived from two main sources: Fordham and Sarver's 2001 U.S. Uses of Force data set and the COW data set.[47] These data sets both identify U.S. international crises and both include incidents where violence occurs as well as incidents where threats were made but no violence occurs. Both data sets are ideal for distinguishing between serious threats of force and routine movements of military forces or diplomatic disagreements. The different definitions and coding rules of the data sets allows for robust findings and increased confidence in the analysis.

The Fordham and Sarver data set details 506 incidents involving U.S. uses of force between 1870 and 1995. The data set follows the coding rules of Barry Blechman and Stephen Kaplan's 1978 U.S. Use of Force data set, which defines use of force as "a physical change in the disposition (location, activity, and/or readiness) of some part of the armed forces."[48] Fordham and Sarver, like Blechman and Kaplan, do not aggregate incidents into one dispute, but unlike Blechman and Kaplan, they also include "martial" uses of force, incidents where the U.S. was "physically imposing [its] will" and when "decision makers must have sought to avoid a significant contest of violence."[49]

Perhaps the most extensively used data set in international relations, the COW data set uses wars as its unit of analysis. While it does not have all of the explicit measures unique to this study (e.g., measures at the operational or tactical level, which are necessary to code unilateral uses of force), the unit of analysis, structured along dyadic wars, and its data contents are ideal given the systemic nature of hegemonic theory. The COW MID list, in particular, quantifies a "militarized interstate dispute" as a series of explicit temporal interactions between states involving the threat, display, or actual use of force.[50] Notably, it excludes measures of cooperation or nonmilitary conflict (e.g., trade barriers), and its ordinal scale uses one unit increments to separate each of the conflict steps.[51]

The Crisis Dyad[52]

The Fordham and Sarver data set is ideal for first identifying the crisis dyad, given its adherence to a sequential crisis process, a necessary condition for testing in this book.

Identifying and Coding the Crisis Dyad

In identifying the crisis dyads, I begin by using Fordham and Sarver's "U.S. Uses of Force, 1870-1995" descriptive list to label each "major" U.S. use of force from 1937 to 1995.[53] The "major" uses of force are based on Fordham's coding of Blechman and Kaplan's classifications: (1) use of strategic or theater nuclear unit plus at least one major force component, (2) two or three major force components but not strategic nuclear units, and (3) either one major force component or strategic unit used.[54]

Once I have identified the crisis dyad, I next need to label U.S. action in the crisis dyad as unilateral or multilateral. It is best to start this process using established research, in which there are four broad categories: (1) unilateralism, (2) UN-sponsored multilateralism, (3) three-or-more-state multilateralism, and (4) two-or-more-state multilateralism.[55] The more minimalist, two-state definition operationalizes multilateralism as *procedural* or *operational.*[56]

To fully answer my research question and to use the most demanding test possible, I use the minimalist, two-state definition of multilateralism. Using this minimalist definition of multilateralism allows me to consistently define unilateralism as a U.S. use-of-force action without any military ally (e.g., NATO) or political international support (e.g., UN or OAS). This is a universally accepted definition of unilateralism.[57] Using such a restricted definition also permits greater confidence in the findings.

The best method to define an action as unilateral is to develop coding rules to examine each individual crisis. So, I first develop coding rules based on Martha Finnemore's, Luck's, and Tago's *operational* and *procedural* dimensions.[58] The operational dimension defines multilateralism as military coalitions with unified command and control and joint operational coordination and execution of military operations. The procedural dimension defines multilateralism as the international community's political and diplomatic endorsement, including formal authorization of the U.S. military action. Procedural multilateral events are possible but rare events. The majority of U.S. uses of force are unilateral or operational multilateralism.[59] Per table 3.1, these dimensions can be illustrated in a 2 × 2 table.

As illustrated in figure 3.1, I construct a decision matrix to operationalize these definitions of operational multilateralism, procedural multilateralism, and unilateralism. In quantifying each of the three types of force, I use the crisis dyad as the unit of analysis and examine each incident at the strategic and tactical levels.

I use a variety of historical and data set sources to answer the decision matrix questions. In particular, I use data from the works of Blechman and Kaplan, Philip Zelikow, Richard Grimmett, James Hickey, and William Leary, as well as Fordham and Sarver's "U.S. Uses of Force, 1870-1995" list and Adam Siegel's 1991 "The Use of Naval Forces in the Post-War Era: U.S. Navy and U.S. Marine Corps Crisis Response Activity, 1946-1990" list.[60] I use the answer to these questions—procedural multilateralism, operational multilateralism, or unilateralism—to comprise the *U.S. action* variable.[61]

Table 3.2 is a frequency count of the three crisis data sets (USUFAD, ICB2, and U.S. Uses of Force data set) from table 1.1 broken into full unilateralism, operational multilateralism, procedural multilateralism, and both operational

TABLE 3.1
Dimensions of Unilateral-Multilateral Uses of Force

		Procedural	
		Multilateral	Unilateral
Operational	Multilateral	Political and Military Multilateralism	Military Multilateralism and Political Unilateralism
	Unilateral	Political Multilateralism and Military Unilateralism	Political and Military Unilateralism

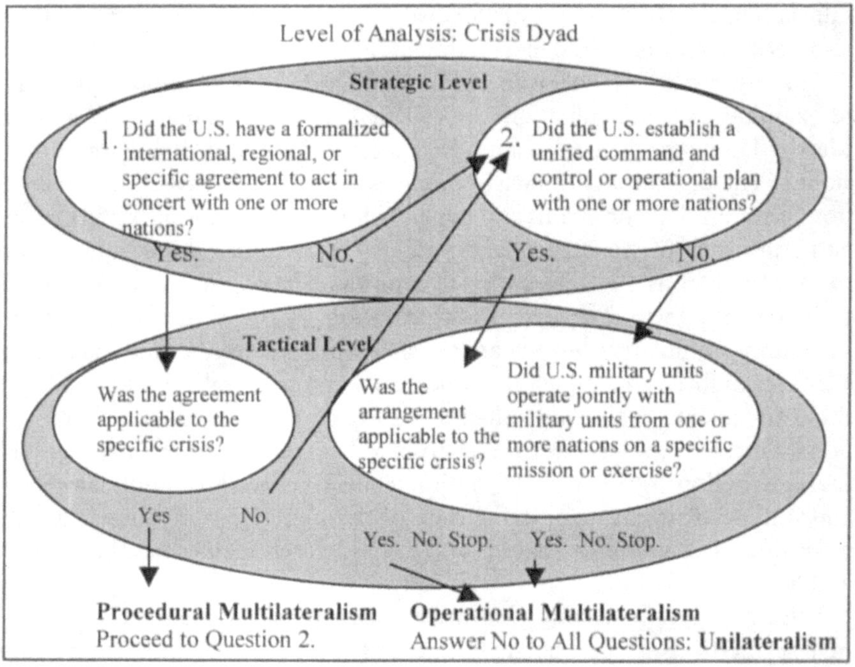

FIGURE 3.1
Decision Matrix for Coding Unilateral/Multilateral Uses of Force

and procedural multilateralism. Notably, the USUFAD reflects Tago's coding rules, while the ICB2 and U.S. Uses of Force data set reflect a frequency using my coding rules. The continued dominance of full unilateralism and the rarity of procedural multilateralism cases is evident in all three data sets.

Dependent Variable

Using the *U.S. action* variable, I construct the dependent variable in two steps, which is consistent with the sequential decision-making assumption of this book. First, I use the COW MID dispute level to code whether military force was used in the crisis. Second, if force was used, I code unilateral incidents from the *U.S. action* variable as a *unilateral* dependent variable.

Use of Force

The Fordham and Sarver data set and its listing of "major" uses of force is a misnomer, as U.S. involvement might not have resulted in an actual military conflict. I need more restrictive post-hoc data that measure the level of conflict;

TABLE 3.2
Frequency Count of Full Unilateral, Procedural Multilateral, and Operational Multilateral Uses of Force

	USUFAD[a]				*ICB2*				*U.S. Uses of Force*			
Years	*U*[b]	*PM*[c]	*OM*[d]	*POM*[e]	*U*	*PM*	*OM*	*POM*	*U*	*PM*	*OM*	*POM*
Interwar Period (1937–1938)	—	—	—	—	1	0	0	0	1	0	0	0
World War II (1939–1945)	—	—	—	—	1	0	2	0	4	0	1	1
Cold War (1946–1990)	141	1	12	12	22	2	11	14	81	7	23	25
Post-Cold War (1991–)	26	0	4	16	4	0	3	4	6	0	0	9
Presidents												
Republican Presidents	82	0	7	13	14	0	7	8	56	4	14	20
Democratic Presidents	85	1	9	15	14	2	9	10	36	3	10	15
Total Crises/Uses of Force	167	1	16	28	28	2	16	18	92	7	24	35

[a] No Data Available for 1937–1945
[b] U = Full Unilateralism
[c] PM = Procedural Multilateralism
[d] OM = Operational Multilateralism
[e] POM = Procedural and Operational Multilateralism

so, I use the Expected Utility Generation and Data Management Program (*EUGene*) software to obtain the COW MID data set's overall hostility level score to code the U.S. involvement.[62]

I code this involvement, *force*, as a dichotomous dependent variable: no force used or force used. I code a one (force used) for a COW MID dispute level (hostlev) of 2 or higher (2 = threat to use force, 3 = display of force, 4 = use of force, 5 = war). For a COW MID dispute level of 1 or lower (0 = no hostility, 1 = no militarized action), I code a zero as no force used. This construction of the Fordham—Cow MID *force* variable adequately accounts for the first stage decision of whether a president decides to use force or not.

Unilateral Use of Force

If the *force* variable is coded one, I use the coding of each crisis dyad (unilateral, procedural multilateralism, or operational multilateralism) to code the *unilateral* dependent variable.[63] If *U.S. action* was procedural multilateralism, operational multilateralism, or both, I code a zero. If *U.S. action* was unilateral, I code a one.

Explanatory Variables

An explanation of a unilateral use-of-force decision consists of two international explanations: military revolutions and situational factors. Military revolutions is comprised of three factors—preponderance, technology, and force employment—that serves as a CIMR index. Situational factors involve variables unique to each crisis dyad: the Monroe Doctrine and the crisis trigger (humanitarian and national security crises).

Military Revolutions

One of the significant contributions of *Acting Alone* is the idea that a military revolution index serves as an alternative to the traditional measure of military capability, the CINC index. In fact, following Biddle's and Corbetta and Dixon's concerns about the inadequacies of the CINC index, I test whether the CINC index correlates with a unilateral/multilateral action.[64] To construct a military revolution variable, I use Biddle's work as a starting point.

Notably, Biddle is a leading critic of the current revolution in military affairs (RMA), but regardless, I agree with Biddle's three categories—preponderance, technology, and force employment—to measure and operationalize military capability.[65] All three are important determinants of battlefield success. As shown in figure 3.2, I believe that military revolutions are measured using these three components.

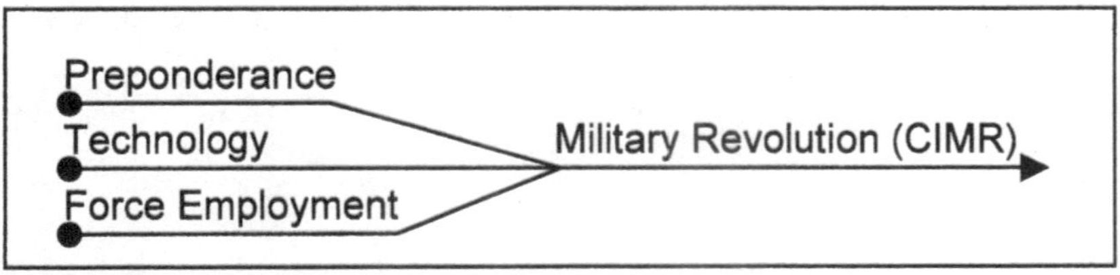

FIGURE 3.2
Components of Military Revolutions

A nation must be willing to spend ample resources on its military, develop and utilize the latest technological innovations, and employ its forces consistent with the operating paradigm. The U.S. has been at the forefront of these military revolutions since the Civil War, and its victories in war and battle is empirical evidence of successful incorporation of these three elements.[66]

Preponderance Gap

One of the most popular and simplest single indicator of military power is Gross National Product (GNP). A.F.K. Organski, Jacek Kugler, and Steven Rosen, among other researchers, prefer a single GNP indicator, as there is a high positive correlation between GNP and the six measures of the CINC score.[67] Given one of the fundamental elements of hegemonic theory (in particular hegemonic stability theory) is economic dominance, the U.S. should maintain a significant gap between it and its potential adversary. Gilpin writes, "It is obvious that there is a generally positive correlation between the material wealth of a society and its military power; wealthier states tend to be more powerful."[68] So, following Biddle, I account for preponderance, based on the assumption that "economic strength is a necessary precondition for military strength."[69]

As Kelly Kadera cites, reliable GNP data suffer from temporal and spatial problems. Reliable GNP information for preindustrial nations and for nations before 1950 is problematic.[70] Based on this, I use annual Gross Domestic Product (GDP) data from Angus Maddison's "World Population, GDP, and Per Capita GDP, 1-2003 AD" data set.[71] I first calculate the U.S. percentage of the world's total GDP:

$$\%\ GDP_{US} = \frac{GDP_{US}}{\Sigma\ GDP_{world}} \qquad [3.1]$$

where:

GDP_{US} is U.S. GDP in millions of dollars (1990) and
$\Sigma\ GDP_{world}$ is the sum of the world's total GDP in millions of dollars (1990).

I then calculate the target country's percentage of the world's total GDP:

$$\% \, GDP_{TargetCountry} = \frac{GDP_{TargetCountry}}{\sum GDP_{world}} \quad [3.2]$$

where:

$GDP_{TargetCountry}$ is the target country's GDP in millions of dollars (1990).

I use the % GDP_{US} and % $GDP_{TargetCountry}$ scores to calculate the *preponderance gap* variable for each unit of analysis:

$$\text{Preponderance Gap}_{CrisisDyad} = \frac{\% \, GDP_{US}}{\% \, GDP_{TargetCountry}} \quad [3.3]$$

Given the lack of GDP data before 1950, I run my model from 1937 to 1995 without a *preponderance gap* variable to determine the significance of the target country force employment, technology gap, and other variables. I then run it from 1950 to 1995 with a *preponderance gap* variable, and the result is a more robust finding.

Technology Gap

In *Win, Lose, or Draw*, Allan Stam writes of the indeterminate role technology plays in war and of the confusing nature of whether a particular weapon favors the offense or defense.[72] He writes, "It is not so much the absolute level of technology present during a war that affects the outcome but rather the relative degree of technical skill and technological investment that the two sides possess."[73] Training and technology are expensive, "approaching the cost of actually fighting a war;" so, a state that spends more on its soldiers should achieve military victories.[74]

Stam, Paul Huth, Scott Bennett, and Christopher Gelpi argue technology can be operationalized as additional spending per soldier, which captures training, equipment, and technology costs.[75] So, I follow their lead and measure technology in the same manner. I use the COW data set to first create a U.S. technology score:

$$\text{Technology}_{US} = \frac{\text{Military Expenditures}_{US}}{\text{Military Personnel}_{US}} \quad [3.4]$$

where:

Military Expenditures_{US} is the total military budget in current year U.S. dollars and

Military Personnel_{US} is the number of personnel in thousands.

I then calculate the technology score for the target country in the same manner:

$$\text{Technology}_{\textit{TargetCountry}} = \frac{\text{Military Expenditures}_{\textit{TargetCountry}}}{\text{Military Personnel}_{\textit{TargetCountry}}} \qquad [3.5]$$

Finally, I calculate the *technology gap* variable based on the technology ratio of the U.S. and the country it is engaged with in a crisis:

$$\text{Technology Gap}_{\textit{CrisisDyad}} = \frac{\text{Technology}_{\textit{US}}}{\text{Technology}_{\textit{TargetCountry}}} \qquad [3.6]$$

Target Country Force Employment[76]

As stated in the argument for a CIMR index, a military must be employing its force on the correct operating paradigm in order to compete on the global stage. While Biddle argues that military actions are less about revolution and more about force employment, I believe, at least from a strategic viewpoint that a nation's military must be prepared to fight a war consistent with the era.[77] Based on the literature, presidents will be wary of using force against an opponent that has transformed its military to meet the existing military paradigm but have fewer reservations about acting unilaterally against a military not using or not possessing the capabilities to use the latest force employment tactics.

The military revolutions that are applicable to the period of study of *Acting Alone* are as follows: (1) land warfare and naval revolutions, (2) mechanization, aviation, and information revolution, (3) nuclear revolution, and (4) the current RMA.[78]

Land Warfare and Naval Revolutions. First, the land warfare and naval revolutions from the mid-nineteenth century to World War I involved railroads, telegraphs, rifled muskets, and metal-hulled ships with turbine engines. Information was transmitted quickly, allowing military forces to concentrate quickly. Defensive trenches became standard as a counter to the murderous volume of fire from machine guns and improved artillery.[79]

Mechanization, Aviation, and Information Revolution. The mechanization, aviation, and information revolution occurred from World War I to World War II. In this revolution, mechanized warfare (e.g., Blitzkrieg) and aircraft carrier warfare became the dominant paradigms for offensive-minded militaries.[80] The use and exploitation of radios and radar made those dominant paradigms possible.[81] Winning wars became "a contest between machines," and this meant keeping ahead of one's opponent in all areas: scientifically, industrially, and economically.[82] So, from 1914 to 1945, I code a one for the target nation if it possessed tanks, aircraft carriers, and/or radar at the start of the crisis.[83]

Nuclear Revolution. The nuclear revolution accompanied the onset of the Cold War. When the U.S. built the first atomic bombs and dropped them on Hiroshima and Nagasaki in August 1945, the nature of warfare changed completely. To John Bolton, U.S. possession of nuclear weapons was "unilateralism in its most compelling form."[84] Nuclear weapons obliterate a potential defense, ensuring a "nuclear balance of terror."[85]

This balance assured that no country could use force to the extreme; so instead, the major powers concentrated on dispersion, which requires wireless communications and the miniaturization of electronics. This quest for electronic innovation resulted in electronic warfare, guided weapons, new military organizations (e.g., U.S. nuclear submarine fleet), and eventually integrated networks of ground, sea, air, and space systems all connected to the "heart" of the network—the command center.[86] So, from 1946 to 1990, I code a one for the target nation if it possessed nuclear weapons at the start of the crisis.[87] The nations, being coded a one, are Russia, China, and Israel. Russia achieved nuclear power status in 1949.[88] China achieved nuclear status in 1964.[89] Israel is alleged to have had nuclear weapons in 1967.[90]

Current RMA. The end of the Cold War signaled the U.S. launch of its current RMA. RMA involves using advanced technologies with a strategy that calls for quick and decisive victory with minimal casualties.[91] More specifically, RMA involves using digital and information technology, sophisticated and automated command and control, and stand-off, precision-strike weapons with synchronized, rapid, global military operations to make quick, simultaneous attacks against an enemy's strategic centers.[92] The U.S. remains at the forefront of this revolution, as most other countries struggle over whether to adapt it.[93]

Most scholars note the overwhelming victory in the 1991 Gulf War as the first evidence of the U.S. military's RMA.[94] For the first time, the U.S. defied the Clausewitzian principles of destroying an enemy's forces first with its strategic "decapitation" air campaign designed to kill or isolate Hussein and force Iraqi forces to withdraw from Kuwait without a ground battle.[95]

The U.S. victory, achieved in 42 days and with only 240 dead, is regarded as "a triumph of concepts and doctrine" with the U.S. employing "revolutionary changes in combat" and bringing "dissimilar weapons of forces" to bear against the Iraqis.[96] Daryl Press finds that superior U.S. technology and training were *each* sufficient conditions for overwhelming victory.[97] The signal from the war was clear, as cited by India's defense minister: "Don't fight the United States unless you have nuclear weapons."[98]

TABLE 3.3
U.S. Battle Deaths in Principal Wars and Selected Military Operations, 1991 to 2009

War/Operation	*Date*	*Battle Deaths*
Operation Desert Shield/Desert Storm (Iraq)	January 16–April 6, 1991	147
Operation Restore Hope/UNOSOM (Somalia)	December 1992–May 1993	29
Operation Uphold Democracy (Haiti)	September 1994–April 1996	4
Operation Allied Force (Kosovo)	March–June 1999	0
Operation Enduring Freedom (Afghanistan)	October 7, 2001–July 4, 2009	482
Operation Iraqi Freedom (Iraq)	March 19, 2003–July 4, 2009	3,451
Total Number of Battle Deaths		4,113

Source: Information from DoD Personnel and Procurement Statistics, http://siadapp.dmdc.osd.mil/personnel/CASUALTY/castop.htm.

The lopsided victory demonstrates the main advantage of RMA: disengaged combat. In disengaged combat, a general can fight the enemy "without ever placing his (or her) forces within range of most enemy weapons."[99] U.S. tanks and helicopters, using new "operational concepts," destroyed Iraqi forces at will from safe distances.[100] Disengaged combat offsets the public's intolerance for risk-taking and casualties in use-of-force decisions, an intolerance often associated with the CNN effect or the media's repeated airing of casualties.[101]

Minimal casualties and superior military capabilities are both necessary conditions for a president's decision to use force.[102] In meeting these conditions, presidents face a paradox: use superior U.S. military technology, training, and skills to wage campaigns alone or work with the international community. For presidents, quick and low cost victories are essential because "only decisive results are worth having," and with RMA, presidents, as illustrated in table 3.3, can achieve unilateral military victory in minimal time and at minimal cost with overwhelming strategic and tactical advantages against an adversary.[103]

So, from 1991 to the present, I code a one for the target nation if its military had global reach capability and it possessed a disengaged combat capability (e.g., cruise missiles or Unmanned Combat Air Vehicles) at the start of the crisis.[104]

Situational Factors

An international explanation of unilateralism requires operationalizing the following factors: (1) Monroe Doctrine and (2) crisis triggers.

Monroe Doctrine

As discussed, the U.S. should maintain its main sphere of influence, the Western hemisphere, unilaterally. The *americas region* is an explanatory variable to test the Monroe Doctrine. A U.S. opponent located in the Americas (or Western hemisphere) is coded a one and the other regions, Europe, Middle East, Africa, and Asia are coded zero. The Western hemisphere countries tested in this chapter are as follows: Cuba, Haiti, Dominican Republic, Guatemala, Panama, Nicaragua, Grenada, and El Salvador.

Crisis Triggers: National Security, Regime Change, and Humanitarian[105]

Following Patrick James and Oneal's 1991 finding that the severity of crisis is important, I also account for the type of crisis.[106] Using the same historical and data set sources as used in "The Crisis Dyad" section and as illustrated in figure 3.3, I code a crisis as a national security, regime change, or humanitarian event.

Control Variables

An explanation of unilateralism also requires inclusion of control variables, in particular those that offer a domestic explanation. For my control variables, I include factors that account for domestic, international, and target characteristic explanations. For domestic factors, I include the following variables:

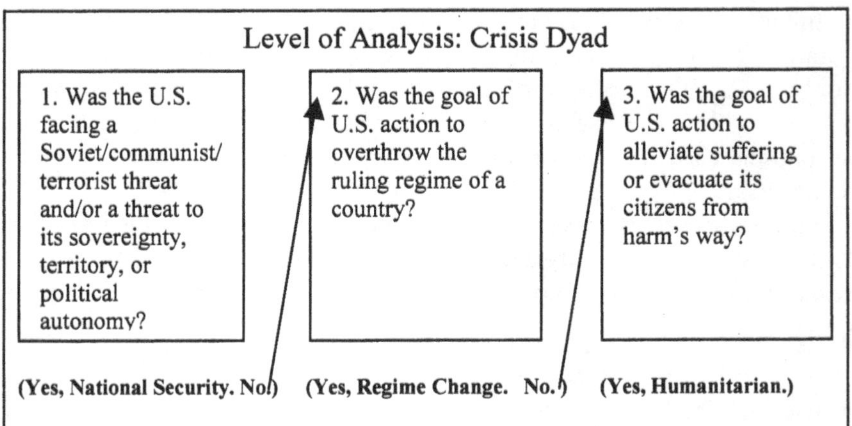

FIGURE 3.3
Decision Matrix for Coding of Crisis Triggers

(1) president's approval rating, (2) public support for force, (3) misery index, (4) divided government, and (5) Republican or Democrat president. For international factors, I include a Cold War and initiator variable. For target characteristic factors, I include the following variables: (1) relative capabilities, (2) rivalry, (3) regime type, and (4) alliance.

Domestic Factors

As stated in the opening paragraphs of *Acting Alone*, the ultimate decision for a president is whether or not to use U.S. military force. Recent research discounts a realist black box approach to explaining state behavior; instead, it emphasizes a domestic political influence on the decision to use force *or* not to use force.[107] This domestic-based explanation needs to be included as a control, and in including domestic variables, I use the variables of earlier research.[108]

For a set of domestic controls, I include the following variables: (1) a divided government measure, (2) a misery index score, (3) president's approval rating, (4) a Republican or Democrat president measure, and (5) public support for force. Presumably, presidents may seek to boost their approval ratings by using force abroad, especially if they are suffering from low ratings and/or a high misery index.[109] Or, the public may "order" a politically weak president (held to follow the whims of the public) to use force.[110]

The *divided government* variable accounts for the possibility that if the opposing party controls Congress, a president may have a more difficult time using unilateral force.[111] A divided government is identified with a one and a unified government with a zero. The *misery index* score, obtained from the U.S. Bureau of Labor Statistics and the U.S. Census Bureau, is a summation of unemployment and inflation.[112] The *president's approval rating* variable, based on Gallup poll data, assumes that a president's approval rating is directly linked to military intervention, casualties, and U.S. prestige and results abroad.[113] The *Republican president* quantifies possible partisan use-of-force decisions with Republican presidents coded one and Democrats zero.[114]

The *public support* variable requires a more complex operationalization in order to reflect the level of American public support for the use of military force in response to an international crisis.[115] I construct the *public support* variable using Gallup poll data.[116] In searching the opinion poll data, I used keyword searches, such as *military*, *force*, *troops*, and the name of the target nation that the U.S. faced in a crisis. I only used polls that preceded a president's use-of-force decisions, and not post hoc evaluations that measure opinion after the president decided to use force.

In using these polls that preceded a president's decision to use force, I rely on two types of polls questions. First, I use questions that ask respondents about a specific crisis and whether or not force should be used. For example, when Germany invaded France in World War II, the Gallup organization asked the following question in May 1940, "What (should the United States do if Germany defeats England and France)?" Seven percent responded: "U.S. should get into it now, should not let the Allies get defeated, fight, help the Allies" and 2 percent responded: "Declare war on Germany, go to war with Germany." So, I code a 9 percent approval rating for using U.S. force against the Germans for the 1940 English-U.S. crisis dyad in the Fordham—COW MID data set.

Second, if the former question was not available, I use questions that ask respondents speculative questions about situations that may occur. If the situation occurs within five years of the speculative question, I use the question given that it is the most recent poll. For example, the Gallup organization asked the following question in January 1969, "If a situation like Vietnam were to develop in another part of the world, do you think the U.S. should or should not send troops?" Twenty-five percent of the respondents thought the U.S. "should" send troops; so, I use this 25 percent and generalize to the 1973 Laos-U.S. and Cambodia-U.S. crisis dyads in the Fordham—COW MID data set.

International Factors

The second set of variables accounts for characteristics of the international system. The *Cold War* variable identifies the period from January 1949 to December 1991 (marking both the banning of the Communist Party in Russia and the formal independence of the Soviet Republics). The Cold War period is coded with a one, and the pre- and post-Cold War period is coded with a zero. A president may have been less likely to use force for fear of a tit-for-tat response from the Soviets.

The *initiator* variable accounts for the fact that a president may be responding to an opponent's aggressive act or he may be taking the initiative against an opponent.[117] A president responding to a crisis is probably more likely to use force. The variable, taken from the COW MID data set (orig), codes a one for the initiator or originator of the crisis and a zero otherwise.

Target Characteristics

The third set of variables accounts for characteristics of the target. I first include the traditional measure of power, the CINC index, based on the capabilities literature. I use the target capabilities and relative capabilities for one of my control models.[118] The *target capabilities* is simply the CINC score of the target country. The *relative capabilities* of the U.S. and its opponent are derived from the CINC index as follows:

$$\text{Relative Capabilities}_{\mathit{CrisisDyad}} = \frac{\text{CINC}_{\mathit{US}}}{\text{CINC}_{\mathit{TargetCountry}}} \quad [3.7]$$

For my *rival* variable, I use James Klein, Goertz, and Diehl's 2004 New Rivalry data set, and I specify the U.S. opponent in the crisis dyad as a rival or not a rival.[119] Goertz and Diehl define rivalries as "a relationship in which both sides deal with issues using the military tools of foreign policy."[120] Conflicts between the rivals must be understood within a historical context of conflicts and should not be weighed as independent events. The "interconnection of disputes" explains the initiation of conflict among rivals, and it provides the basis for understanding how a side bargains during a conflict.[121] If a rival is forced into a bargaining situation with the U.S., then it makes a decision to escalate according to strategic considerations.[122] A rival's strategic choice is based on its anticipation of subsequent U.S. behaviors.[123]

Losing a conflict may not shorten a president's tenure in office, but appeasing a rival does.[124] In an established dyadic rivalry, threats and force are common methods of dealing with the conflict, in which previous crises lead to subsequent crises.[125] Dovish leaders that the public views as granting unreciprocated concessions to a rival are likely to be punished politically.[126] In these cases, presidents need to understand the "interconnection of disputes" with a rival, how the U.S. military is used as a show of strength and resolve, and then not give the perception of backing down.[127]

Crises with rivals are more likely to lead to military actions, and so I include rivalry as a control variable in the first stage decision to use force. I code a one for U.S. rivals, which are listed in table 3.4.[128]

The democratic peace theory needs to be taken into account with a *regime type* variable. Democratic peace theory, in which democracies rarely, if at all, fight each other, has become a lawlike theory in international relations.[129] In particular, scholars find that democracies are more willing to negotiate with one another, rather than fight given the potential high costs.[130] Thus, a *regime type* variable is included as a control, taken from Monty Marshall and Keith Jaggers's 2002 Polity IV democracy-autocracy data set.[131] This variable is coded along an ordinal scale with ten being the strongest democracy and negative ten being the strongest autocracy.

Bueno de Mesquita, in *The War Trap*, examines the crucial component of third parties.[132] He concludes it is not a third party's capabilities that matter to a leader's risk attitude, rather it is the value of these third parties that matter.[133] In general, a third party needs to be considered as potentially having an

TABLE 3.4
U.S. Rivalries

Rival	*Years*
Canada	1974–1997
Cuba	1912–1934; 1959–1996
Nicaragua	1909–1926; 1982–1988
Ecuador	1952–1981
Peru	1955–1992
Czechoslovakia	1953–1961
Yugoslavia/Serbia	1992–2000
Bulgaria	1941–1951
Romania	1940–1951
Russia/USSR	1918–1920; 1946–2000
Libya	1970–1996
Iran	1979–1997
Iraq	1987–2001
Egypt	1956–1973
Syria	1970–1996
China	1926–1972
North Korea	1950–2000
North Vietnam	1961–1973

impact on a crisis: if other states join the target nation, the potential increased military capability may influence a president's use-of-force calculation. Thus, an *alliance* variable for the target is included and is coded along an ordinal scale (1=defense pact, 2=neutrality, 3=entente, 4=no agreement). The scores are operationalized as a dummy variable with a defense pact being coded one and zero otherwise.[134]

Statistical Tests

So far, I have formulated hypotheses, detailed two prominent data sets, and offered coding rules and sources for my dependent, explanatory, and control variables. In particular, I offered the details of my book's three most significant contributions: (1) coding rules that allow for a universally valid unilateral definition and dependent variable; (2) construction of a CIMR index based on measures of preponderance, technology, and force employment; and (3) data sets that support a sequential decision model that predicts and explains a president's unilateral decision.

Next, I use a heckman probit model to test a president's use-of-force decision and his unilateral use-of-force decision as a sequential process. I explain why a maximum likelihood procedure is necessary for testing the two decisions, and

I offer models of the two decisions. For my results, I detail the marginal impact of each variable on separate probit models (the decision to use force and the decision to use unilateral force) and on the unified model of unilateral use-of-force decision making. I then focus on the unilateral decision findings and the significance of the military revolution and situational explanations.

The Probit Framework

Given the dichotomous dependent variables utilized in this book, I use a non-linear model. I code a one for a decision to use force (and zero otherwise) for the first stage decision, and I code a one for a unilateral use-of-force decision (and zero otherwise) for the second stage decision. Specifically, I use a maximum likelihood estimation (MLE) procedure. MLE consists of estimating the parameters so as to increase (or maximize) the probability of observing the dependent variable.[135] In using MLE, I have two available models, logit and probit, that I can use to estimate the probability that a president will choose to act unilaterally, given the hegemonic power of the U.S.

The first is a logit model, which has the following form:

$$\text{Pr (unilateral use of force decision)} = \frac{1}{1 + e^{-(\beta 0 + \beta 1 X\,\mathrm{I})}} \qquad [3.8]$$

where:

e is the base of the natural logarithm and

$\beta 0 + \beta 1 X\mathrm{I}$ are the independent variables in the equation being estimated.

The second is a probit model, which has the following form:

$$\text{Pr (unilateral use of force decision)} = \Phi\,(\beta 0 + \beta 1 X\,\mathrm{I}) \qquad [3.9]$$

where:

Φ is the cumulative distribution function of the standard normal distribution and

$\beta 0 + \beta 1 X\mathrm{I}$ are the independent variables in the equation being estimated.

Both the logit and probit specifications produce "qualitatively similar results" with "no compelling reason" to select one over the other.[136] The conditional probability of reaching a zero or one is slower with logit, and researchers tend to favor it for its mathematical simplicity.[137] But, given that I will be using a heckman probit model, I use a probit model for consistency.

Statistical Models

In examining how a president employs U.S. uses of force from 1937 to 1995, I use the international crisis as the unit of analysis, a design that negates many temporal aggregation and dynamics problems.[138] For the first decision, I simply use the variables of Charles Ostrom and Brian Job, James and Oneal, Karl DeRouen, Fordham, and David Brule and Alex Mintz to control for a use-of-force decision.[139] This decision favors a domestic-based decision, while controlling for other significant findings (e.g., rivalry and democratic peace theory) as explained earlier in this chapter and in Chapter 2. The use-of-force decision model is as follows:

Model: force (force or no force) = A + β1*misery index* + β2*presidential approval* + β3*republican president* + β4*public support* + β5*initiator* + β6*target regime type* + β7*rival* + β8*cold war* + β9*alliance* + εi [3.10]

As explained in the "A New Model of Unilateral Use-of-Force Decision Making" section in Chapter 2, I model a president's decision as a sequential process with emphasis on the second decision of whether to use unilateral or multilateral force. As hypothesized, the *technology gap*, *preponderance gap*, *americas region*, and *national security crisis* variables should be positively correlated with unilateral force, while the *target force employment*, and *humanitarian crisis* variables should be negatively correlated with unilateral force. The unilateral use-of-force decision model is as follows:

Model: unilateral (unilateral force or multilateral force) = A + β1*target force employment* + β2*technology gap* + β3*preponderance gap* + β4*americas region* + β5*national security crisis* + β6*humanitarian crisis* + β7*divided government* + εi [3.11]

To test the robustness of the full model, it is necessary to see how some alternative models fare.[140] First, I replace the CIMR index variables with the CINC score, measured with a *relative capabilities* and a *target capabilities* variable.[141] The alternative unilateral use-of-force decision model is as follows:

Model: unilateral (unilateral force or multilateral force) = A + β1*relative capabilities*/ β1*target capabilities* + β2*americas region* + β3*national security crisis* + β4*humanitarian crisis* + β5*divided government* + εi [3.12]

Next, given the possibility of high correlation between GNP and the CINC scores as cited in the "Preponderance Gap" subsection of this chapter, it is best to run separate models using only the *preponderance gap* variable in one model and only the *technology gap* variable in the other model.[142] The control unilateral use-of-force decision models are as follows:

Model: unilateral (unilateral force or multilateral force) = A + β1*target force employment* + β2*preponderance gap* + β3*americas region* + β4*national security crisis* + β5*humanitarian crisis* + β6*divided government* + εi [3.13]

Model: unilateral (unilateral force or multilateral force) = A + β1*target force employment* + β2*technology gap* + β3*americas region* + β4*national security crisis* + β5*humanitarian crisis* + β6*divided government* + εi [3.14]

Empirical Results

The results of the statistical tests are illustrated in tables 3.5-3.12.[143] Overall, the results lend strong support to an international, power-based explanation of U.S. unilateralism as detailed in Chapter 2.

Predicting Use-of-Force Decisions

Per table 3.5, I first perform probit regression analyses on the data from 1937 to 1995 and from 1950 to 1995, using the *force* dependent variable derived from the Fordham—COW MID data sets. This is a test of the use-of-force model in equation 3.10. For this model (and with all of the other models), I use robust standard errors to correct for "clustering" or inconstant variation across dyad groups (i.e., panel data). The results offer little support for a domestic-based decision to use force and bolster a realist, international explanation.

In fact, only the target characteristic and international factor variables are significant. An opponent being a rival, an opponent being in a defense pact, and the Cold War is significant for both data sets. Interestingly, the *regime type* variable are significant for the 1937 to 1995 data (and insignificant but also in the wrong direction for the 1950 to 1995 data).[144]

Given the nonlinear nature of MLE coefficients, using the coefficients to determine how the dependent variables changes, as is done with ordinary least squares (OLS) analysis, would be erroneous. Rather, the proper method to determine the strength of the coefficients is to use a technique called marginal effects. Calculating the marginal effect an independent variable has on the

TABLE 3.5
Probit Models. U.S. Crises, Fordham (2001) – COW MID Data Set: Probit Estimates with Robust Standard Errors Adjusted for Clustering on Dyads

	1937–1995		*1950–1995*	
Variable	*Force*	*Unilateral*	*Force*	*Unilateral*
Misery Index	0.039		0.016	
	(0.067)		(0.085)	
Presidential Approval	0.005		−0.001	
	(0.019)		(0.023)	
Democrat or Republican President	0.297		0.389	
	(0.418)		(0.509)	
Public Support for Force	0.007		0.003	
	(0.006)		(0.010)	
Initiator	†		†	
Regime Type	0.041***		0.011	
	(0.015)		(0.022)	
Rival	3.013***		2.796***	
	(0.540)		(0.520)	
Cold War	−1.300**		−1.052*	
	(0.586)		(0.697)	
Alliance	1.407***		1.548***	
	(0.553)		(0.583)	
Target Country Force Employment		−0.852**		−1.434***
		(0.372)		(0.449)
Preponderance Gap				−0.000*
				(0.000)
Technology Gap		0.586		1.958***
		(0.499)		(0.772)
Americas Region		0.509**		0.542***
		(0.232)		(0.210)
National Security Crisis		0.069		−0.152
		(0.366)		(0.373)
Humanitarian Crisis		0.154		−0.219
		(0.592)		(0.635)
Divided Government		−0.156		0.036
		(0.311)		(0.320)
Constant	−1.745	0.111	−1.411	0.157
	(1.640)	(0.470)	(1.904)	(0.498)
N	120	142	107	125
Wald Chi-Square(df)	90.89(8)	13.94(6)	69.57(8)	24.18(7)
Log Pseudo Likelihood (full)	−36.586908	−93.382897	−32.009596	−79.823647
Pseudo R2	0.5291	0.0312	0.5361	0.0595
Prob > Chi-Square	0.000	0.0303	0.000	0.0011

Note: Numbers in parentheses are standard errors. *p < .10; **p < .05; ***p < .01 (one-tailed tests)
† This variable predicts failure perfectly and is dropped (see text).

dependent variables requires holding all of the independent variables minus one constant at their mean. The marginal impact of each predictor variable can then be determined.

As illustrated in table 3.6, the impact of the *rival*, *alliance*, and *cold war* variables on the decision to use force is dramatic. Moving the rival variable from zero (no rivalry) to one (rivalry) increases the probability of a president using force by 84.9 percent (1937 to 1995) and 82.9 percent (1950 to 1995). The impact of the rival variable supports the findings of Goertz and Diehl and Michael Colaresi and William Thompson.[145] Presidents are more prone to use force against rivals, perhaps wanting to avoid paying a political price for appearing to appease them.

The probability of a president using force against an opponent with an alliance increases by 49.2 percent and 54.6 percent, respectively. This is an interesting but not unexpected finding, given the conclusions of several researchers. A president may make the decision to use force based on the unreliable nature of alliances, as Woosang Kim and James Morrow argue.[146] Or, the president may believe the contribution of alliance members will be "irrelevant," as Malone argues about NATO's capabilities in the 2001 Afghanistan campaign.[147] Or, as Bueno de Mesquita concludes, a president may simply not include third party's capabilities as a significant factor in his decision making.[148] Regardless of the reason, presidents do not seem to consider an opponent's possible increased allied strength as a deterrent.

The probability of a president using force during the Cold War decreases by 47 percent and 39 percent, respectively. Presidents seemed less likely to use force during the Cold War, possibly fearing a response from the Soviets. This supports neorealism and the stability of a bipolar world.[149] It contributes to the notion that an international, not domestic (or even state level) analysis explains state behavior and conflict.[150] The significance of the Cold War effect is also compatible with the unilateral use-of-force decision-making theory because the U.S., as hegemon, had reached an equilibrium position necessary to maintain its governance of the system. As a result, there was less challenge to its authority and less conflict, but the U.S., if it used force, still tended to use it unilaterally.

As an opponent's autocratic-democratic score moves from low to high (i.e., the opponent becomes more democratic), the probability of a president using force increases by a marginal 1.2 percent for the 1937 to 1995 data. This tempers the significance of the *regime type* variable. As Corbetta and Dixon suggest, regime type may pertain to dyads, but it does not affect "monadic decisions to take part in disputes."[151] Moreover, the significance of regime type can be further marginalized due to the fact that democratic peace findings largely pertain to dyadic movements from non-crisis to crisis, which is not a focus of this book.

TABLE 3.6
Marginal Effects of Independent Variables on Decision to Use Force

	1937–1995				*1950–1995*			
Variable	*Min. Value*	*Max. Value*	*Std. Dev.*[a]	*% Change*	*Min. Value*	*Max. Value*	*Std. Dev.*	*% Change*
Misery Index	3	20.2	3.838	0.012	3	20.2	3.790	0.005
Presidential Approval	24	82	12.161	0.002	24	79	11.845	−0.000
Dem. or Rep. Pres.	0	1	0.493	0.087	0	1	0.474	0.118
Public Support	3	82	19.534	0.002	3	82	18.877	0.001
Initiator	0	1	0.413	—	0	1	0.417	—
Regime Type	−10	10	19.161	0.012	−10	10	12.521	0.004
Rival	0	1	0.500	0.849	0	1	0.501	0.829
Cold War	0	1	0.334	−0.470	0	1	0.291	−0.390
Alliance	0	1	0.418	0.492	0	1	0.430	0.546

[a] Standard Deviation for a dichotomous variable is misleading, given the variable can only be one of two values.

Predicting Unilateral Use-of-Force Decisions

Per table 3.5, I perform probit regression analyses with correction for clustering on the dyads on the data from 1937 to 1995 and from 1950 to 1995, using the *unilateral* dependent variable derived from the Fordham—COW MID data sets. The data from 1950 to 1995 is tested using the unilateral use-of-force model in equation 3.11, but a lack of GDP data precludes using a *preponderance gap* variable in testing the data from 1937 to 1995.[152] The results offer support for a power-based decision to use unilateral force.

In the full model for both time periods, *target country force employment* and *americas region* are significant and in the expected direction. *Technology gap* is significant and in the expected direction for the 1950 to 1995 data and in the expected direction for the 1937 to 1995 data. Interestingly, *preponderance gap* is significant in the wrong direction, and it seems to have little, if any, effect on a president's unilateral decision.

As illustrated in table 3.7, as an opponent's force employment moves from low to high, the probability of a president using unilateral force against that opponent decreases by 32.7 percent (1937 to 1995 data) and by 49.5 percent (1950 to 1995 data). This is strong support for Biddle's finding and his argument that force employment is a significant, yet overlooked, third measure of military power.[153] The simplicity of the operationalization of force employment in this book, coded a one if a nation possessed the capability to use the latest technological innovations, bridges the gap between Biddle's more sophisticated measure and the realist mistake of assuming that force is employed optimally.[154]

If the opponent is in the Western hemisphere, the probability of unilateral force increases by 18.8 percent and 19.8 percent, respectively. This is strong support for the Monroe Doctrine. It suggests that realists should follow the Corbetta and Dixon, Stepanova, and James and Oneal lead and better delve into the details of an international explanation for uses of force.[155] The specifics of the situation are often overlooked in realist doctrine as realists assume a unitary actor model and uniform responses to conflicts (i.e., a use-of-force response can be calculated based on a combination of U.S. interests and capabilities).[156] Rather, the Meernik and Waterman finding that "peculiarities" of the crisis is important should be reflected in future realist studies.[157]

For every one unit change in the *technology gap* variable, the probability of unilateral force increases by 22.8 percent and 75.9 percent. This is strong support for Stam and his belief that the dyadic technological balance is what determines the outcome of a conflict.[158] Presidents, perhaps, in deciding to act unilaterally or multilaterally against a technologically weak opponent may use past multilateral campaigns as *the* reason to act unilaterally, given the problems of burden-sharing, inaction, collaboration and cooperation, and reciprocity. Multilateral arrangements mean increased transaction costs and with technologically

TABLE 3.7
Marginal Effects of Independent Variables on Decision to Use Unilateral Force

	1937–1995				*1950–1995*			
Variable	*Min. Value*	*Max. Value*	*Std. Dev.*[a]	*% Change*	*Min. Value*	*Max. Value*	*Std. Dev.*	*% Change*
Target Country Force Employ.	0	1	0.245	−0.327	0	1	0.233	−0.495
Preponderance Gap	—	—	—	—	2.349	6462.287	675.743	−0.000
Technology Gap	0.000	2.696	0.301	0.228	0.000	1.238	0.190	0.759
Americas Region	0	1	0.409	0.188	0	1	0.417	0.198
National Security Crisis	0	1	0.418	0.027	0	1	0.430	−0.058
Humanitarian Crisis	0	1	0.276	0.059	0	1	0.281	−0.086
Divided Government	0	1	0.490	−0.060	0	1	0.481	0.014

[a] Standard Deviation for a dichotomous variable is misleading, given the variable can only be one of two values.

ill-prepared allies, a president may simply decide to act unilaterally against an opponent that does not spend resources on its military.[159]

There are two perplexing results, involving the *preponderance gap* and the crisis trigger variables, that suggest a separate probit model may not be accurately capturing a president's unilateral decision.[160] A shift in the preponderance gap has zero percent effect on a president's unilateral decision. The zero percent effect means presidents are not considering the economic strength of an opponent before acting unilaterally. Wealthier states may equate with a stronger military, as Gilpin believes, but the gap may be so wide between U.S. GDP and an opponent's GDP that it doesn't factor into a president's calculation.[161]

The crisis trigger also does not seem to matter as presidents are more likely to use unilateral force in the 1937 to 1995 period and less likely to use unilateral force in the 1950 to 1995 period, regardless if it is a national security or humanitarian crisis. This does not entirely discount an international explanation for a unilateral use-of-force decision (a president may still be making a power-based calculation regardless of the situation), but it is an issue to study further with the unified model.

The Heckman Probit Model

The foundation of this book is the assertion that a president's decision to use unilateral force is a subset of the use-of-force decision. A unilateral use-of-force observation cannot be made without first observing a use-of-force decision. This means the separate probit models (table 3.5) are theoretically incorrect, as they assume two separate, unrelated decisions are being made. The heckman probit model, on the other hand, controls for this interdependent relationship between use of force and how force is used and avoids selection effects.[162] In short, it is ideal given the nature of the two-stage, discrete-choice panel data.[163]

The necessity of a selection model can be understood pragmatically. Presidents do not use force randomly, and they do not blindly select unilateral or multilateral force. They instead use a strategic decision process and choose to use force and how to employ force based on a series of factors. Eisenhower's decision *not* to use force at Dien Bien Phu offers a prime example of a decision that is coded a zero for the selection equation (i.e., the use-of-force decision), and Bush's decision to use multilateral force in the 1991 Gulf War is coded a one for the selection equation and a zero for the unilateral use-of-force decision (i.e., the outcome equation).

It is best to illustrate the estimations of heckman probit model by beginning with the two separate bivariate probit models:

$$y_1^* = X_1\beta_1 + u_1 \qquad [3.15]$$

$$y_2^* = X_2\beta_2 + u_2 \qquad [3.16]$$

where:

y_1^* is the decision to use force,
y_2^* is the decision to use unilateral force, and
u is the error term.

Normally, the assumption is that the two probit models are independent of one another, so that $\text{Cov}[u_1, u_2] = 0$. But, the unilateral use-of-force decision model assumes the two models are related:

$$\text{Cov}[u_1, u_2] = \rho \qquad [3.17]$$

where:
ρ is the correlation parameter denoting the extent that the error terms covary.

Based on these assumptions, I can estimate the following probabilities:

Selection equation

$$y_1 = 0 \qquad \Pr(y_1 = 0) = \Phi(-X_1\beta_1) \qquad [3.18]$$

Outcome equation

$$y_1 = 1, y_2 = 0 \qquad \Pr(y_1 = 1, y_2 = 0) = \Phi(X_1\beta_1) - \Phi_2(X_1\beta_1, X_2\beta_2, \rho) \qquad [3.19]$$

$$y_1 = 1, y_2 = 1 \qquad \Pr(y_1 = 1, y_2 = 1) = \Phi_2(X_1\beta_1, X_2\beta_2, \rho) \qquad [3.20]$$

where:

$\Phi(X_1\beta_1)$ is the univariate standard normal cumulative distribution function and
$\Phi_2(X_1\beta_1, X_2\beta_2, \rho)$ denotes the bivariate standard normal cumulative distribution function with correlation coefficient ρ.

The log-likelihood function can then be formulated as follows:

$$\log L = \sum_{i=1}^{N}\{y_{i1}y_{i2}\log \Phi_2(X_1\beta_1, X_2\beta_2; \rho) + y_{i1}(1 - y_{i2})\log[\Phi(X_1\beta_1) - \Phi_2(X_1\beta_1, X_2\beta_2; \rho)] + (1 - y_{i1})\log \Phi(-X_1\beta_1)\} \qquad [3.21]$$

Empirical Results of the Unified Model

First, it is best to see how well a unilateral use-of-force decision can be associated with a use-of-force decision.[164] The ancillary parameter rho measures the correlation of the residuals from the two models (equations 3.10 and 3.11). As illustrated in table 3.8, the two equations for the 1937 to 1995 data are strongly associated, rho = 1, which is significant (chi-square = 6.34, df = 1, p =.01). The two equations for the 1950 to 1995 data are also strongly associated, rho = 1, which is significant (chi-square = 13.11, df = 1, p =.00). This suggests a president's use-of-force decision is related to his unilateral use-of-force decision.

So, using a heckman probit model corrects for problems unrecognized in the separate probit models. Notably, the *preponderance gap* and *national security crisis* trigger variables are in the wrong direction or insignificant in the separate models, but both variables are significant and in the expected direction in the unified model. This demonstrates that a president is using preponderance as a measure and is factoring in the type of crisis in his unilateral decision.

As an additional test of the robustness of the unified model, I want to test the positive correlation between use-of-force and unilateral decisions (i.e., the sequential nature of the model); so, I reverse the model. I test the unilateral model as the selection equation (equation 3.11) and the force model as the outcome equation (equation 3.10). Perhaps, a president decides to act unilaterally and then decides to use force?

I perform a heckman probit regression analysis with correction for clustering on the dyads on the data from 1950 to 1995, using the *force* dependent variable derived from the Fordham—COW MID data sets.[165] I must exclude using a *humanitarian crisis* and *initiator* variable to test the data. First, in the unilateral model (equation 3.11), the *americas region* variable is the only significant variable in the expected direction. For the force model (equation 3.10), the *cold war*, *rival*, and *misery* variables are significant and in the expected direction.[166] Most importantly, the two equations are strongly negatively associated, rho = -1, which is significant (chi-square = 121.44, df = 1, p =.00). Common unmeasured factors are affecting the outcomes of the two equations in an opposite manner: use-of-force decisions are negatively correlated with unilateral decisions.

All of this reinforces the central foundation of this book, that unilateral use-of-force decision making is a sequential process, and that the heckman probit is the most appropriate model to use. Given this, I now examine the unified model results.

Predicting Unilateral Use-of-Force Decisions

Per table 3.8, I perform heckman probit regression analyses with correction for clustering on the dyads on the data from 1937 to 1995 and from 1950 to 1995, using the *unilateral* dependent variable derived from the Fordham—COW MID data sets. The data from 1950 to 1995 is tested using the unilateral use-of-force model in equation 3.11. But, as I did in the separate probit unilateral use-of-force decision analysis, I must exclude using a *preponderance gap* variable to test the data from 1937 to 1995. The results for both data time periods offer strong support for a power- and international-based unilateral use-of-force decision.

First, in the force model (equation 3.10), the *rival* and *alliance* variables are the only significant variables for both data time periods, signaling that presidents decide to use force based on a target's characteristics and not necessarily based on domestic factors.[167] Though it should be noted that the *initiator* variable is significant for the 1937 to 1995 data, indicating presidents are more likely to use force when responding to a dispute initiator. Also, the *public support* variable is significant for the 1937 to 1995 data, indicating presidents are likely to use force if the public is clamoring for force to be used. The *regime type* variable is significant in the wrong direction as it was for the 1937 to 1995 probit model.

Though I believe the *regime type* variable results can be marginalized as discussed in the table 3.5 and 3.6 results, the wrong direction of the *regime type* variable and its incompatibility with the democratic peace theory deserves further analysis. Following the Corbetta and Dixon belief that regime type does not affect monadic decisions, I believe that rivalry may be confounding the results.[168] As such, I conduct sensitivity analysis on the *rival* variable. In 73 out of the 157 crisis dyads (1937 to 1995) and in 65 out of 140 crisis dyads (1950 to 1995), the U.S. faced a rival. This seems to have a great impact on the results, and if the *rival* variable is excluded from the unified model, both the *presidential approval* and *regime type* variables are signed in the expected direction. The former is significant and is consistent with the diversionary hypotheses, in which presidents are more likely to use force as their approval rating declines.[169] Though insignificant, the *regime type* variable is negative, which is consistent with democratic peace theory.

For the unilateral model (equation 3.11) using data from 1937 to 1995, the *target country force employment*, *technology gap*, *americas region*, and *national security crisis* variables are significant and in the expected direction. For the 1950 to 1995 model (equation 3.11), the *target country force employment*, *preponderance gap*, *technology gap*, and *national security crisis* variables are significant and in the expected direction.[170]

TABLE 3.8
Unified Model. U.S. Crises, Fordham (2001) – COW MID Data Set: Heckman Probit Estimates with Robust Standard Errors Adjusted for Clustering on Dyads

	1937–1995		*1950–1995*	
Variable	*Force*	*Unilateral*	*Force*	*Unilateral*
Misery Index	0.069		0.019	
	(0.066)		(0.080)	
Presidential Approval	0.018		0.011	
	(0.018)		(0.026)	
Democrat or	0.111		0.352	
Republican President	(0.364)		(0.391)	
Public Support for Force	0.010***		0.004	
	(0.004)		(0.009)	
Initiator	7.328***		8.828	
	(0.522)		(.)	
Regime Type	0.037***		−0.007	
	(0.009)		(0.021)	
Rival	2.972***		2.554***	
	(0.488)		(0.414)	
Cold War	−0.641*		0.800**	
	(0.460)		(0.475)	
Alliance	1.216**		1.282***	
	(0.533)		(0.525)	
Target Country Force		−1.057***		−4.796***
Employment		(0.364)		(2.033)
Preponderance Gap				0.001**
				(0.001)
Technology Gap		0.192*		6.874**
		(0.132)		(3.207)
Americas Region		0.783***		0.200
		(0.281)		(0.389)
National Security Crisis		0.315***		0.668***
		(0.114)		(0.266)
Humanitarian Crisis		0.059		†
		(0.821)		
Divided Government		−0.098		−0.108
		(0.463)		(0.487)
Constant	-3.346*	−0.453	-3.844**	−1.480***
	(2.072)	(0.368)	(2.312)	(0.572)
N		150		134
Wald Chi-Square(df)		. (4)		. (6)
Log Pseudo Likelihood (full model)		−76.73777		−62.45884
Rho		1		1
Wald Test of Ind. Equations:				
Chi-Square (df)		6.34(1)		13.11(1)
Prob > Chi-Square		0.0118		0.0003

Note: Numbers in parentheses are standard errors. *p < .10; **p < .05; ***p < .01 (one-tailed tests)
† This variable predicts failure perfectly and is dropped (see text).

As illustrated in table 3.9, two of the three CIMR index variables have a significant impact on a president's unilateral decision.[171] As an opponent's force employment moves from low to high, the probability of a president using unilateral force decreases by 34.1 percent (1937 to 1995) and by 11.7 percent (1950 to 1995). For every one unit change in the *technology gap* variable, the probability of unilateral force increases by 7.6 percent and 92.5 percent, respectively. This is a strong indication that allocating more resources to the military and using innovative tactics and technology does correlate positively with unilateral action. As proposed in Chapter 2, the fact that the U.S., as hegemon, remains at the forefront of military revolutions should be viewed synonymously with unilateral action. Gilpin is correct in stating that "a novel military weapon or technique" can be the impetus for unilateral military force.[172] Quite simply, presidents act unilaterally because they have the military power advantage to do so.

But, as the situational factors demonstrate, presidents use quite more discretion in using unilateral force than realists may give them credit. If the opponent is located in the Western hemisphere, the probability of unilateral force increases by 30.3 percent and 2.9 percent. If the crisis involves national security, the probability of unilateral force increases by 12.2 percent and 6.9 percent, and if it is a humanitarian crisis, the probability of unilateral force decreases by 57.6 percent for the 1950 to 1995 period. The substantive effects of these explanatory variables does support realist doctrine that presidents will act unilaterally to protect U.S. interests and national security, but it sheds more light on the particulars of their decision. As stated before, the Meernik and Waterman finding that "peculiarities" of the crisis are important deserves a more prominent place in realist doctrine.[173]

For the alternative model (equation 3.12 and table 3.10), *americas region* and *national security crisis* are the only unilateral decision variables to attain statistical significance and be signed in the expected direction for all of the models. The *target capabilities* variable is also significant for both time periods.[174] Of the force variables, the *rival*, *cold war*, and *alliance* variables are significant for all of the models. A president seems more likely to use force against a rival and an allied opponent and less likely to use force during the Cold War.

The *relative capabilities* variable is in the expected direction for both time periods, but it fails to attain statistical significance. It also has minimal, if any, impact on a president's decision.[175] This is not good news for international relations researchers that blindly rely on the CINC score as a proxy for military power.

The *target capabilities* variable does attain statistical significance and is in the expected direction for both time periods. For every one unit change in an

TABLE 3.9
Marginal Effects of Independent Variables on Decision to Use Unilateral Force

	1937–1995				*1950–1995*			
Variable	*Min. Value*	*Max. Value*	*Std. Dev.*[a]	*% Change*	*Min. Value*	*Max. Value*	*Std. Dev.*	*% Change*
Target Country Force Employ.	0	1	0.245	−0.341	0	1	0.233	−0.117
Preponderance Gap	—	—	—	—	2.349	6462.287	675.743	0.000
Technology Gap	0.000	2.696	0.301	0.076	0.000	1.238	0.190	0.925
Americas Region	0	1	0.409	0.303	0	1	0.417	0.029
National Security Crisis	0	1	0.418	0.122	0	1	0.430	0.069
Humanitarian Crisis	0	1	0.276	0.023	0	1	0.281	−0.576
Divided Government	0	1	0.490	−0.039	0	1	0.481	−0.015

[a] Standard Deviation for a dichotomous variable is misleading, given the variable can only be one of two values.

TABLE 3.10
CINC Models. U.S. Crises, Fordham (2001)—COW MID Data Set: Heckman Probit Estimates with Robust Standard Errors Adjusted for Clustering on Dyads

	1937–1995				*1950–1995*			
Variable	*Force*	*Unilateral*	*Force*	*Unilateral*	*Force*	*Unilateral*	*Force*	*Unilateral*
Misery Index	0.047		0.041		0.016		0.024	
	(0.052)		(0.055)		(0.074)		(0.081)	
Presidential Approval	0.011		0.011		0.004		0.008	
	(0.016)		(0.015)		(0.026)		(0.028)	
Democrat or Republican Pres.	0.228		0.231		0.371		0.340	
	(0.343)		(0.336)		(0.433)		(0.430)	
Public Support for Force	0.012***		0.010**		0.007		0.006	
	(0.005)		(0.006)		(0.009)		(0.009)	
Initiator	6.993***		9.382***		8.459		9.077	
	(0.569)		(0.765)		(.)		(.)	
Regime Type	0.043***		0.040***		0.012		0.012	
	(0.010)		(0.010)		(0.022)		(0.021)	
Rival	3.127***		3.122***		2.885***		2.904***	
	(0.512)		(0.524)		(0.478)		(0.486)	
Cold War	−1.267***		−1.133***		−1.125*		−1.195*	
	(0.367)		(0.358)		(0.733)		(0.745)	
Alliance	1.438***		1.455***		1.547***		1.549***	
	(0.500)		(0.512)		(0.555)		(0.562)	

Relative Military Capabilities		0.001				0.001		
		(0.002)				(0.002)		
Target Capabilities				−4.388**				−3.771*
				(2.604)				(2.609)
Americas Region		0.756***		0.668**		0.796***		0.651**
		(0.080)		(0.310)		(0.248)		(0.307)
National Security Crisis		0.474*		0.420**		0.746**		0.471**
		(0.335)		(0.243)		(0.422)		(0.219)
Humanitarian Crisis		0.371		0.278				†
		(0.985)		(1.081)				
Divided Government		0.138		0.087		0.325		0.299
		(0.301)		(0.298)		(0.296)		(0.287)
Constant	−2.391*	−0.899***	−2.370*	−0.559**	−1.747	−1.217**	−1.945	−0.719**
	(1.712)	(0.337)	(1.706)	(0.318)	(2.077)	(0.553)	(2.192)	(0.434)
N		154		154		138		138
Wald Chi-Square(df)		. (4)		212.38(5)		16.73 (4)		. (3)
Log Pseudo Lik. (full)		−81.84425		−80.35563		−72.42885		−71.11561
Rho		1		1		1		1
Wald Test Ind. Eq.:								
Chi-Square (df)		1.43(1)		1.38(1)		0.06(1)		0.00(1)
Prob > Chi-Square		0.2318		0.2407		0.8129		0.9609

Note: Numbers in parentheses are standard errors. *p < .10; **p < .05; ***p < .01 (one-tailed tests)
† This variable predicts failure perfectly and is dropped (see text).

opponent's CINC score, the probability of unilateral force decreases by 173.8 percent (1937 to 1995) and 69.3 percent (1950 to 1995). This finding is compatible with *Acting Alone*'s power calculation: the stronger an opponent, the less likely a president is to use unilateral force against it. But, the inconsistencies with the *relative capabilities* variable suggests a CINC score may not be a good fit for measuring military power.

The mixed results of the CINC variables gives greater credence to using the CIMR index variables. The table 3.10 results also help to illustrate the conflicting findings of the military capability literature: findings that fail to identify a positive correlation between military power advantage and outcome success, but identify democracies and "overwhelming preponderance" with equating to conflict success and less conflict in general.[176]

Testing the correlation between the preponderance and technology gap variables (table 3.11) reveals that there is some correlation. While the gap and target country preponderance and technology variables are not correlated, the U.S. technology and preponderance variables are highly correlated.

For the control models (equations 3.13 and 3.14) of table 3.12, the *target country force employment* and *americas region* variables are significant and in the expected direction. For the preponderance gap model, the *preponderance gap* variable is insignificant and in the wrong direction. For every one unit change in the *preponderance gap* variable, the probability of unilateral force increases by zero percent. For the technology gap model, the *technology gap* variable attains statistical significance and is in the expected direction. For every one unit change in the *technology gap* variable, the probability of a president using unilateral force increases by 7.6 percent.

These control model results are consistent with the results from the unified model, suggesting that technology and preponderance (i.e., elements of CINC and GDP) should be viewed as separate measures. The *technology gap* variable in both the unified and control models is capturing the fact that increased spending per soldier matters to a president in his unilateral decision making. The *preponderance gap* variable, on the other hand, is significant in

TABLE 3.11
Correlation Tests of Technology/Preponderance Variables

	Technology Gap
Preponderance Gap	−0.1962
	Target Country Technology
Target Country Preponderance	−0.0418
	U.S. Technology
U.S. Preponderance	0.9683

TABLE 3.12
Technology/Preponderance Gap Models. U.S. Crises, Fordham (2001)– COW MID Data Set: Heckman Probit Estimates with Robust Standard Errors Adjusted for Clustering on Dyads

	Preponderance Gap (1950–1995)		*Technology Gap (1937–1995)*	
Variable	*Force*	*Unilateral*	*Force*	*Unilateral*
Misery Index	0.028		0.069	
	(0.083)		(0.066)	
Presidential Approval	0.008		0.018	
	(0.028)		(0.018)	
Democrat or Republican President	0.345		0.111	
	(0.429)		(0.364)	
Public Support for Force	0.006		0.010***	
	(0.009)		(0.004)	
Initiator	7.744		7.328***	
	(.)		(0.522)	
Regime Type	0.012		0.037***	
	(0.022)		(0.009)	
Rival	2.907***		2.972***	
	(0.485)		(0.488)	
Cold War	−1.180*		−0.641*	
	(0.765)		(0.460)	
Alliance	1.545***		1.216**	
	(0.567)		(0.533)	
Target Country Force Employment		−0.945***		−1.057***
		(0.243)		(0.364)
Preponderance Gap		−0.000		
		(0.000)		
Technology Gap				0.192*
				(0.132)
Americas Region		0.717***		0.783***
		(0.281)		(0.281)
National Security Crisis		0.406		0.315***
		(0.336)		(0.114)
Humanitarian Crisis		†		0.059
				(0.821)
Divided Government		0.304		−0.098
		(0.316)		(0.463)
Constant	−1.982	−0.675*	-3.346*	−0.453
	(2.244)	(0.453)	(2.072)	(0.368)
N		138		150
Wald Chi-Square(df)		. (4)		. (4)
Log Pseudo Likelihood (full model)		−70.47202		−76.73777
Rho		1		1
Wald Test of Ind. Equations:				
Chi-Square (df)		. (1)		6.34(1)
Prob > Chi-Square				0.0118

Note: Numbers in parentheses are standard errors. *p < .10; **p < .05; ***p < .01 (one-tailed tests)
† This variable predicts failure perfectly and is dropped (see text).

one of the unified models and thus deserves a place in the CIMR index, but its non-impact on a president's unilateral decision deserves further study. The variable may be capturing the fact that the U.S. acts unilaterally against less economically powerful countries, in general, but economic factors do not affect a president's decision.

Conclusion

A realist-based explanation for U.S. crisis behavior is strongly supported with the statistical tests of this chapter. International factors not only explain a president's unilateral decision, but they seem also to better explain a president's initial decision to use force. Domestic political factors, in contrast, do not seem to play a significant role in a president's use-of-force decision. As a result, these findings offer strong support for a unified model of unilateral use-of-force decision making.

All of this is in line with the central tenet of *Acting Alone*—presidents, when deciding to use unilateral force, act unilaterally based on a power calculation. Presidents decide to act as the military revolution gap, comprised of force employment and technology, widens between the U.S. and an opponent. While preponderance plays a role in U.S. unilateralism, its impact seems marginal. Presidents are also inclined to consider the situation, whether an opponent is in the Western hemisphere and whether the crisis is national security.

The use-of-force decision sets the stage for the unilateral decision. In 77 of 157 incidents (1937 to 1995) and 69 of 140 incidents (1950 to 1995), the crisis escalated to a use-of-force situation. As has been stated, researchers have largely ignored the unilateral decision, assuming it to be a suboptimal choice, and when they have conducted research on multilateralism, they have failed to model the process sequentially. The result has been to miss the interdependence between a use-of-force and a unilateral decision.

In Chapter 4, I open up the black box of realism and conduct an experiment to better understand the impact of the crisis trigger on a president's unilateral decision. The empirical world (and common sense) dictates that presidents do not blindly make a unilateral force calculation based on military capability alone. But, instead the crisis trigger, an international factor, may be implicitly reflecting how much the president (and domestic audience) values the stakes in a crisis. The lower the stakes, the more likely the president is to want to lower the costs and act multilaterally, and his decision may be based on public opinion, as reviewed in the "Unilateralism: An Ambivalent Public" subsection of Chapter 2. Given this, I test the extent to which the American public can influence a president trying to determine whether to use unilateral force in responding to a national security threat, bringing about a regime change, or intervening in a humanitarian crisis.

Notes

1. 1995 is the end date of the Benjamin Fordham, "U.S. Uses of Force, 1870-1995," Benjamin Fordham Homepage, 2001, http://bingweb.binghamton.edu/~bfordham/list.pdf (August 8, 2009) descriptive list.
2. Benjamin O. Fordham and Christopher C. Sarver, "Militarized Interstate Disputes and United States Uses of Force," *International Studies Quarterly* 45, no. 2 (September 2001): 455-66; Daniel Jones, Stuart A. Bremer, and J. David Singer, "Militarized Interstate Disputes, 1816-1992: Rationale, Coding Rules, and Empirical Patterns," *Conflict Management and Peace Science* 15, no. 2 (Fall 1996): 163-213; D. Scott Bennett and Allan C. Stam, III, "*EUGene*: A Conceptual Manual," *International Interactions* 26, no. 2 (2000): 179-204.
3. Stephen Biddle, *Military Power: Explaining Victory and Defeat in Modern Battle* (Princeton, N.J.: Princeton University Press, 2004); Renato Corbetta and William J. Dixon, "Multilateralism, Major Powers, and Militarized Disputes," *Political Research Quarterly* 57, no. 1 (March 2004): 5-14.
4. Bruce Bueno de Mesquita, *The War Trap* (New Haven, Conn.: Yale University Press, 1981); Bruce Bueno de Mesquita, "The Contribution of Expected Utility Theory to the Study of International Conflict," in *Handbook of War Studies*, ed. Manus I. Midlarsky (Boston: Unwin Hyman, 1989); David Lalman, "Conflict Resolution and Peace," *American Journal of Political Science* 32, no. 3 (August 1988): 590-615; James D. Morrow, "A Rational Choice Approach to International Choice," in *Decision Making on War and Peace: The Cognitive-Rational Debate*, eds. Nehemia Geva and Alex Mintz (Boulder, Colo.: Lynne Rienner Publishers, 1997).
5. RFD, "Unilateral and Multilateral Options in the Execution of Foreign Policy," *International Organization* 23, no. 3 (Summer 1969): 641-754; Richard N. Haass, "Military Force: A User's Guide," *Foreign Policy* 96 (Autumn 1994): 21-37; Lukasz Kamienski, "The RMA and War Powers," *Strategic Insight* (September 2003): 1-5; Robert Gilpin, *War and Change in World Politics* (New York: Cambridge University Press, 1981), 32-34.
6. An unavoidable problem is the fact that the U.S. rarely faces a strong opponent (i.e., a small gap as measured in terms of preponderance, technology, or force employment). This is a potential criticism, and it is perhaps the main reason why presidents are acting unilaterally a majority of the time. However, there is enough variation to allow statistical tests, and this issue does not affect the experiment and case studies chapters.
7. Gilpin, *War and Change*, 28-35.
8. Gilpin, *War and Change*, 34, 37, 139.
9. Gilpin, *War and Change*, 129, 145.

10. Gilpin, *War and Change*, 31-32.

11. Gilpin, *War and Change*, 60, 145.

12. Robert Gilpin, "The Theory of Hegemonic War," *Journal of Interdisciplinary History* 18, no. 4 (Spring 1988): 612.

13. See Zeev Maoz, "Resolve, Capabilities, and the Outcomes of Interstate Disputes, 1816-1976," *Journal of Conflict Resolution* 27, no. 2 (June 1983): 195-229; Frank W. Wayman, J. David Singer, and Gary Goertz, "Capabilities, Allocations, and Success in Militarized Disputes and Wars, 1816-1976," *International Studies Quarterly* 27, no. 4 (December 1983): 497-515.

14. Bueno de Mesquita, *The War Trap*, 36.

15. Gilpin, *War and Change*, 60.

16. Corbetta and Dixon, "Multilateralism, Major Powers"; Ekaterina Stepanova, "The Unilateral and Multilateral Use of Force by the United States," in *Unilateralism and U.S. Foreign Policy: International Perspectives*, eds. David M. Malone and Yuen Foong Khong (Boulder, Colo.: Lynne Rienner, 2003).

17. Gilpin, *War and Change*, 37, 146, 187.

18. Peter J. Hugill, "The American Challenge to British Hegemony, 1861-1947," *Geographical Review* 99, no. 3 (July 2009): 403-25.

19. Gelson Fonseca, Jr., "The United States and Latin America: Multilateralism and International Legitimacy," in Malone and Khong, eds., *Unilateralism*, 321; Donald W. Meinig, *The Shaping of America: A Geographical Perspective on 500 Years of History, Volume 4: Global America, 1915-2000* (New Haven, Conn.: Yale University Press, 2004), 319.

20. James D. Richardson, *Compilation of the Messages and Papers of the Presidents*, Volume 2 (New York: Bureau of National Literature, 1907), 287.

21. David C. Hendrickson, "Preemption, Unilateralism, and Hegemony: The American Tradition?," *Orbis* 50, no. 2 (Spring 2006): 279.

22. Arthur M. Schlesinger, Jr., "Unilateralism in Historical Perspective," in *Understanding Unilateralism in American Foreign Relations*, ed. Gwyn Prins (London: Royal Institute of International Affairs, 2000), 19.

23. Joseph S. Nye, Jr., "The Changing Nature of World Power," *Political Science Quarterly* 105, no. 2 (Summer 1990): 185.

24. Meinig, *The Shaping*, 331.

25. Meinig, *The Shaping*, 319.

26. Hendrickson, "Preemption," 281.

27. Meinig, *The Shaping*, 324-25.

28. Meinig, *The Shaping*, 333-35.

29. Larman C. Wilson, "The Monroe Doctrine, Cold War Anachronism: Cuba and the Dominican Republic," *Journal of Politics* 28, no. 2 (May 1966): 322; Carlos Gibson and Celso Pastor, "American Regionalism and the United Nations," *Annals of the American Academy of Political and Social Science* 360 (July 1965): 120-24.

30. Meinig, *The Shaping*, 384. See Chapter 5 for the Bay of Pigs case study.

31. Gilpin, *War and Change*, 37, 146, 187; Howard J. Wiarda and Lana L. Wylie, "New Challenges in U.S. Foreign Policy," in *Comparative Foreign Policy: Adaptation*

Strategies of the Great and Emerging Powers, ed. Steven W. Hook (Upper Saddle River, N.J.: Prentice-Hall, 2002), 16.

32. Fonseca, "The United States"; Wilson, "The Monroe Doctrine"; Hendrickson, "Preemption"; Wiarda and Wylie, "New Challenges"; Gibson and Pastor, "American."

33. See Barry M. Blechman and Stephen S. Kaplan, *Force Without War: U.S. Armed Forces as a Political Instrument* (Washington, D.C.: The Brookings Institution, 1978); Philip Zelikow, "The U.S. and the Use of Force: A Historical Summary," in *Democracy, Strategy and Vietnam: Implications for American Policymaking*, eds. George K. Osborn, Asa A. Clark IV, Daniel J. Kaufman, and Douglas E. Lute (Lexington, Mass.: Lexington Books, 1987).

34. Kanti Bajpai, "U.S. Nonproliferation Policy After the Cold War," in Malone and Khong, eds., *Unilateralism*, 17.

35. James Meernik and Peter Waterman, "The Myth of the Diversionary Use of Force by American Presidents," *Political Research Quarterly* 49, no. 3 (September 1996): 573-90; Giacomo Chiozza and H.E. Goemans, "International Conflict and the Tenure of Leaders: Is War Still 'Ex Post' Inefficient," *American Journal of Political Science* 48, no. 3 (July 2004): 604-19; Bradley Lian and John R. Oneal, "Presidents, the Use of Military Force, and Public Opinion," *Journal of Conflict Resolution* 37, no. 2 (June 1993): 277-300.

36. See RFD, "Unilateral"; Haass, "Military Force"; John Mearsheimer, "The False Promise of International Institutions," *International Security* 19, no. 3 (Winter 1994-1995): 5-49; Henry Kissinger, *Does America Need a Foreign Policy? Toward a Diplomacy for the 21st Century* (New York: Simon & Schuster, 2001); Joseph S. Nye, Jr., *Understanding International Conflict: An Introduction to Theory and History*, 4th ed. (New York: Longman, 2003); Thomas M. Franck and Nigel S. Rodley, "After Bangladesh: The Law of Humanitarian Intervention by Military Force," *American Journal of International Law* 67, no. 2 (April 1973): 275-305.

37. Sophia Clement, "The United States and NATO: A Selective Approach to Multilateralism," in Malone and Khong, eds., *Unilateralism*, 404.

38. Clement, "The United States," 404.

39. Clement, "The United States," 403.

40. A. Helton, "Reaction and Inattention Within the U.S. Government," in *Multilateralism v Unilateralism: Policy Choices in a Global Society*, eds. John B. Attanasio and Joseph J. Norton (London: The British Institute of International and Comparative Law, 2004), 121.

41. Christine Chinkin, "The State That Acts Alone: Bully, Good Samaritan or Iconoclast?," *European Journal of International Law* 11, no. 1 (2000): 37.

42. Bruce M. Russett and Miroslav Nincic, "American Opinion on the Use of Military Force Abroad," *Political Science Quarterly* 91, no. 3 (Autumn 1976): 430; Mark Duffield and Joe Stork, "Bosnia is the Classic Case of Using Humanitarian Aid as a Smokescreen to Hide Political Failure," *Middle East Report* 187/188 (March—June 1994): 20.

43. Peter Viggo Jakobsen, "National Interest, Humanitarianism or CNN: What Triggers UN Peace Enforcement after the Cold War?," *Journal of Peace Research* 33,

no. 2 (May 1996): 213; Alex de Waal and Rakiya Omaar, "Can Military Intervention Be 'Humanitarian?'," *Middle East Report* 187/188 (March—June 1994): 3; Mark Duffield and John Prendergast, "Sovereignty and Intervention after the Cold War: Lessons from the Emergency Relief Desk," *Middle East Report* 187/188 (March—June 1994): 9-10; Haass, "Military Force," 36.

44. See Helton, "Reaction."

45. James Cockayne and David Malone, "Creeping Unilateralism: How Operation Provide Comfort and the No-Fly Zones in 1991 and 1992 Paved the Way for the Iraq Crisis of 2003," *Security Dialogue* 37, no. 1 (March 2006): 123-41.

46. Cockayne and Malone, "Creeping Unilateralism," 123.

47. Fordham and Sarver, "Militarized Interstate"; Jones, Bremer, and Singer, "Militarized Interstate"; Bennett and Stam, "*EUGene.*"

48. Stephen S. Kaplan and Barry M. Blechman, *Political Uses of the United States Armed Forces, 1946-1976* [computer file] (Ann Arbor, Mich.: Inter-university Consortium for Political and Social Research, 1978); Fordham and Sarver, "Militarized Interstate," 457.

49. Fordham and Sarver, "Militarized Interstate," 460, 462-63.

50. Charles S. Gochman and Zeev Maoz, "Militarized Interstate Disputes, 1816-1976," *Journal of Conflict Resolution* 28, no. 4 (December 1984): 587.

51. It needs to be noted that an ordinal scale does not allow a researcher to be sure of "how much more severe" each step a nation takes is: Kelly M. Kadera, *The Power-Conflict Story: A Dynamic Model of Interstate Rivalry* (Ann Arbor: The University of Michigan Press, 2001), 122-23.

52. A president's decision to enter a crisis is a step in the decision-making process preceding the decision to use force, and I believe I control for this decision with my *initiator* variable (i.e., the decision to initiate a crisis). Out of the potential 6,961 US-opponent dyads from 1937 to 1995, 202 dyads resulted in a MID with 150 of the MID dyads having a score of 2 or higher. The US was an originator 113 out of 150 times. This frequency count supports James Fearon's point that presidents "select themselves" into a crisis based on their ranking of relative capabilities and interests vis-à-vis an opponent: James D. Fearon, "Domestic Political Audiences and the Escalation of International Disputes," *American Political Science Review* 88, no. 3 (September 1994): 586. So, I believe the decision to be involved in a crisis and the decision to use force are closely related but separate, distinct decisions: William Reed, "A Unified Model of Conflict Onset and Escalation: Capabilities, Democracy, and Status Quo Evaluations," *American Journal of Political Science* 44, no. 1 (January 2000): 84. By focusing on just the decision to use force and the decision to use unilateral force, I am attempting to control for selection effects. In other words, tracing a president's decision to enter a crisis, to use force, and then to use unilateral force would be too complex to model, as explaining the behavior of 92 unilateral dyads out of 6,961 total dyads would omit too many explanatory variables.

53. The descriptive list (Fordham, "U.S. Uses") can be obtained from Fordham's website at http://bingweb.binghamton.edu/~bfordham/list.pdf (August 8, 2009). The descriptive list is pulled from Fordham and Sarver's 2001 data set (Fordham and Sarver, "Militarized Interstate"), which is available online at http://bingweb

.binghamton.edu/~bfordham/data.html (August 8, 2009). The Fordham and Sarver data set is a compilation of the descriptive list, which is based on the research of many authors including the following: Richard Grimmett, *Instances of Use of United States Armed Forces Abroad, 1798-2004* (Washington, D.C.: Congressional Research Service, 2004); Harry Alanson Ellsworth, *One Hundred Eighty Landings of United States Marines, 1800-1934* (Washington, D.C.: History and Museums Division, Headquarters, United States Marine Corps, 1934; reprint, Washington, D.C.: History and Museums Division, Headquarters, United States Marine Corps, 1974); Milton Offutt, *The Protection of Citizens Abroad by the Armed Forces of the United States* (Baltimore: Johns Hopkins University Press, 1928); Blechman and Kaplan, *Force Without War*; Zelikow, "The U.S."; Benjamin O. Fordham, "The Politics of Threat Perception and the Use of Force: A Political Economy Model of U.S. Uses of Force, 1949-1994," *International Studies Quarterly* 42, no. 3 (September 1998): 567-90.

54. Fordham, "The Politics," 585. Using only the top three levels of force allows for the exclusion of routine troop movements and incidents of ambiguous political significance: Benjamin O. Fordham, "Partisanship, Macroeconomic Policy, and U.S. Uses of Force, 1949-1994," *Journal of Conflict Resolution* 42, no. 4 (August 1998): 426.

55. See Robert O. Keohane, "Multilateralism: An Agenda for Research," *International Journal* 45 (Autumn 1990): 731-64; G. John Ikenberry, "Is American Multilateralism in Decline?," *Perspectives on Politics* 1, no. 3 (September 2003): 533-50; John G. Ruggie, "Multilateralism: The Anatomy of an Institution," *International Organization* 46, no. 3 (Summer 1992): 561-98; Corbetta and Dixon, "Multilateralism, Major Powers"; Christopher Ashby, "Multilateralism vs. Unilateralism: Principle or Policy?," in Attanasio and Norton, eds., *Multilateralism*; Stepanova, "The Unilateral"; Atsushi Tago, "Determinants of Multilateralism in US Use of Force: State of Economy, Election Cycle, and Divided Government," *Journal of Peace Research* 42, no. 5 (September 2005): 585-604.

56. See Tago, "Determinants of Multilateralism."

57. John B. Attanasio, "Introduction: Multilateralism, Unilateralism, and Leadership," in Attanasio and Norton, eds., *Multilateralism*, 14; Ashby, "Multilateralism," 42; Tago, "Determinants of Multilateralism," 587; Ikenberry, "Is American Multilateralism," 547; Malone and Khong, eds., *Unilateralism*. It should be noted that a lack of consensus plagues the unilateral definition debate. Institutionalists argue that non-UN actions, U.S. defection from institutions and norms, and even regional organization actions are unilateral: see Daniel Bodansky, "What's So Bad about Unilateral Action to Protect the Environment?," *European Journal of International Law* 11, no. 2 (2000): 339-47; Cockayne and Malone, "Creeping Unilateralism"; Pierre-Marie Dupuy, "The Place and Role of Unilateralism in Contemporary International Law," *European Journal of International Law* 11, no. 1 (2000): 19-29; Nico Krisch, "Unilateral Enforcement of the Collective Will: Kosovo, Iraq, and the Security Council," *Max Planck Yearbook of United Nations Law* 3 (1999): 59-103; Alan Pellet, "Brief Remarks on the Unilateral Use of Force," *European Journal of International Law* 11, no. 2 (2000): 385-92; Philippe Sands, "American Unilateralism," *Proceedings of the American Society of International Law Annual Meeting* 96 (2002): 85-94; W. Michael Reisman, "Unilateral Action and the Transformations of the World Constitutive

Process: The Special Problem of Humanitarian Intervention," *European Journal of International Law* 11, no. 1 (2000): 3-18; W. Michael Reisman and Scott Shuchart, "Unilateral Action in an Imperfect World Order," in Attanasio and Norton, eds., *Multilateralism*; John G. Ruggie, "Multilateralism: The Anatomy of an Institution," *International Organization* 46, no. 3 (Summer 1992): 561-98; Ruth Wedgwood, "NATO's Campaign in Yugoslavia," *American Journal of International Law* 93, no. 4 (October 1999): 828-34. Realists have a more minimalist, the U.S. acting alone, as a definition of unilateralism: Tago, "Determinants of Multilateralism," 587; Ikenberry, "Is American Multilateralism," 547; Malone and Khong, eds., *Unilateralism*, 3.

58. Martha Finnemore, "Military Intervention and the Organization of International Politics," in *Collective Conflict Management and Changing World Politics*, eds. Joseph Lepgold and Thomas G. Weiss (Albany: State University of New York Press, 1998); Edward Luck, "The United States, International Organization, and the Quest for Legitimacy," in *Multilateralism and US Foreign Policy: Ambivalent Engagement*, eds. Stewart Patrick and Shepard Forman (Boulder, Colo.: Lynne Rienner, 2002); Tago, "Determinants of Multilateralism."

59. Tago, "Determinants of Multilateralism," 586-87.

60. Fordham, "U.S. Uses"; Blechman and Kaplan, *Force Without War*; Zelikow, "The U.S."; Grimmett, *Instances*; James E. Hickey, Jr., "Challenges to Security Council Monopoly Power Over the Use of Force in Enforcement Actions: The Case for Regional Organizations," *IUS GENTIUM* 10 (Fall 2004): 69-121; William Leary, "CIA Air Operations in Laos, 1955-1974," *Studies in Intelligence* (Winter 1999-2000): 71-86; Adam B. Siegel, *The Use of Naval Forces in the Post War Era: U.S. Navy and U.S. Marine Corps Crisis Response Activity, 1946–1990* (Alexandria, Va.: Center for Naval Analyses Research Manual 90-246, 1991). The Siegel list can be found at http://www.history.navy.mil/library/online/forces_cold.htm (August 8, 2009).

61. The *U.S. Action* list with description of coding for each crisis is included as Appendix A.

62. Bennett and Stam, "*EUGene.*"

63. If the *force* variable is coded zero, I code the *unilateral* dependent variable as zero; the same as if the U.S. action was multilateral. This allows me to exclusively examine only unilateral uses of force.

64. Corbetta and Dixon, "Multilateralism, Major Powers," 11; Biddle, *Military Power*, 20-21.

65. Biddle's findings warrant further elaboration: Stephen Biddle, "Victory Misunderstood: What the Gulf War Tells Us about the Future of Conflict," *International Security* 21, no. 2 (Autumn 1996): 139-79; Stephen Biddle, "The Past as Prologue: Assessing Theories of Future Warfare," *Security Studies* 8, no. 1 (Autumn 1998): 1-74; Biddle, *Military Power*. As discussed in Chapter 2, Biddle proposes force employment, unchanged since 1918, as an explanatory variable of success or failure in military conflict. While he attributes the outcome of the 1991 Gulf War to a "synergistic interaction between a major skill imbalance and new technology," he does not believe that the technological changes associated with RMA created a new form of warfare: Biddle, "Victory Misunderstood," 140; Biddle, *Military Power*, 197. To Biddle, so-called technological innovation (increasing striking range and lethality of precision weapons and

better information collection and processing) are simply "extensions of longstanding trends": Biddle, *Military Power*, 197.

I do not dispute Biddle's emphasis on force employment. I agree that a modern system entails effectively reducing exposure to increasing lethality, range (or speed), and surveillance: Biddle, *Military Power*, 52, 197. I also do not take issue with the fact that success has been positively correlated with effective cover and concealment since 1918. But, I argue that a strict moral, political, and military adherence to all but eliminating casualties is a revolutionary concept that became the operating paradigm with the 1991 Gulf War.

Militaries, the U.S. in particular, have wanted to reduce the exposure of their troops, once generals (and politicians) realized that employing Napoleonic tactics was tantamount to dooming troops to a cannon fodder death. For the U.S., this realization occurred with the land warfare revolution: Andrew F. Krepinevich, "Cavalry to Computer: The Pattern of Military Revolutions," *National Interest* 37 (Fall 1994): 37; Martin Van Creveld, *Technology and War: From 2000 B.C. to the Present* (New York: The Free Press, 1989), 172-73. But, this reduction in exposure was an expected utility calculation. Losses occurring from direct assaults (e.g., the D-Day beach landings) were acceptable as long as victory on the battlefield was highly probable.

But, the concept of trying to achieve victory with few, if any, casualties is revolutionary, and a concept that took hold in the 1991 Gulf War. Biddle's identification of a reduced exposure force employment system is identifiable with the current RMA's emphasis on disengaged combat. But, disengaged combat means achieving victory with minimal or possibly no casualties. Presidents can make the decision to fight and win a war, while not putting soldiers' lives at risk. President Clinton's Kosovo decision serves as an ideal example: no ground troops were used and planes were instructed to fly at altitudes above the range of ground fire.

66. See Krepinevich, "Cavalry to Computer"; Richard O. Hundley, *Past Revolutions, Future Transformations: What can the history of revolutions in military affairs tell us about transforming the U.S. military?* (Santa Monica, Calif.: Rand, 1999).

67. A.F.K. Organski and Jacek Kugler, *The War Ledger* (Chicago: University of Chicago Press, 1980); A.F.K. Organski, *World Politics* (New York: Knopf, 1958); Steven Rosen, "War, Power and the Willingness to Suffer," in *Peace, War, and Numbers*, ed. Bruce Russett (Beverly Hills, Calif.: Sage, 1972).

68. Gilpin, *War and Change*, 65.

69. Biddle, *Military Power*, 14. Biddle measures preponderance as a force-to-force ratio and as a force-to-space ratio: Biddle, *Military Power*, 14-15, 71, 155-58, but his analysis involves more of a tactical assessment. He acknowledges that measuring preponderance as GDP (or GNP) is a traditional method for more strategic assessments: Biddle, *Military Power*, 14, 21.

70. Kadera, *The Power-Conflict Story*, 115.

71. Angus Maddison, *Monitoring the World Economy 1820 - 1992* (Paris: OECD, 1995); Angus Maddison, *The World Economy: Historical Statistics* (Paris: OECD Development Centre, 2003); Angus Maddison, *The World Economy: A Millennial Perspective* (Paris: OECD Development Centre, 2001). The data set is available at http://

www.ggdc.net/maddison/Historical_Statistics/horizontal-file_09-2008.xls (August 8, 2009).

72. Allan C. Stam, III, *Win, Lose, or Draw: Domestic Politics and the Crucible of War* (Ann Arbor: The University of Michigan Press, 1999).

73. Stam, *Win, Lose*, 95.

74. Stam, *Win, Lose*, 94-95. Biddle disagrees with Stam's military spending per soldier measure, arguing it is biased in favor of capital-intensive air and naval powers: Biddle, *Military Power*, 251. He measures a country's technology score as the introduction date of tanks/aircrafts weighted by the number of each type: Biddle, *Military Power*, 24. But, as with the preponderance variable, Biddle's assessment is more of a tactical nature, and he agrees that Stam's measure is suitable for a more strategic assessment: Biddle, *Military Power*, 251, 306.

75. Stam, *Win, Lose*; Paul D. Huth, Scott Bennett, and Christopher Gelpi, "System Uncertainty, Risk Propensity, and International Conflict among the Great Powers," *Journal of Conflict Resolution* 36, no. 3 (September 1992): 478-517.

76. A *force employment gap* variable would be ideal, but as the variable is a dummy variable and the U.S. has been at the forefront of military revolutions since the Civil War, the U.S. is coded a one throughout the data set. So, I code a dummy variable for the target country based on whether it is capable of employing its force consistent with the appropriate revolution.

77. Biddle operationalizes force employment using an indirect test involving casualties, duration of troops engaged, and the ground taken: Biddle, *Military Power*, 150-80. As with his preponderance and technology measures, his assessment is of a tactical nature.

78. It should be noted that since the American Civil War, the competitive advantages of military revolutions are becoming increasingly short-lived in terms of time and duration: Krepinevich, "Cavalry to Computer," 40.

79. Krepinevich, "Cavalry to Computer," 37; Van Creveld, *Technology and War*, 172-73.

80. Hundley, *Past Revolutions*, 12; Krepinevich, "Cavalry to Computer," 38; Van Creveld, *Technology and War*, 168-171, 182.

81. Krepinevich, "Cavalry to Computer," 38.

82. Van Creveld, *Technology and War*, 224-25.

83. Hundley, *Past Revolutions*; Krepinevich, "Cavalry to Computer"; Van Creveld, *Technology and War*.

84. John R. Bolton, "Unilateralism Is Not Isolationism," in Prins, ed., *Understanding Unilateralism*, 70.

85. Van Creveld, *Technology and War*, 264.

86. Van Creveld, *Technology and War*, 268-273, 279; Krepinevich, "Cavalry to Computer," 38.

87. Hundley, *Past Revolutions*; Krepinevich, "Cavalry to Computer." Huth, Bennett, and Gelpi find that nuclear weapons do not have an impact on dispute initiation: Huth, Bennett, and Gelpi, "System Uncertainty," 513. A rival's possession of nuclear weapons does not deter a challenger from initiating a dispute, possibly because the challenger does not believe the rival has the resolve to use nuclear weapons: Huth,

Bennett, and Gelpi, "System Uncertainty," 513. But, nuclear weapons remain a potent military capability and must be accounted for in this book.

88. Lawrence Freedman, "Arms Race: Nuclear Arms Race," in *The Oxford Companion to American Military History*, ed. John Whiteclay Chambers, II (New York: Oxford University Press, 1999), 43.

89. Gungwu Wang, "China and the World since 1949," in *The Making of the Twentieth Century*, ed. Christopher Thorne (New York: St. Martin's, 1977), 87.

90. Warner D. Farr, "The Third Temple's Holy of Holies: Israel's Nuclear Weapons," *Counterproliferation Papers Series* 2 (September 1999).

91. Kamienski, "The RMA," 2; Michael J. Mazaar, *The Revolution in Military Affairs: A Framework for Defense Planning* (Carlisle, Pa.: Strategic Studies Institute, 1994), 12.

92. Steven Metz and James Kievit, *The Revolution in Military Affairs and Conflict Short of War* (Carlisle, Pa.: Strategic Studies Institute, 1994), 3; Christopher G. Warner, *Implementing Joint Vision 2010: A Revolution in Military Affairs for Strategic Air Campaigns* (Maxwell AFB, Ala.: Air University Press, 1999), 3; Mazaar, *The Revolution*, 12; Biddle, "Victory Misunderstood," 141.

93. Ahmed S. Hashim, "The Revolution in Military Affairs Outside the West," *Journal of International Affairs* 51, no. 2 (Spring 1998): 431.

94. Krepinevich, "Cavalry to Computer," 30; Biddle, "Victory Misunderstood," 141; Biddle, "The Past as Prologue," 1; Williamson Murray and MacGregor Knox, "Thinking about Revolutions in Warfare," in *The Dynamics of Military Revolution: 1300-2050*, eds. MacGregor Knox and Williamson Murray (Cambridge: Cambridge University Press, 2001), 189; Mazaar, *The Revolution*.

95. Michael R. Gordon and Bernard E. Trainor, *The Generals' War: The Inside Story of the Conflict in the Gulf* (Boston: Little, Brown, and Company, 1995), 78-80; Robert A. Pape, *Bombing to Win: Air Power and Coercion in War* (Ithaca, N.Y.: Cornell University Press, 1996), 222, 250; Daryl G. Press, "The Myth of Air Power in the Persian Gulf War and the Future of Warfare," *International Security* 26, no. 2 (Fall 2001): 12.

96. Murray and Knox, "Thinking about Revolutions," 189; Thomas A. Keaney, "The Linkage of Air and Ground Power in the Future of Conflict," *International Security* 22, no. 2 (Autumn 1997): 149; Daryl G. Press, "Lessons from Ground Combat in the Gulf: The Impact of Training and Technology," *International Security* 22, no. 2 (Autumn 1997): 137.

97. Press, "Lessons from Ground," 138.

98. Samuel P. Huntington, "The Clash of Civilizations?," *Foreign Affairs* 72, no. 3 (Summer 1993): 46.

99. Mazaar, *The Revolution*, 12.

100. Mazaar, *The Revolution*, 11-12; Murray and Knox, "Thinking about Revolutions," 189.

101. Jakobsen, "National Interest," 213; Mazaar, *The Revolution*, 11.

102. Kamienski, "The RMA," 2-3.

103. Edward N. Luttwak, "Toward a Post-Heroic Warfare," *Foreign Affairs* 74, no. 3 (May—June 1995): 121; Kamienski, "The RMA," 2; Qingguo Jia, "In Search of Absolute Security: U.S. Nuclear Policy," in Malone and Khong, eds., *Unilateralism*, 204.

104. Van Creveld, *Technology and War*; Krepinevich, "Cavalry to Computer"; Murray and Knox, "Thinking about Revolutions"; Biddle, "Victory Misunderstood"; Biddle, "The Past as Prologue"; Mazaar, *The Revolution.*

105. I code crises as national security, regime change, and humanitarian to most accurately reflect the empirical world. While I am able to test all three crises in Chapter 4, a lack of regime change observations (22) and a lack of literature support for a directional hypothesis means I do not test a regime change variable in this chapter.

Regime change involves the infringement on another nation's sovereignty, a controversial issue perhaps dating back to the 1648 Treaty of Westphalia, which recognized the sanctity of national sovereignty. Ironically, as the Treaty recognized the sovereignty of states as the defining unit of the international system, unequal distribution of power between states also defined the system: Fonseca, "The United States," 325. The fundamental equality of states forms the basis of legitimacy and should limit unilateralism: Fonseca, "The United States," 329. This probably explains why the American people are reluctant to want force to be used to foster regime change. As such, presidents may want to use multilateral force when using the military for regime change.

On the other hand, the normative values restraining democratic states does not apply to how they act toward autocracies: Nils P. Gleditsch and H. Hegre, "Peace and Democracy–Three Levels of Analysis," *Journal of Conflict Resolution* 41, no. 2 (April 1997): 283-310; Arvid Raknerud and Havard Hegre, "The Hazard of War: Reassessing the Evidence for the Democratic Peace," *Journal of Peace Research* 34, no. 4 (November 1997): 385-404. Presidents, with the public's backing, may unilaterally topple a dictator in order to install a regime friendlier to the U.S.

This ambiguity makes it difficult to formulate a generalizable, directional unilateral-multilateral hypothesis. For reasons supporting the lack of a directional hypothesis, see the "Unilateralism: An Ambivalent Public" subsection in Chapter 2.

106. Patrick James and John R. Oneal, "The Influence of Domestic and International Politics on the President's Use of Force," *Journal of Conflict Resolution* 35, no. 2 (June 1991): 307-32.

107. See Blechman and Kaplan, *Force Without War*; Charles W. Ostrom, Jr. and Brian L. Job, "The President and the Political Use of Force," *American Political Science Review* 80, no. 2 (June 1986): 541-66; James and Oneal, "The Influence"; Karl R. DeRouen, Jr., "The Indirect Link: Politics, the Economy, and the Use of Force," *Journal of Conflict Resolution* 39, no. 4 (December 1995): 671-95; Karl R. DeRouen, Jr., "Presidents and the Diversionary Use of Force: A Research Note," *International Studies Quarterly* 44, no. 2 (June 2000): 317-28; Karl R. DeRouen, Jr., "The Decision Not to Use Force at Dien Bien Phu: A Poliheuristic Perspective," in *Integrating Cognitive and Rational Theories of Foreign Policy Decision Making*, ed. Alex Mintz (New York: Palgrave Macmillan, 2003); Fordham, "Partisanship, Macroeconomic"; Fordham, "The Politics"; John E. Mueller, "A Review: American Public Opinion and the Gulf War: Some Polling Issues," *Public Opinion Quarterly* 57, no. 1 (Spring 1993): 80-91; Alvin Richman, "Poll Trends: American Support for International Involvement," *Public Opinion Quarterly* 57, no. 2 (Summer 1993): 264-76; Alex Mintz, "The Decision to Attack Iraq: A Noncompensatory Theory of Decision Making," *Journal of Conflict Resolution* 37, no. 4 (December 1993): 595-618.

108. Ostrom and Job, "The President"; James and Oneal, "The Influence"; DeRouen, "The Indirect Link"; Fordham, "Partisanship, Macroeconomic"; Fordham, "The Politics"; David Brule and Alex Mintz, "Blank Checks or Marching Order? Public Opinion and Presidential Use of Force in the United States," in *Crossing Boundaries*, ed. Harvey Starr (New York: Palgrave Macmillan, 2006).

109. See Ostrom and Job, "The President"; James and Oneal, "The Influence"; DeRouen, "The Indirect Link"; Fordham, "Partisanship, Macroeconomic"; Fordham, "The Politics."

110. Brule and Mintz, "Blank Checks"; George C. Edwards III, *At the Margins: Presidential Leadership of Congress* (New Haven, Conn.: Yale University Press, 1989).

111. Fordham, "Partisanship, Macroeconomic"; Tago, "Determinants of Multilateralism." This is the only control variable for the unilateral model.

112. The misery index data can be obtained from Fordham, "The Politics," for the years 1949 to 1994 and from the U.S. Bureau of Census at http://factfinder.census.gov/home/saff/main.html?_lang=en and the U.S. Bureau of Labor Statistics at http://www.bls.gov/ for the years 1937 to 1948 and for 1995.

113. The Gallup poll data can be obtained from Fordham, "The Politics," for the years 1949 to 1994 and from The Roper Center via Lexis-Nexis.com for the years 1937 to 1948 and for 1995.

114. Fordham, "Partisanship, Macroeconomic."

115. Brule and Mintz, "Blank Checks"; John E. Mueller, "Trends in Popular Support for the Wars in Korean and Vietnam," *American Political Science Review* 65, no. 2 (June 1971): 358-75; John E. Mueller, *War, Presidents and Public Opinion* (New York: John Wiley, 1973); Scott Sigmund Gartner and Gary M. Segura, "War, Casualties, and Public Opinion," *Journal of Conflict Resolution* 42, no. 3 (June 1998): 278-300.

116. The Gallup poll data can be found through the Roper Center, University of Connecticut.

117. Bruce Bueno de Mesquita and David Lalman, *War and Reason* (New Haven, Conn.: Yale University Press, 1992).

118. See Maoz, "Resolve, Capabilities"; Wayman, Singer, and Goertz, "Capabilities, Allocations"; Huth, Bennett, and Gelpi, "System Uncertainty"; David A. Lake, "Powerful Pacifists: Democratic States and War," *American Political Science Review* 86, no. 1 (March 1992): 24-37; Stuart A. Bremer, "Dangerous Dyads: Conditions Affecting the Likelihood of Interstate War, 1816-1965," *Journal of Conflict Resolution* 36, no. 2 (June 1992): 309-41.

119. James Klein, Gary Goertz, and Paul Diehl, "The New Rivalry Data Set: Procedures and Patterns," Paper presented at the Annual Meeting of the Peace Science Society, Houston, November 2004.

120. Gary Goertz and Paul F. Diehl, "(Enduring) Rivalries," in *Handbook of War Studies II*, ed. Manus I. Midlarsky (Ann Arbor: The University of Michigan Press, 2000), 222.

121. Gary Goertz and Paul F. Diehl, "Enduring Rivalries: Theoretical Constructs and Empirical Patterns," *International Studies Quarterly* 37, no. 2 (June 1993): 148. It should be noted that Gartzke and Simon find different results when they run a Poisson analysis. Their model, which calculates the probability of a dispute between any

pairs of countries being the same year after year, produces as many enduring rivalries as is identified by traditional rival literature: Erik Gartzke and Michael W. Simon, "'Hot Hand': A Critical Analysis of Enduring Rivalries," *Journal of Politics* 61, no. 3 (August 1999): 796.

122. Alastair Smith, "Testing Theories of Strategic Choice: The Example of Crisis Escalation," *American Journal of Political Science* 43, no. 4 (October 1999): 1254.

123. Smith, "Testing Theories," 1255.

124. Michael Colaresi, "When Doves Cry: International Rivalry, Unreciprocated Cooperation, and Leadership Turnover," *American Journal of Political Science* 48, no. 3 (July 2004): 555-70.

125. Goertz and Diehl, "(Enduring) Rivalries," 222, 225; Michael Colaresi and William R. Thompson, "Hot Spots or Hot Hands? Serial Crisis Behavior, Escalating Risks, and Rivalry," *Journal of Politics* 64, no. 4 (November 2002): 1194.

126. Colaresi, "When Doves Cry," 566.

127. Goertz and Diehl, "Enduring Rivalries," 148; Colaresi, "When Doves Cry."

128. Klein, Goertz, and Diehl, "The New Rivalry."

129. See Bruce M. Russett and Harvey Starr, "From Democratic Peace to Kantian Peace: Democracy and Conflict in the International System," in Midlarsky, ed., *Handbook*; Gleditsch and Hegre, "Peace and Democracy"; Zeev Maoz and Bruce M. Russett, "Normative and Structural Causes of the Democratic Peace," *American Political Science Review* 87, no. 3 (September 1993): 624-38.

130. David L. Rousseau et al., "Assessing the Dyadic Nature of the Democratic Peace, 1918-88," *American Political Science Review* 90, no. 3 (September 1996): 512-33; Bruce Bueno de Mesquita et al., "An Institutional Explanation of the Democratic Peace," *American Political Science Review* 93, no. 4 (December 1999): 791-807.

131. Monty G. Marshall and Keith Jaggers, *Polity IV Data Set* [Computer file; version p4v2002] (College Park, Md.: Center for International Development and Conflict Management, University of Maryland, 2002).

132. Bueno de Mesquita, *The War Trap*.

133. Bueno de Mesquita, *The War Trap*, 36-38.

134. Controlling for an alliance is necessary for the first decision of whether to use force or not. But, an *alliance* variable complicates the unilateral model unnecessarily given the following findings: (1) nations that choose to increase their military power are unsure that the allies will choose to assist them in a conflict; (2) the effect of alliances parallels that of internal capabilities; and (3) internal military buildups are long, slow processes, while alliances tend to be short-term and dynamic affairs that are not easily captured in empirical analyses or in a decision maker's crisis analysis: Kadera, *The Power-Conflict Story*, 43-46; James D. Morrow, "Arms versus Allies: Tradeoffs in the Search for Security," *International Organization* 47, no. 2 (Spring 1993): 208-16; Woosang Kim and James D. Morrow, "When Do Power Shifts Lead to War?," *American Journal of Political Science* 36, no. 4 (November 1992): 908. For tests including an *alliance* variable in the unilateral decision model, see footnote 140.

135. Damodar N. Gujarati, *Basic Econometrics*, 4th ed. (Boston: McGraw-Hill, 2003), 115.

136. Gujarati, *Basic Econometrics*, 614.

137. Gujarati, *Basic Econometrics*, 614.

138. See Sara McLaughlin Mitchell and Will H. Moore, "Presidential Uses of Force During the Cold War: Aggregation, Truncation, and Temporal Dynamics," *American Journal of Political Science* 46, no. 2 (April 2002): 438-52.

139. Ostrom and Job, "The President"; James and Oneal, "The Influence"; DeRouen, "The Indirect Link"; Fordham, "Partisanship, Macroeconomic"; Fordham, "The Politics"; Brule and Mintz, "Blank Checks."

140. I also test the unilateral model using an *alliance* variable (i.e., whether or not the target nation had a defense pact), which is insignificant. In using an *alliance* variable in the unilateral model (equation 3.11 and table 3.5), the likelihood statistics remains the same at -93.4 (1937 to 1995) and at -79.8 (1950 to 1995). For the 1937 to 1995 data, the chi-square increases from 13.94 to 14.13, resulting in a *p*-value that increases from 0.049 to 0.030. The pseudo R-square remains the same at 0.03. The chi-square for the 1950 to 1995 data increases from 24.18 to 24.73, resulting in a *p*-value that decreases from 0.001 to 0.002. The pseudo R-square remains the same at 0.06. Based on these results, *alliance* does not seem to make a significant contribution to the model; so, I exclude the variable.

I also test the force (equation 3.10 and table 3.5), unilateral model (equation 3.11 and table 3.5), and the unified model (equations 3.10, 3.11, and table 3.8) for variation within Democratic and Republican presidents from 1937 to 1995. I create a dummy variable for each president, *fdr*, *truman*, *ike*, *jfk*, *lbj*, *nixon*, *ford*, *carter*, *reagan*, *bush41*, and *clinton*, testing each variable in each model (I dropped the *Republican president* variable). All of the variables are dropped due to collinearity.

141. Using the capabilities of a target relative to the U.S. and then just the capabilities of the target nation allows for a robust test of the CINC score.

142. See Organski and Kugler, *The War Ledger*; Organski, *World Politics*; Rosen, "War, Power." I conduct a correlation test of the two variables later in this chapter.

143. I use the STATA statistical software program to run all of the statistical tests.

144. This issue is addressed and analyzed with the unified model (table 3.8).

145. Goertz and Diehl, "(Enduring) Rivalries"; Goertz and Diehl, "Enduring Rivalries"; Colaresi, "When Doves Cry"; Colaresi and Thompson, "Hot Spots or Hot Hands."

146. Morrow, "Arms versus Allies"; Kim and Morrow, "When Do Power Shifts."

147. David M. Malone, "A Decade of U.S. Unilateralism?," in Malone and Khong, eds., *Unilateralism*, 34.

148. Bueno de Mesquita, *The War Trap*, 36-38.

149. See Kenneth N. Waltz, *Theory of International Politics* (Boston: McGraw-Hill, 1979).

150. See Waltz, *Theory*; Michael Mastanduno, David A. Lake, and G. John Ikenberry, "Toward a Realist Theory of State Action," *International Studies Quarterly* 33, no. 4 (December 1989): 457-74; Steven Forde, "International Realism and the Science of Politics: Thucydides, Machiavelli, and Neorealism," *International Studies Quarterly* 39, no. 2 (June 1995): 141-60.

151. Corbetta and Dixon, "Multilateralism, Major Powers," 11.

152. Given the lack of a *preponderance gap* variable, I also test the model for consistency with a *target country technology* variable (which is simply the technology score for the target country). The variable is significant (coefficient = 6.717, robust standard error = 3.016, significance at p =.05 level), but it is in the wrong direction.

153. Biddle, *Military Power.*

154. Biddle, *Military Power.*

155. Corbetta and Dixon, "Multilateralism, Major Powers"; Stepanova, "The Unilateral"; James and Oneal, "The Influence."

156. See Blechman and Kaplan, *Force Without War*; Zelikow, "The U.S."; Gochman and Maoz, "Militarized Interstate Disputes."

157. Meernik and Waterman, "The Myth."

158. Stam, *Win, Lose.*

159. Douglass C. North, "Transaction Costs, Institutions, and Economic History," *Journal of Institutional and Theoretical Economics* 140, no. 1 (1984): 7-17; James A. Caporaso, "International Relations Theory and Multilateralism: The Search for Foundations," *International Organization* 46, no. 3 (Summer 1992): 599-632; Stephen G. Brooks and William C. Wohlforth, "International Relations Theory and the Case against Unilateralism," *Perspectives on Politics* 3, no. 3 (September 2005): 509-24.

160. The results from the unified model confirm that the national security crisis trigger was not recognized correctly with the separate probit estimates.

161. Gilpin, *War and Change*, 65.

162. See William Reed, "A Unified Model."

163. A Heckman model is another alternative, but it assumes a dichotomous dependent variable for the selection equation and a continuous dependent variable for the outcome equation: James Heckman, "Sample Selection Bias as a Specification Error," *Econometrica* 47, no. 1 (January 1979): 153-62.

164. As with the separate probit models, I use estimated robust standard errors to control for heteroscedasticity across dyad groups.

165. The model becomes unstable for the 1937 to 1995 data, as STATA is unable to output the results. The instability of the 1937 to 1995 models and having to drop variables in the 1950 to 1995 model limits the conclusions that can be drawn from this regression. Nonetheless, this was an interesting discovery and is further discussed in the "Directions for Future Research" section in Chapter 6.

166. In the two models, the *preponderance gap*, *alliance* and *presidential approval* variables also attain statistical significance but not in the expected direction.

167. The *cold war* variable is also significant for both time periods, but it is in the negative direction for the years 1937 to 1995 and in the positive direction for the years 1950 to 1995.

168. Corbetta and Dixon, "Multilateralism, Major Powers."

169. See Ostrom and Job, "The President"; DeRouen, "The Indirect Link"; DeRouen, "Presidents"; Fordham, "Partisanship, Macroeconomic."

170. The *humanitarian crisis* variable fails to attain statistical significance in either data set. It is in the wrong direction for the 1937 to 1995 data and is dropped for predicting failure perfectly for the 1950 to 1995 data.

171. The *preponderance gap* variable is significant and in the expected direction, but the probability of a president acting unilaterally increases by zero percent.

172. Gilpin, *War and Change*, 63.

173. Meernik and Waterman, "The Myth."

174. In order to run the 1950 to 1995 relative capabilities model, I needed to drop the *humanitarian crisis* variable, which was predicting failure perfectly.

175. As the relative gap capability between the U.S. and an opponent widens, the probability of a president making a unilateral decision increases by zero percent for the years 1937 to 1995 and for the years 1950 to 1995.

176. See Wayman, Singer, and Goertz, "Capabilities, Allocations"; Lake, "Powerful Pacifists"; D. Scott Bennett and Allan C. Stam, III, "The Declining Advantages of Democracy: A Combined Model of War Outcome and Duration," *Journal of Conflict Resolution* 42, no. 3 (June 1998): 344-66; Bremer, "Dangerous Dyads."

4

Does the Type of Crisis Matter?

An Experimental Test

Introduction

For the second method of this three-method book, I conduct an experimental test. Experimentation remains an alternative methodology in political science, as it raises questions of internal and external validity.[1] But its contribution in reducing the impact of bias, control in testing the research question, and precise measurement of the research question is invaluable.[2] Most importantly for this book, it offers an explanation (i.e., causal analysis) of why a unilateral decision is made.[3]

Though typically applied to case studies, I use Eckstein's critical case method and select extreme values of domestic- and international-based explanatory variables for my experiment.[4] In doing so, I create a condition that controls for the Chapter 2 domestic and military power explanations and allows me to determine how well my theory of unilateral use of decision making performs. My theory specifies an international level explanation for unilateral use of force, and while I focus primarily on military power, I need to determine whether the other significant, international level explanation—the situational factor—has explanatory power. So, I expose 360 Texas A&M student subjects to one of four possible manipulations of public opinion and military power independent variables and to one of three possible international crisis scenarios. In each crisis, the difficulty of the mission and level of public support varies and the participant has to respond and rate support for either an American unilateral or multilateral force option.

The experiment results confirm the statistical test (and the case study) results. The situational factor, encapsulated in the crisis trigger, significantly affects a president's unilateral use-of-force decision. The more severe the crisis, the more likely a president is to make a unilateral decision. I reach this conclusion first by describing the study. Second, I offer a research design. Third, I discuss the results and analyze how important the crisis trigger is to a president's unilateral use-of-force decision.

The Study

As presented in Chapter 3, this book tests several hypotheses relating to unilateralism, military power and situational factors. In this chapter, I address two extensions of those hypotheses:

1. How important is the crisis trigger?
2. Why is the crisis trigger important?

My theory of unilateral use-of-force decision making cites the importance of realism and power-based international factors, and the results of the statistics chapter confirm a president makes his calculation based on a military power advantage. But, I also find that situational factors are important, and this chapter tests to see just how important the crisis trigger is and why the crisis trigger is important.

More specifically, the experiment offers an explanation for hypothesis 5a (presidents are more likely to use unilateral force when facing a national security crisis) and 5b (presidents are less likely to use unilateral force when facing a humanitarian crisis). The U.S., as hegemon, has the power to act unilaterally whenever it wishes, but the crisis trigger represents a fundamental variable in Bueno de Mesquita's expected utility calculation: how much a president values the policies of his own nation vis-à-vis a potential opponent's value of his policies.[5] The president will make a calculation based on how much he values the stakes involved in a crisis, a calculation based on how vital the crisis is to U.S. security and interests. A diminishing utility to U.S. national security should correspond with fewer decisions to act unilaterally. For crises other than those involving national security, the president is going to seek to lower the casualty and financial costs as much as possible, even if it means increasing transaction costs (i.e., delays, logistic problems, less interoperability, etc.) due to working with multilateral partners.

A hegemon has the power to act unilaterally, but it does not mean the hegemon will act unilaterally all the time. Rather, the hegemon will govern the system, establish the rules based on its values, and it will be willing to enforce the rules (and ensure its dominant position) through a mixture of unilateral and multilateral military actions.[6] The key point is that the hegemon, in this case, the president, decides how to enforce the rules of the system, and for the president, this is an expected utility decision. The crisis, and how the American people view the crisis, will play a large role in a president's decision.

While Gilpin views the state as a unitary actor, he does not entirely discount the role a nation's society plays in its foreign policy. He writes, "Powerful groups set constraints on and may even determine the actions of state authority."[7] To Gilpin, Western values (the right to property, the rules of war, the sanctity of sovereignty), as protected by the U.S., serve as the foundation of the international system.[8] So, American domestic interests may pressure a president to act militarily to right a humanitarian wrong or to overthrow a brutal dictator that is violating international norms. But, as regime change and humanitarian interventions are outside of "vital interests," a president may appease domestic constituents (who want others in other nations to have the same rights and values they have) and lower the costs by acting multilaterally. As Gilpin states, a method to reduce costs is to reduce international commitments (i.e., multilateral partners share the costs), and so, it may be in a president's interests to act multilaterally in certain types of crises not considered vital to U.S. sovereignty.[9]

These crises, not vital to U.S. sovereignty and most likely to politically benefit a president through multilateral action, are humanitarian and regime change.

As cited in Chapters 2 and 3, humanitarian operations should be negatively correlated with unilateral force. Presidents wanting to avoid the perception of the U.S. acting as a bully, not wanting to unilaterally violate another state's sovereignty, wanting to respond to the American public's desire for an international effort, and wanting to lower the costs will act multilaterally.[10]

Regime change crises should also be correlated negatively with unilateral action. Presidents recognize that the American public does not prefer force to be used for regime change.[11] Presidents also want to uphold, not violate, the 1648 Treaty of Westphalia and the sanctity of national sovereignty.[12] After all, the key to U.S. hegemony is reflecting the "values common to a set of states."[13] So, when a president acts to change a regime's leadership to suit U.S. interests, he will seek to act on behalf of an international mandate with a multinational coalition.

However, when it comes to national security, the president will find strong domestic support for unilateralism. Thus, national security threats will correlate positively with unilateral action. American exceptionalism cites a willingness to act unilaterally, as Americans are reluctant to rely on international assistance in guaranteeing national security.[14] The U.S. military is also reluctant to rely on ally militaries for assistance.[15] Most importantly, the president may recognize hegemonic "prestige" is on the line and that the U.S. must be willing to enforce its dominance of the international system unilaterally. After all, a state that "retrenches" or makes concessions signals its waning power, which may bring about more conflict.[16]

Experimental Method

Using 360 Texas A&M University students, I am able to test whether domestic politics and military power impact a president's unilateral decision given a set of situational factors (i.e., the crisis trigger). Each crisis scenario assumes a decision to use force has been made, and each scenario involves one of four possible decisional contexts, ranging from a "most-likely" case for unilateral force with a significant military power gap vis-à-vis an opponent and significant popular support for unilateralism to a "least-likely" scenario with a militarily strong opponent and weak popular support for unilateralism.

Subjects

One hundred and twenty Texas A&M University students participated in each of the three studies. The students were randomly assigned to one of four different experimental conditions for one experimental situation: the humanitarian, regime change, or national security situation.

Design

The study employed a 2 × 2 between groups factorial design. There were two constructions of the dependent measure. In the first construction, subjects chose one of two decision alternatives: act alone (unilateral force) or partner with others (multilateral force). In the second construction, subjects ranked their support from 0 (no support) to 10 (high support) for their choice of unilateral or multilateral force. The main independent measure placed subjects in one of two decision dimensions: domestic political and power or relative military capability. Several additional manipulations were assessed in order to ascertain the internal validity of the experiment.[17]

Research Instrument

Subjects assumed the role of the public and were asked how the president should respond to a given crisis. Subjects were presented with a crisis scenario. Subjects were informed that one of the following crises—a humanitarian crisis, a regime change crisis, or a national security threat—had arisen and the U.S. president, after exhausting all possibilities, must choose to use unilateral or multilateral force.

The two independent variables, the domestic political dimension and the "power" or relative military capability dimension, were manipulated as follows. For the domestic political dimension, half of the subjects were told that "over 70 percent of the public supports the president in his decision to act alone and use unilateral force." The other half of the subjects were told that "less than 30 percent of the public supports the president in his decision to act alone and use unilateral force."[18] For the power dimension, half of the subjects were told that "the U.S. military, acting alone is facing a poorly trained, poorly equipped, and fragmented militia enemy, which is plagued by low morale." The other half of the subjects were told that "the U.S. military, acting alone is facing a well-trained, well-equipped, and tenacious enemy, which is considered to be the most powerful in its region." In meeting the requirements of a between subject design, subjects were introduced to only one out of the three scenarios, and they were introduced to both dimensions in their respective scenario.

In sum, for each scenario, one-quarter of the subjects received high public support and high military capability dimensions, one-quarter of the subjects received high public support and low military capability dimensions, one-quarter of the subjects received low public support and high military capability dimensions, and the remaining quarter received low public support and low military capability dimensions.

Given this information about the dimensions, subjects were then asked to make their dependent variable selection, use unilateral or multilateral force.

Procedure

The instructions and scenario were presented in written form.[19] Subjects were free to take their time reading the introductory materials. The experiment itself took 7-10 minutes. Subjects were debriefed after completing the experiment.

Humanitarian Crisis Results

As presented in table 4.1, the experiment shows a strong negative correlation between intervention in a humanitarian crisis and choosing a unilateral force alternative. When subjects were sensitized to dimensions containing either one of the low support or low probability of military success or both conditions, they were unlikely to choose a unilateral force decision. Specifically, among the four conditions, the highest percentage of subjects chose unilateral force given high public support for unilateral action and high probability of success (63.3 percent). Only a minority of subjects favored a unilateral decision if either there was low public support for unilateral action *or* low probability of unilateral military success (43.3 percent). An even smaller portion of subjects advised using unilateral force, when both dimensions of low public support for unilateral action and low probability of success were present (16.7 percent).

Additional data collected in this experiment offers supplementary information about other questions. For example, subjects that chose the unilateral force option ($M = 5.32$) believed the humanitarian operation was less dangerous than those who chose the multilateral force option ($M = 6.51$) $t(1,49) = 2.60$ $p = .0122$. Unilateral proponents also believed there would be less casualties ($M = 39.6$) than multilateralists ($M = 49$) $t(1,49) = 2.12$ $p = .0396$. Finally, those selecting unilateral force ($M = 5.8$) perceived public support for unilateral force higher than those selecting multilateral force ($M = 4.6$) $t(1,49) = -2.93$ $p = .0052$.[20]

Regime Change Results

As presented in table 4.2, the experiment shows a strong negative correlation between regime change and choosing a unilateral force alternative. Subjects sensitized to dimensions containing low support for unilateral action and low probability of unilateral military success rarely selected a unilateral op-

TABLE 4.1
For the Humanitarian Crisis, Proportion of Students Choosing the Unilateral Force Alternative[a]

		Domestic Political Dimension	
		High Public Support for Unilateral Force	Public Opposition for Unilateral Force
Power Dimension	High Probability of Unilateral Military Success	0.633	0.433
	Low Probability of Unilateral Military Success	0.433	0.167

[a] N in each cell = 30

tion (3.3 percent). But, subjects were more attuned to the military capability dimension as only a minority advised using unilateral force given conditions of high unilateral support but low probability of unilateral military success (30 percent). The subjects were evenly divided about making a unilateral decision given high public opposition to unilateral military action success but high probability of success (50 percent). A majority of subjects advised using unilateral force given dimensions of high public support for unilateral action and high probability of success (56.7 percent).

Additional data collected in this experiment offers supplementary information about other questions. For example, subjects that chose the unilateral force option (M = 8.13) were more confident in their decision than those who chose the multilateral force option (M = 7.35) t(1,39) = -2.69 p = .0105. Unilateral proponents believed the regime change operation was less dangerous (M = 5.5) than those who chose the multilateral force option (M = 6.49) t(1,41) = 2.22 p = .0321. Unilateralists also believed there would be less casualties (M = 345.29) than multilateralists (M = 467.95) t(1,41) = 2.38 p = .0220. Finally, those selecting unilateral force (M = 6.0) perceived public support for unilateral force higher than those selecting multilateral force (M = 4.77) t(1,41) = -2.20 p = .0333.[21]

National Security Results

As presented in table 4.3, the experiment shows a strong positive correlation between national security threats and choosing a unilateral force alternative. When subjects were sensitized to dimensions containing high support for unilateral action (regardless of the probability of unilateral military success),

TABLE 4.2
For Regime Change, Proportion of Students Choosing the Unilateral Force Alternative[a]

		Domestic Political Dimension	
		High Public Support for Unilateral Force	Public Opposition for Unilateral Force
Power Dimension	High Probability of Unilateral Military Success	0.567	0.500
	Low Probability of Unilateral Military Success	0.300	0.033

[a] N in each cell = 30

TABLE 4.3
For National Security Threat, Proportion of Students Choosing the Unilateral Force Alternative[a]

		Domestic Political Dimension	
		High Public Support for Unilateral Force	Public Oppos tion for Unilateral Force
Power Dimension	High Probability of Unilateral Military Success	0.733	0.500
	Low Probability of Unilateral Military Success	0.600	0.200

[a] N in each cell = 30

the majority favored a unilateral force decision. Specifically, among the four conditions, the highest percentage of subjects chose unilateral force given high public support for unilateral action and high probability of success (73.3 percent). Even subjects facing dimensions of high public support for unilateral action but low probability of unilateral military success still advised making a unilateral decision (60 percent). The subjects were evenly divided about making a unilateral decision, even given the high probability of unilateral military success (50 percent). Some subjects still advised using unilateral force even when facing dimensions of low public support for unilateral action and low probability of success (20 percent).

Additional data collected in this experiment offers supplementary information about other questions. For example, subjects that chose the unilateral force option ($M = 5.74$) perceived public support for unilateral force higher than those selecting multilateral force ($M = 4.37$) $t(1,58) = -3.05$ $p = .0035$. Unilateralists also believed this to be less of a regime change crisis ($M = 3.44$) than multilateralists ($M = 4.95$) $t(1,58) = 2.79$ $p = .0072$.[22]

Discussion

Per table 4.4, the three studies show that military power and domestic politics seem to have about the same effect on subjects. Specifically, only a minority of subjects with a condition of high probability of unilateral military success favored a unilateral decision (47.8 percent), and about the same percentage facing high support for unilateralism but low probability of success also wanted a unilateral decision (44.4 percent). If both the high public support for unilateral force and high probability of unilateral success dimensions were

TABLE 4.4
The Proportion of Students Choosing the Unilateral Force Alternative[a]

		Domestic Political Dimension	
		High Public Support for Unilateral Force	Public Opposition for Unilateral Force
Power Dimension	High Probability of Unilateral Military Success	0.644	0.478
	Low Probability of Unilateral Military Success	0.444	0.133

[a] N in each cell = 30

available, then the majority of subjects did favor a unilateral decision (64.4 percent). A small portion of subjects still favored unilateral action even with low public support and low probability of success (13.3 percent).

Additional data collected in this experiment offers supplementary information about other questions. For example, subjects that chose the unilateral force option (M = 7.86) were more confident in their decision than those who chose the multilateral force option (M = 7.52) $t(1,149) = -2.34$ $p = .0209$. Unilateral proponents believed the use-of-force actions were less dangerous (M = 5.72) than those who chose the multilateral force option (M = 6.59) $t(1,152) = 4.36$ $p < .0001$. Finally, those selecting unilateral force (M = 5.83) perceived public support for unilateral force higher than those selecting multilateral force (M = 4.6) $t(1,152) = -8.35$ $p < .0001$.[23]

The subjects acted in the hypothesized direction. Presidents are less likely to act unilaterally in crises, such as in humanitarian operations and regime change, in which there is lower confidence in the mission, more risk, and the public is calling for multilateral action.[24] But, presidents will act unilaterally when facing national security threats. The public is supportive of the president using unilateral force to protect the nation, even when facing potentially high casualties.[25]

The national security results are interesting. The president seems to follow the advice of the public and use unilateral force regardless of military capabilities. The president was willing to use unilateral force 60 percent of the time if the public wanted unilateral force, even though there was low probability of unilateral success. This percentage drops to 50 percent if the public is opposed to unilateral force, even though there was a high probability of unilateral success.

The other two scenarios basically show an interactive effect between public support and military capabilities, suggesting the president makes a decision based on an expected utility calculation. In the humanitarian scenario, only 43 percent of respondents wanted unilateral action, if either there was public opposition to unilateralism or low probability of unilateral military success. In the regime change scenario, only 30 percent of the subjects wanted unilateral action, even when advised that 70 percent of the public supports unilateral action. In both scenarios, the unilateral proponent subjects made a cost-benefit calculation, as evident in the fact that they perceived the missions as less dangerous, having less casualties, and more public support for unilateral action than the multilateral proponent subjects. This generalizes well to expected utility, in which presidents want to increase the "benefit" side by adding allies.[26]

The main follow-up question of whether or not the crisis trigger is important can be answered in the positive. The results demonstrate *why* the president is less inclined to use unilateral force when facing humanitarian and regime change triggers but more inclined to use unilateral force when facing a national security threat. Domestic politics is linked inexorably to the crisis trigger and plays a role in the crisis decision. Unilateral proponent subjects, regardless of the crises, seemed to be more confident in their decision, believed the crises less dangerous, and perceived higher public support for unilateral action than the multilateral-choosing subjects. This suggests a president will likely want to take fewer risks with less severe crises and will choose to disseminate the costs through allied partners in order to protect himself from domestic political costs.

The results shed some light on the unilateral-multilateral debate, as explained in the "Unilateralism: An Ambivalent Public" subsection of Chapter 2. The public, as demonstrated by the subjects in this experiment, tends to vary its support for unilateral action depending on the situation. For national security threats, the public orders the president to act unilaterally even with potentially high casualties and prolonged conflicts, but it is less supportive of unilateral force whenever the nature of the threat becomes ambiguous or the significance of the conflict less vital to protecting the nation.

Conclusion

This chapter specified under what conditions a president makes a decision to use force unilaterally or multilaterally. The evidence sheds light on why the crisis trigger is important. The intention of the experiment was to look inside the black box realist thesis of this book and see why the president may or may not make a unilateral decision. A foreign leader trying to anticipate U.S. actions must not only calculate military capabilities, but he must also calculate how much the U.S. values the stakes of a particular crisis. The higher the stakes, the more severe the crisis, the more the U.S. is willing to act unilaterally.

In each of the three crises, the president is making an expected utility calculation. The crisis trigger is clearly important with the president willing to follow public opinion and act unilaterally in a national security crisis, even when facing a strong opponent. But, in facing other crises (i.e., the humanitarian and regime change operations), the president seems to want to lower the "cost" of the conflict by adding allies. The multilateral option, in general, correlated with the perception that the public wasn't supporting a unilateral action, as well the situations being perceived as more dangerous and having a higher casualty count.

In Chapter 5, I use case study examinations of the 1991 Gulf War, the 1961 Bay of Pigs invasion, and the 1989 Panama invasion to highlight the importance of international and situational factors. In determining the accuracy of the theory of unilateral use-of-force decision making, I test the hypotheses that a unilateral decision will be positively correlated with a wide gap in military power, an opponent located in the Western hemisphere, and a national security threat. For each case, I summarize the events of the case, review domestic political factors, explain the crisis trigger, detail the military power of involved actors, trace the president's decision-making process, and assess how well the theory fares.

Notes

1. Donald T. Campbell and Julian C. Stanley, *Experimental and Quasi-Experimental Designs for Research* (Chicago: Rand McNally, 1966); Douglas G. Mook, "In Defense of External Invalidity," *American Psychologist* 38, no. 4 (April 1983): 379-87; David O. Sears, "College Sophomores in the Laboratory: Influences of a Narrow Data Base on Social Psychology's View of Human Nature," *Journal of Personality and Social Psychology* 51, no. 3 (1986): 515-30.

2. Rose McDermott, "Experimental Methods in Political Science," *Annual Review in Political Science* 5 (June 2002): 33, 38-39; Gary King, Robert O. Keohane, and Sidney Verba, *Designing Social Inquiry: Scientific Inference in Qualitative Research* (Princeton, N.J.: Princeton University Press, 1994).

3. Rose McDermott, "Experimental Methodology in Political Science," *Political Analysis* 10, no. 4 (Autumn 2002): 326.

4. Harry Eckstein, "Case Study and Theory in Political Science," in *The Handbook of Political Science, Vol. 7: Strategies of Inquiry*, eds. Fred Greenstein and Nelson Polsby (Menlo Park, Calif.: Addison-Wesley, 1975).

5. Bruce Bueno de Mesquita, *The War Trap* (New Haven, Conn.: Yale University Press, 1981), 36.

6. Robert Gilpin, *War and Change in World Politics* (New York: Cambridge University Press, 1981), 156.

7. Gilpin, *War and Change*, 16.

8. Gilpin, *War and Change*, 34-37.

9. When discussing reducing costs, Gilpin is referring to the actions of a declining hegemon, and Gilpin in 1981 believed the U.S., while still a hegemonic power, "retrenched" and reduced its international commitments. Gilpin's analysis is dated, but his main point that the U.S. assesses its international commitments based on a cost calculation is consistent with the methodology of this book and serves as the basis for this experiment: Gilpin, *War and Change*, 232-33.

10. Steven Kull, "The FP Interview: Vox Americani," *Foreign Policy* 126 (September—October 2001): 28-38; Steven Kull, "Public Attitudes Toward Multilateralism," in *Multilateralism and US Foreign Policy: Ambivalent Engagement*, eds. Stewart Patrick and Shepard Forman (Boulder, Colo.: Lynne Rienner, 2002); Jeremy Rabkin, "When Can America Be Bound by International Law?," in *Understanding Unilateralism in American Foreign Relations*, eds. Gwyn Prins (London: Royal Institute of International Affairs, 2000); A. Helton, "Reaction and Inattention Within the U.S. Government," in *Multilateralism v Unilateralism: Policy Choices in a Global Society*, eds. John B. Attanasio and Joseph J. Norton (London: The British Institute of International and Comparative Law, 2004); Christine Chinkin, "The State That Acts Alone: Bully, Good Samaritan or Iconoclast?," *European Journal of International Law* 11, no. 1 (2000): 31-41; James Cockayne and David Malone, "Creeping Unilateralism: How Operation Provide Comfort and the No-Fly Zones in 1991 and 1992 Paved the Way for the Iraq Crisis of 2003," *Security Dialogue* 37, no. 1 (March 2006): 123-41.

11. See Bruce W. Jentleson, "The Pretty Prudent Public: Post Post-Vietnam American Opinion on the Use of Military Force," *International Studies Quarterly* 36, no. 1 (March 1992): 49-73; Bruce W. Jentleson and Rebecca L. Britton, "Still Pretty Prudent: Post-Cold War American Public Opinion on the Use of Military Force," *Journal of Conflict Resolution* 42, no. 4 (August 1998): 395-417; John R. Oneal, Brad Lian, and James H. Joyner, Jr., "Are the American People 'Pretty Prudent'? Public Responses to U.S. Uses of Force, 1950-1988," *International Studies Quarterly* 40, no. 2 (June 1996): 261-79.

12. Gelson Fonseca, Jr., "The United States and Latin America: Multilateralism and International Legitimacy," in *Unilateralism and U.S. Foreign Policy: International Perspectives*, eds. David M. Malone and Yuen Foong Khong (Boulder, Colo.: Lynne Rienner, 2003).

13. Gilpin, *War and Change*, 34.

14. RFD, "Unilateral and Multilateral Options in the Execution of Foreign Policy," *International Organization* 23, no. 3 (Summer 1969): 641-754; Richard N. Haass, "Military Force: A User's Guide," *Foreign Policy* 96 (Autumn 1994): 21-37; John Mearsheimer, "The False Promise of International Institutions," *International Security* 19, no. 3 (Winter 1994-1995): 5-49; Henry Kissinger, *Does America Need a Foreign Policy? Toward a Diplomacy for the 21st Century* (New York: Simon & Schuster, 2001); Joseph S. Nye, Jr., *Understanding International Conflict: An Introduction to Theory and History*, 4th ed. (New York: Longman, 2003); Thomas M. Franck and Nigel S. Rodley,

"After Bangladesh: The Law of Humanitarian Intervention by Military Force," *American Journal of International Law* 67, no. 2 (April 1973): 275-305.

15. Sophia Clement, "The United States and NATO: A Selective Approach to Multilateralism," in Malone and Khong, eds., *Unilateralism.*

16. Gilpin, *War and Change,* 194.

17. I assessed the subjects' perception of the power dimension with questions about the danger and expected casualty count and of the domestic political dimension with a question about the level of public support. Finally, I asked the subjects to recall the main reason for the military operation.

18. The 70 percent and 30 percent public support numbers represent the range of poll numbers taken from actual crises. For example, more than 70 percent of Americans supported using troops in Iraq in 1990, in Iraq in 1993-1994, and for humanitarian purposes in early 1993 in Bosnia. However, only about 30 percent of Americans supported using troops in Somalia after the October 1993 killing of American soldiers, prior to the invasion of Haiti in 1994, and for bringing about regime change in Bosnia in early 1993: Jentleson and Britton, "Still Pretty Prudent," 396, 401, 404-5.

19. A copy of the instructions and three scenarios is included as Appendix B.

20. There were no statistical differences in terms of the subjects rating the type of crisis situation (national security threat, regime change, or humanitarian). Both the multilateral and unilateral subjects almost unanimously recalled the scenario as a humanitarian operation. Also, there was no statistical difference in terms of level of confidence in their decision. Both groups were confident in their decision ($M > 7.6$).

21. There were no statistical differences in terms of the subjects rating the type of crisis situation (national security threat, regime change, or humanitarian). Both the multilateral and unilateral subjects recalled the scenario as a humanitarian and regime change operation.

22. There were no statistical differences in terms of perceptions of danger and casualties. Moreover, both the multilateral and unilateral subjects ranked the scenario highly as a national security crisis. Also, there was no statistical difference in terms of level of confidence in their decision. Both groups were confident in their decision ($M > 7.5$).

23. There were no statistical differences in terms of the subjects' expected casualties or in recalling the type of crisis situation (national security threat, regime change, or humanitarian).

24. See Jentleson, "The Pretty Prudent Public"; Jentleson and Britton, "Still Pretty Prudent"; Oneal, Lian, and Joyner, "Are the American"; Mark Duffield and Joe Stork, "Bosnia is the Classic Case of Using Humanitarian Aid as a Smokescreen to Hide Political Failure," *Middle East Report* 187/188 (March—June 1994): 18-23.

25. See Jentleson, "The Pretty Prudent Public"; Jentleson and Britton, "Still Pretty Prudent"; Oneal, Lian, and Joyner, "Are the American"; RFD, "Unilateral"; Haass, "Military Force."

26. Bueno de Mesquita, *The War Trap*; John E. Mueller, "A Review: American Public Opinion and the Gulf War: Some Polling Issues," *Public Opinion Quarterly* 57, no. 1 (Spring 1993): 80-91.

5

Opening Up the "Black Box" of a President's Unilateral Decision

Case Studies of the 1991 Gulf War, 1961 Bay of Pigs Invasion, and 1989 Panama Invasion

Introduction

HOW ACCURATE IS THE THEORY OF UNILATERAL USE OF FORCE decision making? To answer this question, I employ a case study method. Case studies, defined as "an intensive study of a single unit for the purpose of understanding a larger class of (similar) units," are often held in "low regard" in scientific research.[1] Case studies are criticized on grounds of selection bias and lack of generalizability, but they offer some unique advantages over the statistical and experimental tests conducted in this book.[2]

I use my three selected cases to test my theory of unilateral use of force decision making, as part of an evidence-oriented strategy that describes complex social phenomena.[3] These case studies offer a trade-off, providing accuracy at the expense of generalizability.[4] The accuracy amounts to in-depth knowledge of the data, giving a "feel and flavor" of the subject being tested.[5]

In testing my case studies, I use a process-tracing method, in which I open up the "black box" of factors influencing a president's decision.[6] Using this method, I should find evidence of how a president makes his decision. First, a disparity in military capabilities between the U.S. and its opponent should be correlated with unilateralism, as presidents tend to be realists and will rely exclusively on the U.S. military, if a victory can be assured quickly and with minimal costs.[7] Second, U.S. unilateralism should be especially pronounced in the Western hemisphere, according to the tenets of the Monroe Doctrine.[8] If these factors have strong explanatory power, then the process-tracing case studies should provide a robust test of my predictions.[9]

Using this process-tracing method, I select three cases based on the extreme values of the dependent variable. The first case is the 1991 Gulf War, which is often represented as the ideal multilateral case. The second case is the 1961 Bay of Pigs operation, which represents a "middle ground" unilateral-multilateral case. The third case is the 1989 Panama invasion, which represents the ideal unilateral case. In all three cases, I demonstrate that the theory of unilateral use of force decision making fares well. Presidents Kennedy and Bush decided to act unilaterally or multilaterally based on a cost calculation of military power, the type of crisis, and the location of the crisis. Both presidents acted unilaterally or multilaterally with little regard to domestic politics.

For each case, I begin with an introduction and summary of the crisis events. Second, I review the domestic politics aspect of the case. Third, I explain the crisis trigger. Fourth, I detail the military power of the U.S. and crisis opponent as well as any other parties involved in the dispute. Fifth, I trace the president's decision-making process, including the two decisions—using force and using unilateral or multilateral force. Finally, I conclude with an assessment of the case and how well the theory fares.

1991 Gulf War (Multilateral Case)

As cited by proponents in the earlier chapters, the 1991 Gulf War represents an ideal case in multilateralism with its legitimacy, burden-sharing, and capability aggregation.[10] The 1991 Gulf War is coded as a procedural and operational multilateral case, and it represents one of the few times the UN has authorized force. But, this perception of an ideal multilateralism case is wrong. Rather, the U.S., as hegemon, directed a coalition to restore stability in a region that threatened its (and others) national security interests. I examine this perception with a test of the hypotheses.

As hypothesized in this book, the less the gap in military capability between the U.S. and an opponent, the more likely a president is to decide to use multilateral force. However, as also hypothesized, crises involving national security should be correlated with unilateralism. These competing hypotheses are not incompatible with one another. Rather, we should see President Bush decide to use force without regard to the level of coalitional support and strength, take action consistent with a hegemon protecting its interests, and then persuade a coalition to join it to lower the high expected costs without regard to domestic political influences.

For this case, I review the main events of the 1991 Gulf War. Second, I detail the domestic politics surrounding the crisis, including the particulars of public opinion and congressional involvement. Third, I explain why the Gulf

War was a national security type of crisis. Fourth, I detail the military power of the U.S., the coalition nations, and Iraq in both quantitative and qualitative terms. Fifth, I consider the president's decision in terms of unilateralism and apply the president's decision process to the sequential model of this book. I trace Bush's decision making from deciding to use force on August 3rd to deciding to use multilateral force on October 30th.

Summary of the 1991 Gulf War Events

The U.S.-Iraq relationship began to deteriorate in early 1990 with a Voice of America broadcast calling Hussein a "tyrant" and the State Department compiling a list of Hussein's human rights violations. Hussein, in turn, made matters worse, when he executed a British journalist and threatened Israel with chemical weapons.[11] Despite giving the perception to U.S. Ambassador April Glaspie on July 25, 1990, of no impending invasion, Hussein invaded Kuwait on August 2nd and quickly seized control of the country.[12]

On August 6, 1990, President Bush ordered elements of the 82nd Airborne Division to defend Saudi Arabia at the request of King Fahd bin Abd al-Aziz Al Saud.[13] Bush, while sending U.S. troops to the region, worked with the UN to pass 12 resolutions condemning Iraq's invasion. UN Security Council Resolution 678, issued on November 29, 1990, was the final and most demanding resolution, authorizing the use of "all necessary means" to force Iraq from Kuwait beginning on January 12, 1991.[14]

In a last ditch effort to avoid conflict and in a conversation resembling the Melian Dialogue, Secretary of State James Baker and Iraqi Foreign Minister Tariq Aziz met in Geneva on January 9th. Aziz, believing the U.S. would not want to pay the price of a protracted war, warned Baker, "You are a power which possesses strong weapons . . . I sincerely and without pretention tell you that the nineteen million Iraqis, including the Iraqi leadership, are convinced that if war erupts with you, we will win." To which, Baker reminded Aziz of the futility of fighting the world's greatest power, "Please do not let your military commanders convince you the strategy used against Iran will succeed here. You will face a completely different force. Midnight of January fifteenth is a very real date."[15]

Bush did not wait long after the January 15th deadline: the U.S. began its air and missile attack on Iraq on January 16, 1991. The 39-day air attack, consisting of four phases, was devastating. In the first phase, coalition aircraft quickly disrupted Iraq's command, control, and communication networks, destroyed its air defenses, targeted nuclear, chemical, and biological weapons centers, knocked out most of Iraq's electric, water, military, and oil production infrastructure, destroyed its roads, bridges, and railroads, and shot down three dozen poorly flown Iraqi jets. The second and third phases consisted of attacking Iraq's military forces in Kuwait and interdicting its supplies.[16]

Hussein tried to fight back with a less-than-conventional method: firing al-Hussein Scud missiles at Israel, Saudi Arabia, and Bahrain, setting Kuwait's oil wells on fire, launching terrorist strikes against the coalition, and sending two Iraqi divisions on a surprise attack against coalition Arab units. All of these attempts failed miserably.

By mid-February, Hussein began to negotiate in order to save his army from complete destruction. Morale and logistic problems alone had reduced his force from 550,000 to 350,000. But, the coalition rejected Hussein's offers and launched a massive ground assault along with the fourth phase of the air assault on February 24th. The U.S. sent the Marines on a diversionary attack into southeastern Kuwait and sent its armored VII Corps on a vast outflanking maneuver to the extreme west of Iraqi forces. Iraqi counterattacks against the Marines and armored formations resulted in total defeat of the Iraqi forces.

To prevent being surrounded, Hussein sent five Republican Guard divisions and three armored and mechanized divisions to the south and east to provide a "screen" for troops to withdraw from Kuwait. The Iraqi troops fought hard on February 25th and 26th, but they were simply "outnumbered, outgunned, and outmatched in every way."[17] Believing that the Republican Guard was destroyed and the exit routes from Kuwait cut off, Bush ordered a halt to the ground offensive on the morning of February 28th.[18] The 1991 Gulf War was a total victory for the U.S. and its allies.

Domestic Politics

One of the basic premises of this book is that international considerations, not domestic politics, explain a president's unilateral-multilateral decision. This should be the case even with a multilateral decision. While Bush had favorable public opinion and a Congress that eventually voted to support using military force, it is clear Bush was going to act without regard to domestic political influences.

In the days following Iraq's invasion of Kuwait, U.S. public opinion support for sending U.S. troops to the region increased from 6 percent (August 3-4, 1990) to 78 percent in favor of sending U.S. troops to defend Saudi Arabia (August 9-12, 1990).[19] Public support for using force remained strong, even though subjects were aware that the war could result in potentially 10,000 American casualties.[20] From a domestic standpoint, Bush faced Democratic control of Congress, had an approval rating of 62 percent, had a misery index of 11.3 percent, and was facing a rival in Iraq. But, domestic politics had little, if any, effect on Bush's decision to use force.[21]

Since the beginning of the crisis, Bush argued to Congress that he needed the freedom to be able to threaten force in order to deal effectively with Hussein from a diplomatic standpoint. He did inform Congress in writing of his August deployment of U.S. troops, but he purposely avoided triggering the 90-day clock of the War Powers Resolution.[22] He also used the 12 UN resolutions as a method to convey the international legitimacy of his actions and to discount any domestic opposition.[23]

Throughout the crisis months (August to January), Bush decided he would use force regardless if Congress voted or how Congress voted. Elizabeth Drew labeled Congress as "irrelevant" to Bush's use of force decision making.[24] Congress did pass a resolution on January 12th authorizing force, but Bush made it clear he would have acted without congressional support.[25] Bush wrote in his diary of Congress's harm to America's responsibility for defeating Hussein, "Our role as a world leader will once again be reaffirmed, but if we compromise and if we fail, we would be reduced to total impotence, and that is not going to happen. I don't care if I have one vote in the Congress."[26] Bush's statement is confirmed by the fact he authorized Operation Desert Shield on December 29th, two weeks before the congressional vote. He told allied ambassadors shortly before Christmas, "If I have to go [to war], it's not going to matter to me if there isn't one congressman who supports this, or what happens to public opinion. If it's right, it's gotta be done."[27]

Crisis Trigger

Using the coding rules established in Chapter 3, the 1991 Gulf War would be classified as a national security crisis. Bush viewed Iraq's invasion as a destabilizing factor in the Gulf, given Hussein's bullying could affect America's oil and other interests in the region. In carrying out National Security Directive (NSD) 26 (October 2, 1989) and NSD 54 (January 15, 1991), Bush made it very clear why Iraq's invasion would not be tolerated: "Access to Persian Gulf oil and the security of key friendly states are vital to U.S. national security."[28] As hegemon, the U.S. needed to act to right the "tilt" toward instability, and its leadership, very simply, was a necessary condition for forcibly removing Hussein from Kuwait.[29]

National Security

As Glaspie informed Hussein at their July 25th meeting, the U.S., as a superpower, was "concerned" about Iraq massing troops on its border with Kuwait.[30] The U.S. concern in the region was based on a very simple premise: the free flow of oil.[31] Hussein's possession of Kuwait and potential invasion of

Saudi Arabia could amount to Hussein controlling about 20 percent of global oil production, a monopolizing of oil prices that the U.S. was not willing to tolerate.[32]

Oil was one problem and Iraq's destabilizing antagonism was another problem. In the first National Security Council (NSC) meeting after the invasion of Kuwait, Bush focused the meeting on how best to reduce Iraq's military strength.[33] Bush also focused on convincing Saudi Arabia and other Arab allies of the threat Iraq posed to their national security.[34] The defense of Saudi Arabia was deemed critical to the whole regional balance of power.[35]

Scowcroft described what was required of the U.S.: (1) contain Iraq, (2) slow its conventional and unconventional military capability developments, and (3) force its withdrawal from Kuwait.[36] If the U.S. failed to act, it "would be encouraging a dangerous adversary in the Gulf at a time when the United States had provided a de facto commitment to Gulf stability."[37]

Military Power

The 1991 Gulf War is a simple case of the U.S. estimating the amount of military power necessary to defeat Iraqi forces and then raising the levels of U.S. and coalition power to meet that estimate. Using the CIMR scores, the U.S. clearly had an advantage and in hindsight probably did not need additional military power, but as described in the "Decision to Use Multilateral Force" subsection, Bush and the military commanders were worried about a high casualty rate. As such, Bush made a second decision on October 30th to increase coalition strength, and in the end, non-U.S. forces comprised 37 percent of the troop strength and 24 percent of the aircraft strength.[38]

U.S. Military Power

As shown in table 5.1, in terms of preponderance, the U.S. CINC score in 1990 was 0.141 and its GDP was 5.803 trillion or 21 percent of the world's GDP. In terms of technology, the U.S. spent an average of $133,028 per soldier.

TABLE 5.1
Military Power in 1990

Crisis Actors	*Preponderance (CINC Score)*	*Preponderance (GDP)*	*Technology (Spending/ Soldier)*	*Force Employment (Dummy Variable)*
U.S.	0.141	$5.803 trillion	$133,028	1
Coalition	0.308	$10.915 trillion	$87,107	1
Iraq	0.013	$44.583 billion	$6,194	0

In terms of force employment, the U.S. received a dummy variable of one, given its ability to conduct warfare consistent with the nuclear revolution.

The U.S. would prove it had the most powerful military in the world, and based on a doctrine of "overwhelming strength" and as shown in table 5.2, the U.S. contributed a great deal of its military resources to the Persian Gulf War effort.[39]

Coalition Military Power

In terms of preponderance, the coalition CINC score in 1990 was 0.308 and its GDP was 10.915 trillion or 40.3 percent of the world's GDP.[40] In terms of technology, the coalition countries spent an average of $87,107 per soldier. In terms of force employment, the coalition countries received a dummy variable of one, given its ability to conduct warfare consistent with the nuclear revolution.

While sizable contributions were limited to a handful of countries (notably, the British, French, Canadians, Italians, and Egyptians), the coalition countries contributed about 205,000 troops, more than 60 ships, 750 aircraft, and 1,200 tanks.[41] Other nations provided financial and logistical support (e.g., Germany and Japan).[42] Reports vary on the individual contributions, but table 5.3 is an approximation of the totals.[43]

TABLE 5.2
U.S. Military Forces

Type	*Total*
Air Forces	
Fixed-Wing Combat	1,376
Tankers	285
Airlift	175
Sea Forces	
Aircraft Carriers	6 battle groups with more than 400 aircraft
Battleships	2 surface action groups
Submarines	13
Amphibious	43
Land Forces	
Troops	532,000
Tanks	2,300 M1A1-series tanks
Artillery	1,032 M109 howitzers, M110 howitzers, M270 MLRS (Multiple-Launch Rocket System)
Armored Fighting Vehicles (AFVs)/ Armored Personnel Carriers (APCs)	More than 2,200 Bradley fighting vehicles and M113 APCs

TABLE 5.3
Coalition Military Forces

Country	*Type*	*Total*
Air Forces		
Argentina	Transports	3
Bahrain	Fighters	24
Canada	Fighters, Electronic Warfare (EW), Helicopters	31
France	Fighters, Tankers, EW, Helicopters	67
Italy	Fighters, Transports	12
Kuwait	Fighters, Transports, Helicopters	67
New Zealand	Transports	3
Oman	Fighters	20
Qatar	Fighters	20
Saudi Arabia	AWACS (Airborne Warning and Control Systems), Tankers, Transports	255
United Arab Emirates (UAE)	Fighters	50
UK	Fighters, Tankers, Transports, Helicopters, Reconnaissance and Patrol Aircraft	158
Sea Forces		
Argentina	Destroyer, Frigate	2
Australia	Destroyers, Frigates, Replenishment	5
Bahrain	Corvettes, Missile and Patrol Crafts	8
Belgium	Minesweepers, Frigate, Support	4
Canada	Destroyers, Oiler	3
Denmark	Frigate	1
France	Destroyers, Frigates, Replenishment, Hospital, Minesweepers, Electronic Intelligence	13
Greece	Frigate	1
Italy	Frigates, Support, Minesweepers, Helicopter Assault, Destroyer	10
Kuwait	Patrol Boats	2
Netherlands	Frigates, Minesweepers	5
Norway	Cutter	1
Oman	Missile and Patrol Crafts	12
Poland	Hospital, Salvage	2
Portugal	Transport	1
Qatar	Missile and Patrol Crafts	9
Saudi Arabia	Frigates, Minesweepers, Missile and Torpedo Crafts	25
Spain	Frigates, Transport	4
UAE	Corvettes, Missile and Patrol Crafts	17
UK	Destroyers, Frigates, Replenishment, Minesweepers, Survey, Oilers, Submarines	18

Country	Total
Land Forces	
Afghanistan	300 Mujahedeen Soldiers
Australia	2 Surgical Teams
Bahrain	3,500 Soldiers
Bangladesh	6,000-man Bangladesh Brigade, 1st East Bengal Infantry Battalion
Czechoslovakia	200-man Chemical Defense Unit, 150-man Field Hospital
Egypt	40,000-man II Corps
France	20,000-man 6th Light Armored Division
Honduras	150 Soldiers
Hungary	Medical Team
Kuwait	Al-Fatah, Haq, and Khulud Brigades, 15th and 35th Mechanized Brigades
Morocco	6th Mechanized Battalion
Netherlands	Field Hospital, 3 Patriot Missile Batteries
New Zealand	Field Hospital
Niger	480-man Infantry Battalion
Oman	Omani Brigade
Pakistan	7th Armored Brigade, Infantry Battalion
Poland	Field Hospital
Qatar	7,000-man Mechanized Task Force
Romania	Medical Team
Saudi Arabia	5 Armored and Mechanized Brigades
Senegal	Infantry Battalion
Sierra Leone	Medical Team
South Korea	Medical Team
Sweden	Field Hospital
Syria	9th Armoured Division, 45th Commando Brigade
UAE	Mechanized Battalion
UK	1st Armoured Division

Iraqi Military Power

In terms of preponderance, the Iraqi CINC score in 1990 was 0.013 and its GDP was 44.583 billion or 0.002 percent of the world's GDP. In terms of technology, Iraq spent an average of $6,194 per soldier. In terms of force employment, Iraq received a dummy variable of zero, given its inability to conduct warfare consistent with the nuclear revolution.

Iraq's military force was considered formidable, plentifully equipped, and battle-tested.[44] Iraq had the fourth largest army and sixth largest air force in the world, and though it was a Third World country, its military was that of a First World nation.[45] Hussein, believing he could deter the U.S. and underestimating the role of air power, took on a defensive strategy, a strategy based

TABLE 5.4
Iraqi Military Forces

Type	*Total*
Air Forces	
Fixed-Wing Combat	750
Sea Forces	
Missile Boats	13
Patrol, Minelaying, and Specialized	150
Land Forces	
Troops	955,000-man Army with 50 Regular Army Divisions and 8 Republican Guard Divisions
Tanks	5,500
Artillery	3,000
AFVs/ APCs	11,000

on goading the U.S. into a war of attrition. By the start of Operation Desert Storm, Hussein had deployed 51 of his 66 divisions to the Kuwaiti theater. This was a force of about 550,000 men, 3,475 tanks, 3,080 armored personnel carriers (APCs), and 2,475 artillery pieces.[46] But, as a whole, Hussein could bring far more forces to bear if necessary.[47] Reports on Iraq's military strength vary, but it was approximately as shown in table 5.4.[48]

Bush's Decision Making

The U.S. had failed to deter Iraq, due to not acting as a hegemon should. Deterrence requires credible signaling, and the U.S., with its "policy of inaction," failed to respond to Iraq's aggressive stance toward Kuwait.[49] When Iraq massed troops on Kuwait's border, the U.S. should have made strong military moves (e.g., sending aircraft carriers to the Gulf), but it failed to act, and Hussein read the inaction as a sign of weakness.[50] Believing America suffered from a post-Vietnam malaise, Hussein dismissed the U.S. as "impotent" and "afraid of conflict."[51] Bush was then put in a position of "rolling back" the destabilizing effect of Iraq's invasion and reasserting America's leadership as a hegemon.

Per figure 5.1, Bush made his initial decision to use force on August 3rd, due in large part to a meeting with Prime Minister Margaret Thatcher. He made a second decision to use multilateral force on October 30th, due to numerous military briefings on the strength of Iraq's military and the high expected costs of removing Iraq from Kuwait.

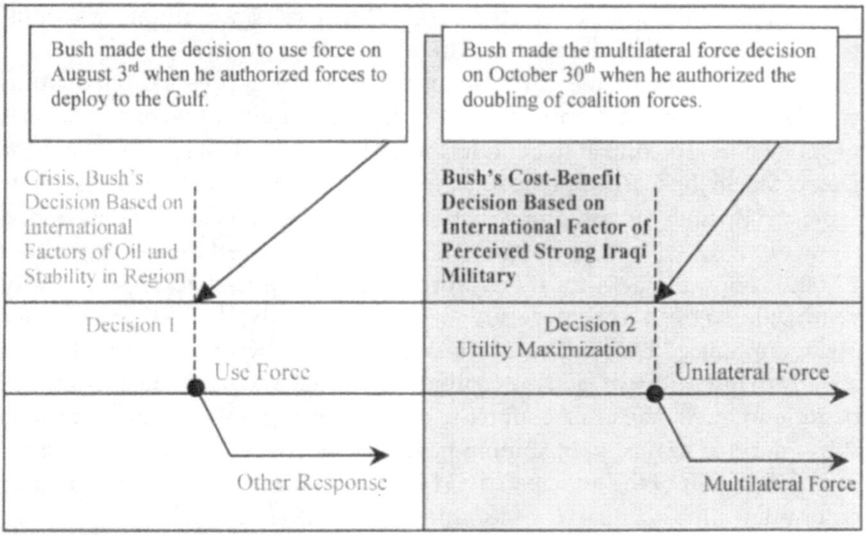

FIGURE 5.1
Sequential Model of Bush's Gulf War Use-of-Force Decision Making

By November, Bush and military commanders had decided that 234,000 coalition troops (of which 150,000 were American) were inadequate for a decisive ground offensive. So, on November 8th, Bush announced plans to increase coalition military strength, and by the start of the ground war, there were an estimated 844,650 troops (of which 532,000 were American) and 2,614 aircraft (1,990 were American) to face off against an estimated million Iraqi troops and 750 Iraqi aircraft.[52]

A Unilateral Use-of-Force Operation?

As stated in the introduction of this case study and in the earlier chapters of this book, the 1991 Gulf War is trumpeted as a multilateral case of legitimacy, burden-sharing, and capability aggregation. The legitimacy argument is valid as the UN passed 12 resolutions and nearly 50 countries participated in military action against Iraq. The legitimacy of the military operation seemed to drive the burden-sharing, though it had little to do with the normative values of restoring sovereignty and more to do with the individual contributing countries' "self respect."[53]

Bush pressed the allies to contribute troops and money, and they contributed based on something akin to peer pressure.[54] Lawrence Freedman and Efraim Karsh describe the non-U.S. military contributions as designed to achieve "the maximum of political profile with the minimum of risk."[55]

Freedman and Karsh describe the non-U.S. financial contributions as simplistic U.S. demands that allies reach into their wallets.[56]

Bush's decision to use multilateral force was a simple expected utility calculation: the more troops, the better the probability of victory. So, Bush prodded allies to contribute, and in the early precarious stages of Operation Desert Shield, he worked tirelessly (and successfully) to build the coalition up rapidly.[57] By mid-August, France had ordered its Persian Gulf fleet to cooperate with the U.S. Navy. By August 21st, Egypt announced the deployment of 12,000 troops, Syria sent armored forces, and the nine-state Western European Union agreed to provide support. Belgium, Italy, the Netherlands, and Spain announced the sending of warships to assist the French and UK ships already in the Gulf.[58] In fact, the coalition naval fleet was assembled so fast and became so large that some countries, believing it was a wasted effort to send ships, decided against contributing naval power.[59] In the end, allies contributed $48 billion of the anticipated $54 billion cost, and the UK, in particular, committed almost a quarter of its army to the war effort.[60]

So, the 1991 Gulf War coalition was a multilateral operation, but it was also an operation that masked American hegemony and American interests.[61] Bush and the U.S. military made all of the key decisions: (1) orchestrating diplomatic activities through the UN, (2) using force against Iraq, (3) building a coalition to increase military capabilities, (4) pressuring coalition members for military and financial support, (5) drawing up the Operation Desert Shield and Desert Storm air and land tactical plans, (6) retaining command and control over the operations, and (7) deciding when to end military operations against Iraqi forces. This is consistent with the manner in which a hegemon operates: build and lead coalitions.

The Decision to Use Force

Based on intelligence reports of Iraqi troops massing on Kuwait's border, Bush initially authorized Operation Ivory Justice and dispatched two KC-135 refueling planes and one C-141 to the UAE on July 24, 1990, to help them defend against a potential air attack. This was an operation, not specifically designed to warn Iraq, but rather to signal to U.S. allies in the Gulf that the U.S. would support them.[62] Based on the coding rules and if used in the statistics chapter, this action alone would be coded a multilateral use of force. But, a detailed analysis of the decision allows one to see how Bush systematically asserted U.S. military power, while lowering the anticipated war costs with allies.

The initial reaction to Iraq's August 2nd invasion of Kuwait was to freeze Iraq's assets and pass a UN Security Council resolution demanding the withdrawal of Iraq from Kuwait.[63] But, no military force was planned. Bush presided over a NSC meeting, in which the consensus was "too bad about Kuwait, but it's just a gas station."[64] Bush told the press that day that he was not "contemplating" using force.[65] Bush then left for a conference at the Aspen Institute in Aspen, Colorado.

At the conference, he met with Thatcher who argued that Iraq's invasion was analogous to the Falkland Islands, and the U.S., as hegemon, must take responsibility to unite the world and defeat Hussein. She urged Bush "not to go wobbly" and that Hussein must be stopped.[66] Along with UK support, Thatcher assured Bush that the French would offer military assistance. *This meeting with Thatcher on August 3rd was the defining moment.* Bush emerged from the meeting and told the press, "We're not ruling any options in, but we're not ruling any options out."[67] In any case, Iraq's "naked aggression" would not stand.[68]

With Thatcher's strong support, Bush took the lead and stated in his memoirs: "It would be up to American leadership" to restore Kuwait's sovereignty.[69] At an NSC meeting that day, National Security Advisor Brent Scowcroft, Deputy Secretary of State Lawrence Eagleburger, and Defense Secretary Dick Cheney echoed Thatcher's thoughts and urged a rollback strategy.[70] So, essentially from August 3rd on, removing Iraqi forces from Kuwait was the goal.[71]

Bush summed up the transition from doing nothing militarily on August 2nd to embracing a rollback strategy on August 3rd:

> I had decided in my own mind in the first hours that the Iraqi aggression could not be tolerated. During my press remarks at the outset of the first NSC meeting [August 2nd], I did say that I was not contemplating intervention that perhaps inadvertently led to some confusion about my intent. I did not intend to rule out the use of force. At that juncture I did not wish explicitly to rule it in. But following the series of meetings [August 3rd meetings with Thatcher and NSC], I came to the conclusion that some public comment was needed to make clear my determination that the United States must do whatever might be necessary to reverse the Iraqi aggression.[72]

By August 4th, the Pentagon had begun deployment of three aircraft carrier groups, the battleship *Wisconsin*, two F-15 squadrons, two Army divisions, the 101st Airborne, the 24th Mechanized Infantry Division, and the 7th Marine Amphibious Force. In total, 125,000 troops were ready for deployment.[73] U.S. Central Command (CENTCOM) Commander General Norman Schwarzkopf suggested that the U.S. quickly deploy the 82nd Airborne to Saudi Arabia as a signal of resolve. Their deployment on August 7th marked the start of Operation Desert Shield (this was officially termed C-Day).[74]

Once Bush made the decision to use force, there is no evidence that he ever doubted his decision. Drew and Christopher Hitchens regard Bush's August 5th press conference and late September White House meeting with exiled Kuwaiti Emir Sheikh Jabir al-Ahmad al-Sabah as realpolitik moments of signaling.[75] Bush was not going to compromise with Hussein. He and Scowcroft made it clear that the U.S. was prepared to use military force to restore the balance in the Persian Gulf in a manner that protected the U.S. interests. The U.S. may have failed to deter Hussein from invading Kuwait, but it was now set on a course to restore its power and influence in the region.[76]

The Decision to Use Multilateral Force

If the goal was to use military force to remove Iraq from Kuwait, the U.S. would need massive amounts of troops, aircraft, and ships (i.e., military power).[77] The operation remained essentially a U.S. operation throughout August and September. The Air Force devised an air campaign, termed Instant Thunder, that would quickly "decapitate" Iraq's leadership. The campaign would destroy Iraq's leadership and military infrastructure before destroying its forces on the ground. It was an "outside-in" strategy and would be a revolution in itself (providing a blueprint for the "shock and awe" air campaign of the 2003 Gulf War).[78]

If the air campaign had been decided in early September, the ground campaign would be predicated on the expectation (and fear) of heavy losses. The initial option called for an attack directly against the center of Iraqi forces, and in briefing Bush on October 11th, the plan was dismissed as a non-starter, given the high expected casualty rate. Scowcroft compared the CENTCOM plan to the bloody attrition battles of the Civil War.[79] Cheney, in vetoing the plan, told JCS Chairman Colin Powell, "I can't let Norman [Schwarzkopf] do this high diddle diddle up-the-middle plan. I just can't let him do it."[80] Instead, a variation of Cheney's original left hook plan, which was designed to outflank the Iraqis far further to the west than the JCS had ever envisioned, was accepted in November.[81]

The fear of high casualties was the defining moment for Bush's second decision on October 30th, when he authorized a doubling of coalition forces to assure victory and disperse costs. No matter the land campaign plan; the losses were anticipated to be high. Schwarzkopf believed dislodging Iraqi forces would be "costly and bloody" with as many as 20,000 casualties.[82] The Marines, charged with an attack into Kuwait, would be outnumbered by three to one and by more than five to one in tanks.[83] A total of 150 planes were expected to be lost during the air campaign.[84] Civilian think tanks predicted possibly over 15,000

American casualties with up to 10,000 killed. Statistical models predicted casualties as high as 40,000.[85]

The U.S. clearly had military superiority, but President Bush, military experts, and even Hussein expected a large number of U.S. casualties. In what was to be the "Mother of All Battles," Hussein had warned Glaspie that the U.S. was "a society that cannot accept 10,000 dead in one battle."[86] On the domestic front, Senator Edward Kennedy cited the impending high costs, "[T]he 45,000 body bags the Pentagon sent to the region are all the evidence we need of the high price in lives and blood we will have to pay."[87]

With 250,000 troops in place, Powell advised Bush on October 30th that the U.S. was at "a fork in the road."[88] It could either build troops up for an offensive or rotate troops out. Based on a doctrine of overwhelming force, Powell requested that the VII Corps be deployed from Europe, three carrier battle groups deploy to the theater, the amount of Air Force planes and Marines be doubled, and the reserve be activated. He concluded by informing Bush that if he chose the buildup option, the forces would not be in place before January 15th. Bush responded, "Defense should go ahead and move its forces."[89] But, the administration waited until after the November 7th elections to make the announcement of the reinforcement decision.[90] Scowcroft summed up the reasoning for the delayed announcement, "The timing of the decision to reinforce the troops was determined by practical military considerations, but the timing of the announcement of the increase was driven by political ones."[91]

With a total force of 844,650 troops in place and having authorized Operation Desert Storm on December 29th, the attack began, as scheduled, at 3:00 am (Iraq time) on January 17th.[92]

Assessment

The 1991 Gulf War, an unlikely case for unilateral action, is consistent with the theory of unilateral use-of-force decision making. While the Gulf War was a remarkable and quick victory with minimal casualties for the U.S. and its coalition, Bush's decision making follows pre-war planning and analysis that estimated Iraq to have a strong military. Bush decided to use force on August 3rd, but after consultations with his advisers, he decided to lower the estimated costs by doubling the number of U.S. and coalition troops on October 30th. Throughout the decision-making process, as Bush has acknowledged, Congress (and its vote) played a marginal role.

The national security nature of the crisis and the predicted correlation with unilateralism did not happen, but we did see Bush decide to act as consistent with a hegemon. Iraq threatened U.S. access to oil and represented a threat to the stability of the region; so, Bush was going to act with or without coalition support. The U.S. did have an advantage with the CIMR scores (force employment, technology, and preponderance), but a fear of a tenacious Iraqi military caused Bush to significantly increase military strength. Bush worked to assemble a coalition, which constituted about a third of the fighting force and had a CINC and CIMR score higher than that of the U.S.!

Bay of Pigs (Unilateral Case)

If ever there was a case that presents a "most likely" case for the unilateral use-of-force decision-making theory, it is Kennedy's Bay of Pigs. Kennedy's Bay of Pigs decision was almost entirely devoid of a domestic political influence and almost entirely based on American hegemonic prestige. The Bay of Pigs would be coded as full unilateralism, but the "most likely" case becomes less obvious when Kennedy's decision making is examined in the context of the Cold War. The seemingly straightforward regime change crisis with unilateral force becomes a national security crisis with attempts to make the overthrow of Castro look multilateral.

As hypothesized, the greater the gap in military capability between the U.S. and an opponent, the more likely a president is to decide to use unilateral force. Crises in the Western hemisphere and those involving national security should also be correlated with unilateralism. So, then why did Kennedy try to make the overthrow of Castro look multilateral (i.e., having Cubans use the force)? Kennedy's decision is especially surprising, given the administration believed it had military superiority and a high probability of success. The answer rests with the Soviets and Kennedy's fear of their possible intervention. We should see Kennedy decide to use unilateral force without regard to domestic politics, take action consistent with a hegemon protecting its sphere of influence, and act unilaterally but try to give the perception of multilateralism to lower the probability (and resultant high costs) of Soviet military intervention.

I examine this case in the same manner as the 1991 Gulf War. First, I review the main events of the 1961 Bay of Pigs operation. Second, I detail the domestic politics surrounding the crisis, including the particulars of public opinion and congressional involvement. Third, I explain why the Bay of Pigs was a regime change *and* national security type of crisis. Fourth, I detail the military power of the U.S., the Cuban Brigade (the exiles), Cuba, and the Soviet Union in both quantitative and qualitative terms. Fifth, I consider the president's decision in terms of unilateralism and apply the president's decision process to the sequential model of this book. I trace Kennedy's decision making from deciding to use force on April 14th to deciding to use unilateral force on April 19th.

Summary of the Bay of Pigs Events

The Bay of Pigs is a remarkable case in failure.[93] Advised by outgoing President Eisenhower not to allow the Castro government to survive, President-elect Kennedy approved plans on November 29, 1960, to continue Central Intelligence Agency (CIA) training of Cuban exiles in Guatemala with the intention of using the exiles to invade Cuba.[94] The plan from the outset was not to use the U.S. military, *but* CIA personnel (i.e., U.S. citizens) were actively involved and participated in the operation.[95]

The Bay of Pigs operation began on April 15, 1961, when B-26 bombers disguised as the Revolutionary Air Force (FAR) bombed three Cuban airports in an attempt to knock out Castro's air force. After intelligence photos showed that only five Cuban aircraft had been destroyed in the April 15th bombings and that Castro still had several T-33s and Sea Furies operational, CIA Deputy Director General C.P. Cabell and CIA Deputy Director of Plans Richard Bissell pleaded through Secretary of State Dean Rusk to have Kennedy approve air strikes to cover the April 17th Monday morning beach landings. Kennedy rejected the request believing it would be politically bad for the U.S. in terms of reputation.[96]

At about 1:00 am on April 17th, an invasion force of some 1,400 anti-Castro Cuban fighters (known as the Cuban Brigade 2506) began to land at two beaches: Blue Beach at Giron and Red Beach at Playa Larga.[97] The U.S. Navy coordinated the launching of the invasion force. It provided destroyer escorts, a landing ship dock (LSD) *San Marcos*, two landing craft infantry (LCIs), three landing craft utility (LCUs), four landing craft vehicles and personnel (LCVPs), and a landing craft mechanized (LCM). CIA and U.S. Navy crews launched the vessels at sea, got off, and Cuban crews got on to take the crafts to the two-targeted beaches.[98]

At 4 am on the 17th, Cabell made a second request to use U.S. jets from the *Essex* to cover the loading and withdrawal of the beach landing vessels. Kennedy not only rejected the request, but he ordered the carrier to move farther out to sea.[99] The denial would prove to be costly. Cuban jets strafed the landing parties throughout the morning of the 17th. By the end of the day, the Cuban air force had shot down three Brigade B-26s, and sank two ships (the *Houston* and *Rio Escondido*) and one landing craft. A 20,000-man Cuban army had also advanced to the beach to meet the invaders.

The attacking Cuban planes were so effective that ships in the landing area were ordered back out to sea past the twelve-mile limit and to resupply under Navy protection. CIA agent Gray Lynch, on one of the landing ships, recalled passing the twelve-mile mark, being under attack, requesting protection from the Navy ships *Eaton* and *Murray*, and having his request denied.[100] Kennedy had ordered that no carrier ship operate closer than 50 miles from the Cuban shore, no aircraft closer than 15 miles, and no more than four aircraft could be "on station" at one time.[101]

Throughout the invasion, Kennedy repeatedly denied requests to use U.S. aircraft, but under pressure at an impromptu meeting in the early morning hours of April 19th, Kennedy authorized six unmarked jets from the *Essex* to provide air cover from 6:30 to 7:30 am for Brigade B-26s.[102] The jets were not to seek air combat or attack ground targets. Through a mix-up, the jets arrived too late to protect the B-26s and two B-26s were shot down.[103]

The Cuban Brigade was effectively abandoned, and the operation was over by the afternoon of the 19th. In the end, 114 Brigade fighters were killed and 1,189 fighters taken prisoner. The failure not only emboldened Castro, who declared Cuba "socialist" (i.e., communist), but it also emboldened Khrushchev to provide "all necessary help" to defend Cuba.[104]

Domestic Politics

Newly elected president, Kennedy was intent on proving himself a Cold Warrior the equal of his predecessor.[105] The Bay of Pigs was his first test, and as he believed, he wasn't typical of his fellow liberal Democrats, that as he often chided, lacked "balls" or were likely to be "grabbing their nuts" on an operation like the Bay of Pigs.[106] Kennedy favored a mano a mano style and did not back down to challenges. In fact, he enjoyed them and often sought out opponents to defeat.[107]

From a domestic standpoint, Kennedy had Democratic control of Congress, had an approval rating of 80.5 percent, had a misery index of 8.02 percent, and was facing a rival in both the Cubans and Soviets. Given this favorable domestic standing, Kennedy was not to be deterred.

His first task was to overcome any bureaucratic inefficiencies. Special Assistant for National Security McGeorge Bundy once commented that the president told him, "By gosh, I don't care what it is, but if I need some material fast or an idea fast, CIA is the place I have to go."[108] The operation planning laid on his desk by the CIA, an agency he admired, was so secretive and so efficient that the president made the decision to plan and carry out the operation without fully consulting with Congress, the Joint Chiefs of Staff, the UN (even the U.S. ambassador to the UN Adlai Stevenson was not fully consulted), or the Cuban Brigade fighters.[109]

The operation was also remarkable in how uninvolved the public was in having any influence on the decision process. Kennedy did not inform the public of his intentions, but he did assume the public would be against using the U.S. military. A July 16-21, 1960 Gallup poll, in which only 3 percent of Americans supported sending U.S. troops to Cuba, seems to confirm Kennedy's assumptions.[110] The *New York Times* regularly reported on the operation planning, and while Kennedy grew angry about the leaks, the public response was mild to say the least.[111]

Kennedy's fellow Democrats also had little influence on his decision. Senator William Fulbright delivered a memo to Kennedy on March 30th, urging him not to invade Cuba. Fulbright argued against the legitimacy of a unilateral attack, saying it violated the OAS charter and hemispheric treaties and would be denounced at the UN as imperialism. The memo did not sway Kennedy. In fact, it probably had a negative effect because Kennedy was "more militant" after reading the memo.[112]

Crisis Trigger

Using the coding rules established in Chapter 3, the Bay of Pigs operation would be classified as a regime change crisis. This makes sense given the removal of Castro was the primary objective, even if national security was the end goal. But, the case study method allows the benefit of studying the nuances of a not-so-easily defined empirical world. Regime change was the objective of the operation, but national security was an overarching (and powerful) influence on Kennedy's decision making. In a sense, the crisis trigger parallels Kennedy's sequential decision with regime change influencing his decision to use force and national security influencing his decision to use unilateral force.

Regime Change

Both Presidents Eisenhower and Kennedy were intent on not allowing communist expansion into the Americas. This was a strong twentieth century interpretation and unilateral enforcement of the Monroe Doctrine.[113] Kennedy partisans suggest that Kennedy was goaded into the Bay of Pigs operation out of fear of Republicans potentially capitalizing on the situation, if he did not use Eisenhower's trained fighters to overthrow Castro.[114] But, Kennedy had always been clear, that he would not allow the Soviets (or Communists) to "push" where U.S. prestige was involved.[115]

The Bay of Pigs operation can be traced back to March 17, 1960, and was based on the "Guatemala model," in which the CIA overthrew the Guatemalan government in the course of one week in 1954.[116] The Guatemalan operation succeeded based on a combination of untraditional methods: CIA propaganda, a force of 150 exiles, Americans flying P-47 fighters, a drunk Guatemalan fighter pilot encouraging his colleagues to defect, and CIA-chosen President Castillo Armas driving across the border from Honduras in a station wagon to assume control of the government.[117]

Even as the Bay of Pigs operation turned into a disaster, Kennedy had Rusk warn the Soviets not to intervene on behalf of Castro, as the U.S. would protect the Western hemisphere from "external aggression."[118]

National Security

To understand his decision-making process, one must understand that the Bay of Pigs was both a regional issue (U.S.-Cuba hostilities) and a global issue (U.S.-Soviet competition).[119] The protection of America's sphere of influence (i.e., keeping a communist regime from ruling in the Western hemisphere) was Kennedy's overt problem and one that drove his Bay of Pigs planning. But, the Soviet threat was a strategic problem, and it drove Kennedy's decision making before and during the Bay of Pigs operation.

Kennedy did not understand Khrushchev and was intimidated by him. But at the same time, Kennedy wanted to prove he was not weak, and as such, he took a dual track approach to Khrushchev. Kennedy ordered military officials to remove anti-Soviet language from their speeches, and he sent Khrushchev a letter appealing for a "harmonious relationship."[120] But, in a January 30, 1961, speech, Kennedy declared an "hour of maximum danger," in which the Communists were expanding into Latin America, the Soviets were determined to dominate the world, and domestic problems paled in comparison to the strategic threats.[121]

Khrushchev, facing his own domestic pressures, responded to Kennedy's militancy with a threat against Berlin. He charged Bonn on February 17th with making military preparations and threatened that the Soviets were determined to achieve a German peace treaty.[122] The Soviet threat against Berlin limited Kennedy's use of military power against Cuba. If Kennedy used the U.S. military to invade Cuba, Khrushchev may do the same thing in Berlin. If the Soviets attacked Berlin, Kennedy, who was compelled to defend Berlin (through NATO), would either have to decide on superpower confrontation or appeasement.[123]

Seeing this choice, Kennedy believed it necessary to remove Castro, but he did not want to risk a confrontation with Castro's ally, the Soviet Union. Kennedy, in meeting with Brigade members after the invasion, informed them that he believed the mission could have succeeded without U.S. help. More importantly, he told them that the U.S., as hegemon, had many responsibilities in its struggle against communism, and that using U.S. troops would have had negative ramifications.[124]

The Soviets understood the strategic implications as well. Khrushchev was livid upon hearing about the invasion. He informed Kennedy that the invasion was at the "backing of the Americans," and he would provide Castro "all necessary assistance" unless Kennedy called off the operation.[125] More privately, Khrushchev was surprised that Kennedy did not use U.S. troops to invade Cuba. The Soviets would not have allowed an unfavorable dictator to remain in their sphere of influence, and there was little Khrushchev could have done to save Castro.[126] Given this failing, Khrushchev decided that Kennedy was weak, and he tested Kennedy in Berlin and at the Vienna Summit.[127]

Soon after the invasion, Kennedy met separately with former President Eisenhower and Vice President Nixon to discuss the failure of the operation. Kennedy told Eisenhower he did not provide air cover for fear of the Soviets taking Berlin. Eisenhower admonished him, "That is exactly the opposite of what should really happen. The Soviets follow their own plans, and if they see us show any weakness, that is when they press us the hardest."[128] Nixon advised Kennedy to press hard, to find a legal justification to use U.S. troops to invade the country. Kennedy responded, "There is a good chance that, if we move on Cuba, Khrushchev will move on Berlin. I just don't think we can take the risk."[129] Nixon left the meeting believing Kennedy was a "chicken" for canceling the air strikes and for not wanting to attack Cuba with U.S. troops.[130]

The Bay of Pigs disaster did not deter Kennedy from trying to remove Castro; Kennedy actually increased efforts to remove the "thorn" in his side. Attorney General Robert Kennedy declared the toppling of Castro as the administration's "top priority" and started "Operation Mongoose," which included assassination schemes.[131]

Military Power

Military Power between the U.S. and Soviets dictated Kennedy's decision making during the Bay of Pigs. The U.S. had a superior military advantage vis-à-vis Castro, but the Soviets had a superior military advantage vis-à-vis NATO troops in Berlin.[132] Given this, it is necessary to examine all four of the actors involved in the Bay of Pigs operation: (1) the Cuban Brigade, (2) Castro's Cubans, (3) the U.S., and (4) the Soviets.

Once again the case study method offers an advantage over the statistical method. Military power can be defined using components of the CIMR, and it can be defined using a more qualitative tactical measure of the aircraft, soldiers, tanks, and weapons used. For each crisis actor, I first list the CIMR components and then I list the actual military power each actor could have brought or did bring to bear in the crisis.

Cuban Brigade Military Power

The Cuban Brigade does not have preponderance, technology, or force employment scores, given that the crisis dyad fails to meet the use of force standard in the Fordham—COW MID data set.[133] However, the operation as a whole cost $46 million and about 1,511 fighters were trained, meaning the average spending per soldier was $30,443.[134] The Cuban Brigade CINC score would have been zero, and the force employment would have had a dummy of zero.

The Brigade fighters stormed the beach aboard two LCIs, three LCUs, four LCVPs, and seven commercial freighters.[135] With the exception of three of the freighters, each vessel had 50-caliber machine guns, and the LCIs also included two 75-mm rifles. Each Brigade soldier carried their personal weapon, and as a whole, the invasion force was armed with a large number of Browning automatic rifles, machine guns, mortars, recoilless rifles, rocket launchers, and flame-throwers. There were also five M-41 tanks, 12 heavy trucks, an aviation fuel tank truck, a tractor crane, a bulldozer, two large water trailers, and numerous small trucks and tractors. Eleven B-26s were available for close air support and interdiction during the beach landings.[136]

U.S. Military Power

Per table 5.5, the U.S. CINC score in 1961, in terms of preponderance, was 0.211 and its GDP was 2.094 trillion or 24 percent of the world's GDP. In terms of technology, the U.S. spent an average of $20,723 per soldier. In terms of force employment, the U.S. received a dummy variable of one, given its ability to conduct warfare consistent with the nuclear revolution.

The massive U.S. military advantage led Kennedy to assume that the operation would be successful.[137] But, Kennedy was insistent that U.S. combat forces not be used. He believed U.S. forces to be under strength, and if for some reason, the troops became bogged down in Cuba, he was sure the Soviets would try to take Berlin.[138]

TABLE 5.5
Military Power in 1961

Crisis Actors	*Preponderance (CINC Score)*	*Preponderance (GDP)*	*Technology (Spending/ Soldier)*	*Force Employment (Dummy Variable)*
U.S.	0.211	$2.094 trillion	$20,723	1
Cuban Brigade	0.000	$0	$30,443	0
Cuba	0.004	$14.625 billion	$648	0
Soviets	0.174	$891.763 billion	$14,554	1

Cuban Military Power

In terms of preponderance, the Cuban CINC score in 1961 was 0.004 and its GDP was 14.625 billion or 0.002 percent of the world's GDP. In terms of technology, Cuba spent an average of $648 per soldier. In terms of force employment, Cuba received a dummy variable of zero, given its inability to conduct warfare consistent with the nuclear revolution.

The Kennedy administration tended to underestimate the strength of Castro's military in the short term, but it was concerned that in the long term, Cuba could become a "significant military power" with Soviet aid.[139] By January 1961, the Soviets were shipping large quantities of arms to Cuba and were preparing to train Cuban pilots to fly Soviet-provided MiG jets.[140]

The Joint Chiefs of Staff believed the invasion plan had "a fair chance of ultimate success."[141] The isolated Bay of Pigs region was accessible by only three roads, which the Kennedy administration believed could be defended with a minimal number of Brigade members.[142]

The Cuban air force was estimated to have had a total of 36 aircraft: (1) 17 B-26s, (2) 13 Sea Furies, (3) five T-33s, and (4) one F-51. An after-action report estimates that the Cubans launched seven aircraft against the invasion force: (1) two B-26s, (2) two Sea Furies, and (3) three T-33s.[143] Armed with Soviet Bloc–furnished weapons, the Cuban Revolutionary Army was estimated to have had 32,000 men and the militia was estimated to have had 200,000 men.[144]

Soviet Military Power

In terms of preponderance, the Soviet CINC score in 1961 was 0.174 and its GDP was 891.763 billion or 10.2 percent of the world's GDP. In terms of technology, the Soviets spent an average of $14,554 per soldier. In terms of force employment, the Soviets received a dummy variable of one, given its ability to conduct warfare consistent with the nuclear revolution.

Kennedy's Decision Making

Kennedy's decision making follows the theory of this book. He was a realist committed to using his leadership to protect national interests, and as Assistant for National Security Affairs McGeorge Bundy described, he believed the U.S. "was the locomotive at the head of mankind, and the rest of the world the caboose."[145]

Kennedy also made an expected utility calculation. While he believed the U.S. had a superior military advantage, he did not want to risk a prolonged war. In an April 12th meeting, he stated, "The minute I land one Marine, we're in this thing up to our necks. I can't get the United States into a war and then lose it, no matter what it takes. I'm not going to risk an American Hungary."[146] Instead, he would rely on the Cuban Brigade, and even if they failed initially, they could escape to the hills and carry out a guerrilla campaign.[147]

Kennedy's use-of-force decision and unilateral use-of-force decision followed a sequential process as illustrated in figure 5.2. Though confusion reigned throughout the operation, Kennedy made all of the crucial decisions. In his first decision on using force, Kennedy made a series of tactical decisions with the intention of not explicitly using U.S. force. These were as follows: (1) the decision to weaken the first airstrike on the Cuban air bases; (2) the decision to cancel the second strike for the beach landings; and (3) the decision to have the Brigade land on April 17th. Kennedy eventually made the decision to use U.S. unilateral force (though he tried to minimize U.S. visibility).[148]

In sum, Kennedy made the decision to use force in order to enforce the Monroe Doctrine, to reverse a communist inroad in the Western hemisphere. Once the operation was under way, Kennedy resisted the use of U.S. troops due to concerns about a Soviet response. Avoiding losing Berlin was Kennedy's main priority, and it drove his decisions throughout the operation.[149] When Kennedy did commit U.S. forces, he did so in a way as not to be threatening.

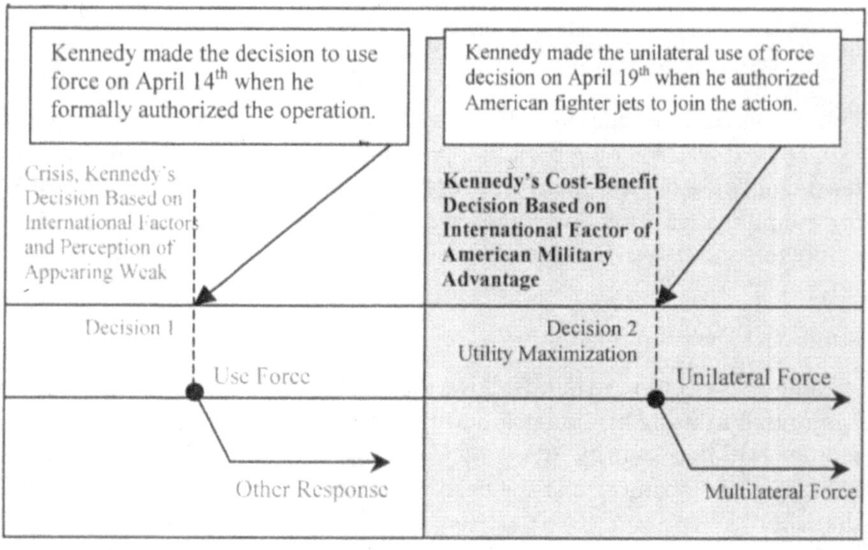

FIGURE 5.2
Sequential Model of Kennedy's Use-of-Force Decision Making

A Unilateral Use-of-Force Operation?

Kennedy's intention was to always use force with Cuban exiles; so, he could technically claim it was not a U.S. action. He made this clear to the public on April 12th: "There will not be, under any conditions, an intervention in Cuba by the United States Armed Forces."[150] However, the world, the American people, and even Brigade members believed it was a unilateral American operation.[151] In fact, Brigade members, upon landing on the beaches, declared themselves as coming from the U.S.[152] Castro called the invasion one in which the U.S. "delivered the planes, the bombs, and trained the mercenaries." He was clear to refer to the Cuban Brigade as U.S. mercenaries and not as Cuban citizens.[153]

The Decision to Use Force

While Kennedy had approved plans to continue training Cuban exiles soon after being elected (November 29, 1960), he continued to ponder whether to go forward with the operation (i.e., decide to use force) throughout the early months of his presidency. Adviser Arthur Schlesinger believed that as late as April 4th, the president was against using force. Kennedy began to see problems with the CIA plans, but more importantly, he was worried that an invasion of Cuba would set back his attempts to gain agreement with the Soviets over Laos. Khrushchev was obsessed with Cuba, and an invasion would have strong negative implications on the U.S.-Soviet relationship.[154]

In meetings on April 4th and 6th, Schlesinger saw the president's reluctance begin to fade, as the CIA convinced him that the Brigade could escape from the beaches into the hills. The costs, both in military and political terms, would be minimal: if the operation failed, the exiles could fight as guerrillas along with other anti-Castro guerrillas already on the island. Kennedy believed it better to have the Cuban exiles fighting in Cuba, than running around the U.S. saying how Kennedy had failed them.[155]

Kennedy is believed to have authorized the invasion on Saturday, April 8th, and on the 11th, Attorney General Robert Kennedy informed Schlesinger that his brother had made up his mind and expected everyone's support.[156] As the invasion date approached, Kennedy felt compelled to move forward with the operation. He did not want to appear weak or to give the perception that Castro was popular.[157]

On April 13th, Kennedy requested an appraisal of the Brigade's capability, and receiving a strong positive appraisal in response, Kennedy was confident in formally authorizing the operation on April 14th.[158] On the 14th, Kennedy called Bissell and informed him to go ahead with the airstrikes on the 15th.

Bissell informed him 16 planes would conduct the operation. But, Kennedy, in authorizing only eight planes, responded, "Well, I don't want it on that scale. I want it minimal."[159] The operation was set to begin.

The Decision to Use Unilateral Force

From the start of the operation, confusion was the modus operandi. The Cuban Brigade was not up to the task, and the president contemplated direct U.S. involvement. For a couple days, Kennedy steadfastly refused to allow U.S. participation, but by the 17th, he began to have second thoughts. In fact, Robert Kennedy believed that his brother would have authorized U.S. involvement as early as the evening of April 17th, but the president was receiving information five to seven hours after the battle incidents were occurring. Upon hearing that ammunition supply ships were needed to ensure the beachhead's survival, Kennedy remarked, "I'd rather be an aggressor than a bum."[160]

By 9 pm on April 17th, the reports of a disastrous operation were being received, but it was too late to try to save the operation.[161] By the morning of the 18th, Kennedy was trying to minimize the damage to U.S. prestige and still trying to minimize U.S. visibility in the operation.[162] By the evening of the 18th, he had concluded that it was useless to continue the operation, even with U.S. aircrews and resupplies.[163] To all around him, Kennedy had accepted the failure and went about his presidential duties, including hosting the annual Congressional Reception that night at the White House.

Deputy National Security Adviser Walt Rostow and Bissell were anything but relaxed. To them, the operation needed to be saved. Rostow shared the sentiments of the CIA and the military, "It was inconceivable to them that the President would let it openly fail when he had all this American power."[164] Rostow scheduled a meeting for midnight at the White House. At 11:58 pm, he and Bissell would meet the president, Rusk, Vice President Lyndon Johnson, Secretary of Defense Robert McNamara, Chairman of the Joint Chiefs of Staff General Lyman L. Lemnitzer, and Chief of Naval Operations Admiral Arleigh A. Burke, all of whom were in formal attire from the reception.[165] Bissell made a case for using jets from the *Essex* to save the operation. Burke readily agreed with Bissell, suggesting that with two jets and one destroyer, the U.S. could defeat Castro's forces. Kennedy was not to be persuaded, "Burke, I don't want the United States involved in this." Burke reminded the president that the U.S. was involved.[166]

Finally, Kennedy was persuaded, he authorized six unmarked jets from the Essex to fly from 6:30 to 7:30 am on Wednesday morning to cover a B-26 attack. The jets could not engage enemy aircraft nor attack ground targets; they could only defend the B-26s. Rusk reminded the president that his decision meant active U.S. involvement. To which, Kennedy responded, "We're already in it."[167] Through a massive communication breakdown, four American-piloted B-26s, including pilots from the Alabama National Guard, arrived over the beachhead before the *Essex* received its authorization to protect the bombers. The B-26s were attacked and four of the American pilots were killed.[168]

Assessment

The Bay of Pigs operation, a likely case for unilateral action, is consistent with the theory of unilateral use of force decision making. While the Bay of Pigs was a complete failure and a complete defeat of unilaterally applied American military action, Kennedy's decision making followed the theory of this book. Kennedy believed the Cuban Brigade could topple Castro's regime and convinced of probable success, he decided to use force on April 14th. Then, in an attempt to save the operation (and perhaps still have success), he ordered the American military to become overtly involved. Throughout the decision-making process, Congress and the public played almost no role at all.

The location of the crisis in the Western hemisphere is consistent with the theory's predicted unilateralism, but the regime change and national security nature of the crisis complicate the case. National security should be consistent with unilateralism. But, the national security trigger was premised on fear of Soviet involvement and fear of a high cost conflict against the superpower with high CIMR scores. So, it is understandable to see why Kennedy wished to conceal U.S. involvement. But, when faced with defeat, Kennedy resorted to dramatically increasing military power through direct U.S. military intervention. This case, while consistent with the theory, serves to enrich the theory as well.

1989 Panama Invasion (Unilateral Case)

The 1989 Panama invasion represents an ideal case in unilateralism. With a dictator threatening U.S. interests (and its citizens) in the Western hemisphere, Bush acted without trying to overcome the obstacles of multilateralism. The invasion is coded as full unilateralism, and it represents the clearest case of how a hegemon should act. Examining the case in detail, though, illustrates the sequential nature of a president's decision, even if it is made in a short span of time. Bush decided to use force and then he asked his advisers on how best to achieve his main objective of removing Noriega from power. Assured of probable unilateral military success, Bush acted without regard to public opinion or congressional involvement.

As hypothesized, a large military gap and a crisis in the Western hemisphere should correlate positively with unilateralism. The Panama invasion is the "most likely" case, in which Bush's decision to act unilaterally should be made unconditionally. Bush's decision should reflect that of a hegemon protecting its sphere of influence. Bush's decision should also involve estimating the costs of toppling the Noriega regime and acting unilaterally if military superiority is assured. The unilateral decision should also be made without regard to domestic political influences.

I examine this case in the same manner as the prior two cases. First, I review the main events of the 1989 Panama invasion (Operation Just Cause). Second, I detail the domestic politics surrounding the crisis, including the particulars of public opinion and congressional involvement. Third, I explain why the Panama invasion was a regime change type of crisis. Fourth, I detail the military power of the U.S. and Panama in both quantitative and qualitative terms. Fifth, I consider the president's decision in terms of unilateralism and apply the president's decision process to the sequential model of this book. I trace Bush's decision making from deciding to use force in the late morning of December 17th to deciding to use unilateral force by the afternoon of the 17th.

Summary of the 1989 Panama Invasion Events

Once an intelligence source for the U.S., Dictator Manuel Antonio Noriega lost favor with the U.S., turned to support Cuba and Nicaragua in the summer of 1987, and was indicted in Florida in February 1988 on drug charges.[169] Noriega was a violent dictator and the Bush administration began to plan and prepare for a military intervention in the event Noriega threatened U.S. interests. These threats to U.S. interests began in March 1988 with a series of hostile Panama Defense Force (PDF) actions toward U.S. forces in Panama. In March, the PDF wounded a Marine corporal's wife with a shotgun blast. In August, an Air Force sergeant and his father were beaten. In November, a Navy petty officer was forced to beg for his life. On March 3, 1989, the PDF detained six American school buses, two loaded with children for several hours.[170]

When Noriega's candidate Carlos Duque lost an election, wrought by fraud and violence, Noriega still declared Duque the winner and had president-elect Guillermo Endara beat with tire irons in front of television cameras on May 10, 1989.[171] In mid-December 1989, Noriega crossed the line, when he declared Panama "at war" with the U.S., murdered a U.S. Marine lieutenant, and beat a Navy lieutenant and his wife.[172]

At 12:45 am on December 20th, Operation Just Cause commenced. U.S. military forces descended upon Panama in the largest military action since Vietnam and the largest air-drop since D-Day. The Army Rangers and 82nd Airborne Division seized Torrijos and Tocumen airfields. The Navy SEALs seized Noriega's personal jet at Paitilla airfield. A C-130 Spectre gunship attacked the PDF's crown jewel, the Comandancia, and two F-117s dropped two 2,000 pound bombs near the PDF barracks in Rio Hato to "scare" the barrack occupants. Army Rangers then seized the PDF barracks. The Rangers, along with Mechanized Infantry and Airborne Infantry, also seized the Comandancia. Delta Force commandos seized Noriega's Radio Nacional broadcast station. The Marines secured the Bridge of the Americas and protected areas around Howard Air Force Base. U.S. forces also secured the Canal and Colon.

The military campaign was intense but brief. The PDF was a non-factor, ceasing to exist by December 24th, and Noriega's *battallones de la dignidad* fought for a couple days and even held out in a mined tunnel at Tinjaita but the U.S. campaign was overwhelming.[173] The quick victory resulted in a manhunt for Noriega, and he was detained on January 3, 1990, when he left the Papal Nunciature (the Vatican Embassy) in Panama.[174] Though 23 U.S. troops were killed, the end result was considered a complete success.[175]

Domestic Politics

Domestic politics had little, if any, influence on Bush's decision to use force. U.S. public opinion support for sending U.S. troops to Panama decreased from 58 percent (May 11-12, 1989) to 26 percent (October 5-6, 1989).[176] From a domestic standpoint, Bush faced Democratic control of Congress, had an approval rating of 71 percent, had a misery index of 10.1 percent, and was not facing a rival in Panama.

Interestingly, Bush faced congressional pressure to remove Noriega. In fact, Congress chided Bush throughout 1988 and 1989 for failing to take decisive action. Senator John McCain and Congressman John Murtha, returning from the 1989 Panamanian elections, found U.S. Southern Command (SOUTHCOM) General Frederick Woerner weak and ineffective. They pressed Bush to replace him, and Bush did so, putting General Maxwell Thurman in charge in September 1989.[177] After the failed Giroldi coup, Senators Jesse Helms and David Boren accused the administration of being a bunch of "Keystone Kops" for failing to take advantage of the coup and remove Noriega.[178]

But generally, Bush did not consult with Congress or ask for its permission to use force. His consultation consisted of calling congressional leaders from 6:00 pm to 6:30 pm on December 19th to inform them of his planned invasion.[179]

Crisis Trigger

Using the Chapter 3 coding rules, the Panama invasion would be classified as a regime change crisis. This makes sense given the removal of Noriega was the primary objective. But, also in a sense, Bush's desire to protect the Americans living in Panama could represent a national security goal.

Regime Change

Bush, in deciding to remove Noriega from power, justified his decision as self-defense, given Noriega's declaration of war and the murder of a U.S. Marine. According to Bush, the U.S. toppled the Noriega regime for three explicit reasons: (1) to save American lives, (2) to bring indicted Noriega to trial and (3) to restore democracy in Panama.[180] Noriega was a fugitive from U.S. justice, and it was up to the U.S. to remove him from power and put in place the rightfully and democratically elected president.[181]

The post-invasion reaction to the regime change was strong. In general, the Latin American response to the invasion was "muted and quite inconsequential," due to the fact Bush had talked to nearly every Latin American leader and informed them of why the U.S. was using military force.[182] But, the UN General Assembly denounced the U.S. action as a "flagrant violation of international law" and the Vatican described U.S. troops surrounding the Papal Nunciature as an "occupying army."[183] Various world leaders criticized Bush for taking unilateral action. But, Bush cared very little about world opinion, as his response to criticism from Soviet General Secretary Mikhail Gorbachev demonstrates: "If they kill an American Marine, that's real bad. And if they threaten and brutalize the wife of an American citizen, sexually threatening the lieutenant's wife while kicking him in the groin over and over again—then, Mr. Gorbachev, please understand, this president is going to do something about it."[184]

Military Power

The decision to act unilaterally seems to have been a rather easy decision for Bush. Powell would later call the Panama invasion a "scrimmage" as opposed to the "NFL" game of the Iraq invasion.[185]

U.S. Military Power

Per table 5.6, the U.S. CINC score in 1989, in terms of preponderance, was 0.150 and its GDP was 5.704 trillion or 21 percent of the world's GDP.

TABLE 5.6
Military Power in 1989

Crisis Actors	*Preponderance (CINC Score)*	*Preponderance (GDP)*	*Technology (Spending/ Soldier)*	*Force Employment (Dummy Variable)*
U.S.	0.150	$5.704 trillion	$131,696	1
Panama	0.0003	$10.215 billion	$10,071	0

In terms of technology, the U.S. spent an average of $131,696 per soldier. In terms of force employment, the U.S. received a dummy variable of one, given its ability to conduct warfare consistent with the nuclear revolution.

As in the 1991 Gulf War, Bush would order the doubling of forces in an effort to have military superiority to carry out an offensive campaign. On December 19th, transports landed troops, doubling the number of U.S. troops in Panama from 13,000 to more than 26,000.[186] All four services participated in the invasion and a special emphasis was given to special forces, which accounted for 4,150 troops of the 26,000 troops.[187]

Panamanian Military Power

In terms of preponderance, the Panamanian CINC score in 1989 was 0.0003 and its GDP was 10.215 billion or zero percent of the world's GDP. In terms of technology, Panama spent an average of $10,071 per soldier. In terms of force employment, Panama received a dummy variable of zero, given its inability to conduct warfare consistent with the nuclear revolution.

Panama, in essence, did not have military but a "glorified police force" with 10,000 men and four poor quality, propeller-driven combat planes. It had no tanks and no missiles.[188] Noriega's main power came from the *battallones de la dignidad*, an "armed rabble" that wore no uniforms and was undisciplined. Richard Koster and Guillermo Sanchez describe the battlioneers as "barbarian nomads of some new dark age, but when it came to a fight, they fought better than the regular PDF units."[189]

Bush's Decision Making

Noriega, like Hussein after him, did not believe Bush would resort to military force. When the reinforcements landed at Howard Air Base in Panama, Noriega wasn't worried. Bush had twice sent reinforcements and nothing happened. The State Department had even labeled the murder of the U.S. Marine an "isolated incident."[190] But, Bush had made the decision to remove

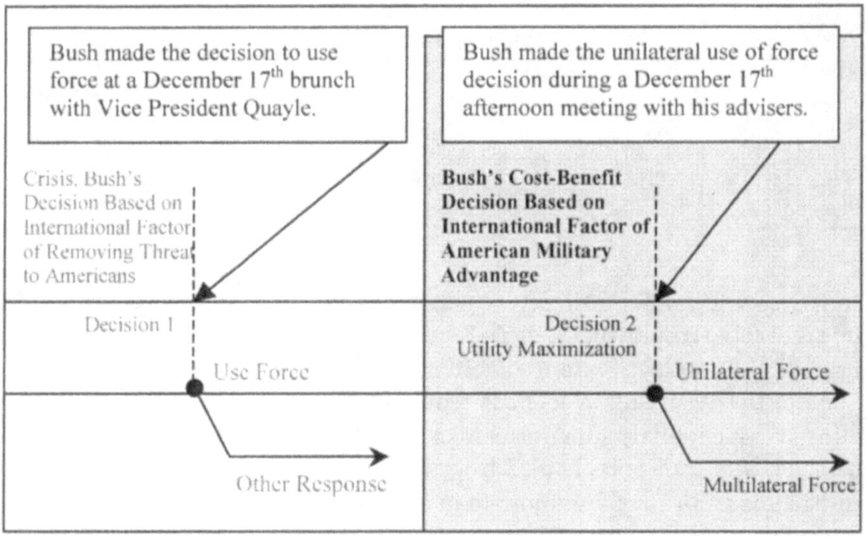

FIGURE 5.3
Sequential Model of Bush's Panama Use-of-Force Decision Making

Noriega, and it was a decision, like his 1991 Gulf War decision, that he did not have second thoughts about.[191] John Dinges describes Bush's order to remove Noriega as being personal, based on the evilness of Noriega, and not a decision driven by ideological differences.[192]

As illustrated in figure 5.3, Bush made the decision to use force during a brunch with Vice President Dan Quayle on December 17th. In an afternoon meeting with his advisers, Bush asked for the best military plan to accomplish his decision to remove Noriega. Powell advised him to use overwhelming unilateral strength. In a matter of hours, Bush had made his two decisions—to use force and to use unilateral force. A multilateral force option was not even discussed.

A Unilateral Use-of-Force Operation?

After the fraud of the 1989 elections, the OAS passed a couple of resolutions deploring Noriega to "respect" the will of the Panamanian people.[193] But, the OAS and the U.S. worked at cross purposes. Both entities wanted Noriega out of office, but the OAS wanted to resolve the situation diplomatically while the U.S. was prepared to act militarily. The OAS sent five delegations to Panama from May 23rd to August to report on how a transfer of power could be achieved. Noriega, not only ignored the OAS resolutions, but he openly referred to the OAS delegations as "idiots." The U.S. was not to be deterred by international inaction. It sent armored vehicle convoys through the streets of Panama and conducted military exercises as a show of strength. Noriega, not believing the threat, simply denounced the U.S. actions as well.[194]

Using the 1983 Grenada invasion as a model, the U.S. simply took action to topple a leader it saw as a threat to its citizens living there.[195] Unlike Grenada, Bush concluded that multilateral diplomacy and military action was useless and a waste of time and effort.[196] In short, Bush never seriously contemplated using multilateral force.

The Decision to Use Force

After the May 10th election fiasco, Bush sent 2,000 troops to Panama as a signal to Noriega. He also sought international assistance and openly appealed on May 13th to the PDF for a coup.[197] But Bush, unlike Kennedy with the Bay of Pigs operation, was not willing to rely on indigenous forces.[198] Major Moises Giroldi had approached the CIA and U.S. military about coordinating a coup. The Bush administration, while wanting to overthrow Noriega, was "wary" of Giroldi's plan and decided not to actively support him.[199] Powell commented, "A great power doesn't throw the weight of its prestige and authority behind some guy who walks in. . . . When the time comes and there is believed to be a requirement to do this, we do it on our agenda for our purposes."[200] Giroldi's October 3rd coup ended in disaster with Noriega executing Giroldi and ten other coup participants.[201]

But in the aftermath of the October coup, Bush decided to take action.[202] Under the cover of routine supply shipments to its Panamanian bases, the U.S. transported equipment for a military offensive, consisting of Apache helicopters and at least four tanks.[203] With planning dating back to Operation Blue Spoon in 1988, the military was prepared for a massive invasion.[204]

Noriega's declaration of war on the U.S. on December 15th and the beating of a Navy officer and his wife on December 16th were too much for Bush. This latter incident, in particular, seemed to have a strong effect on Bush, causing him to authorize Operation Just Cause on December 17th.[205] On December 17th, Bush met Quayle for a brunch and informed him that he had decided to use military force. In authorizing the invasion of Panama, Bush set into motion a doctrine of overwhelming strength that would foreshadow his Operation Desert Storm decision making.[206]

The Decision to Use Unilateral Force

After the brunch, at a 2 pm meeting with his advisers, Bush outlined his three objectives: (1) remove Noriega from power, (2) secure the safety of

Americans in Panama, and (3) restore democracy to Panama.[207] Then, he stated he wanted to use military force and he asked his team, "How can I do that?"[208]

Powell advised Bush to use massive force, consisting of 25,000 troops and Stealth fighter-bombers. Bush asked if a smaller force could accomplish the same objective. Powell responded that Noriega would hide, and in order to prevent Noriega from commanding troops if he emerged from hiding, the PDF would need to be destroyed.[209] A larger force would also reduce the probability of high casualties. *After learning of an estimated 70 U.S. soldiers killed, Bush signed off on the operation, "Let's do it."*[210]

Assessment

The Panama invasion, a likely case for unilateral action, is consistent with the theory of unilateral use-of-force decision making. In fact, the Panama invasion case is the strongest evidence in support of the theory. With a weak military and being located in the Western hemisphere, Panama was an easy target for American military power. The rapidity and ease of Bush's use of force and unilateral use of force decision seems to confirm this notion. After the brutal beating of a Navy officer, Bush made his decision to use force after brunch on December 17th. In a follow-up meeting with advisers, he asked how best to remove Noriega and after being advised to use overwhelming unilateral strength, he authorized the operation on the afternoon of the 17th. As with the other cases, Congress and the public played almost no role in Bush's decision-making process.

The location of the crisis in the Western hemisphere and Panama's weak military is consistent with the theory's predicted unilateralism. Moreover, the case study evidence demonstrates that Bush entirely ignored the possibility of multilateral action. The OAS proved ineffective at diplomacy, and there is little doubt that establishing a multilateral operation would have been plagued by the multilateral problems listed in Chapter 2. This case was selected as an "extreme" example of unilateralism and upon examination, it adds considerable weight in support of the theory.

Conclusion

The case studies, the last of the three methods of this book, were intended to determine the accuracy of the theory of unilateral use-of-force decision making. Taking cases with extreme values of the dependent variable (the 1991 Gulf War and Panama invasion), along with a more complicated case (the Bay of Pigs operation) was designed to test the hypotheses of this book: unilateral military action is positively correlated with a wide gap in military power, an opponent located in the Western hemisphere, and a national security threat.

The three variables performed well in the statistics chapter, and the variables in this chapter performed well with the case study method. Though notably, the case study method has an advantage over the statistics method. It allows a detailed examination (e.g., the 1991 Gulf War was a national security threat and against a strong opponent) of historical events that cannot neatly be generalized to a theory. The other test of this book—that a unilateral decision is premised on international, not domestic factors—was supported in the experiment chapter and reinforced with the case studies of this chapter. The common theme for all three cases was for a president to meet with his advisers and make a unilateral-multilateral decision without regard to domestic pressures.

I, now, turn to the Conclusion chapter. First, I discuss the implications from the statistical, experimental, and case study analyses. For each of the methods, I explain the results and assess the performance of the explanatory variables and the unilateral use-of-force decision-making theory. I then offer potential areas for future research, which includes expanding the data set and constructing more robust operationalizations of the dependent variables. I finish with concluding thoughts about why presidents are deciding to act alone.

Notes

1. John Gerring, "What Is a Case Study and What Is It Good For?," *American Political Science Review* 98, no. 2 (May 2004): 341-42.

2. See Christopher H. Achen and Duncan Snidal, "Rational Deterrence Theory and Comparative Case Studies," *World Politics* 41, no. 2 (January 1989): 143-69; Gary King, Robert O. Keohane, and Sidney Verba, *Designing Social Inquiry: Scientific Inference in Qualitative Research* (Princeton, N.J.: Princeton University Press, 1994); Barbara Geddes, "How the Cases You Choose Affect the Answers You Get: Selection Bias in Political Science," *Political Analysis* 2, no. 1 (1990): 131-50; John Gerring, "What Is a Case Study"; Stephen Van Evera, *Guide to Methods to Students of Political Science* (London: Cornell University Press, 1997).

3. Van Evera, *Guide to Methods*, 35; David Collier, "New Perspectives on the Comparative Method," in *Comparative Political Dynamics*, eds. Dankart A. Rustow and Kenneth P. Erikson (New York: HarperCollins, 1991), 23.

4. Adam Przeworski and Henry Teune, *The Logic of Comparative Social Inquiry* (New York: Krieger Publishing Company, 1970), 17.

5. Bernard E. Brown, "The Case Method in Comparative Politics," in *Cases in Comparative Politics*, eds. Bernard E. Brown and James B. Christoph (Boston: Little,

Brown, 1976), 3; Timothy McKeown, "Case Studies and the Statistical Worldview," *International Organization* 53, no. 1 (January 1999): 174, 178; Bernhard Ebbinghaus, "When Less Is More: Selection Problems in Large-N and Small-N Cross-National Comparisons," *International Sociology* 20, no. 2 (June 2005): 134; James Mahoney, "Strategies of Causal Inference in Small-N Analysis," *Sociological Methods and Research* 28, no. 4 (May 2000): 395; Gerardo L. Munck, "Canons of Research Design in Qualitative Analysis," *Studies in Comparative International Development* 33, no. 3 (September 1998): 36.

6. Christopher Layne, "Kant or Cant: The Myth of the Democratic Peace," *International Security* 19, no. 2 (Autumn 1994): 13.

7. RFD, "Unilateral and Multilateral Options in the Execution of Foreign Policy," *International Organization* 23, no. 3 (Summer 1969): 641-754; Richard N. Haass, "Military Force: A User's Guide," *Foreign Policy* 96 (Autumn 1994): 21-37; Lukasz Kamienski, "The RMA and War Powers," *Strategic Insight* (September 2003): 1-5; Graham T. Allison, "Military Capabilities and American Foreign Policy," *Annals of the American Academy of Political and Social Science* 406 (1973): 17-37.

8. Bruce M. Russett and Miroslav Nincic, "American Opinion on the Use of Military Force Abroad," *Political Science Quarterly* 91, no. 3 (Autumn 1976): 430; Howard J. Wiarda and Lana L. Wylie, "New Challenges in U.S. Foreign Policy," in *Comparative Foreign Policy: Adaptation Strategies of the Great and Emerging Powers*, ed. Steven W. Hook (Upper Saddle River, N.J.: Prentice-Hall, 2002), 16.

9. Van Evera, *Guide to Methods.*

10. See John G. Ruggie, "Multilateralism: The Anatomy of an Institution," *International Organization* 46, no. 3 (Summer 1992): 561-98; Ekaterina Stepanova "The Unilateral and Multilateral Use of Force by the United States," in *Unilateralism and U.S. Foreign Policy: International Perspectives*, eds. David M. Malone and Yuen Foong Khong (Boulder, Colo.: Lynne Rienner, 2003).

11. Lawrence Freedman and Efraim Karsh, *The Gulf Conflict, 1990-1991: Diplomacy and War in the New World Order* (Princeton, N.J.: Princeton University Press, 1993), 28, 31; Jean Edward Smith, *George Bush's War* (New York: Henry Holt and Company, 1992), 45-46, 48.

12. Freedman and Karsh, *The Gulf Conflict*, 53.

13. Richard P. Hallion, *Storm Over Iraq: Air Power and the Gulf War* (Washington, D.C.: Smithsonian Institution Press, 1992), 135.

14. John Keegan, *The Iraq War* (New York: Alfred A. Knopf, 2004), 76; Micah L. Sifry and Christopher Cerf, eds., *The Gulf War Reader: History, Documents, Opinions* (New York: Times Books, 1991), 156.

15. Michael R. Gordon and Bernard E. Trainor, *The Generals' War: The Inside Story of the Conflict in the Gulf* (Boston: Little, Brown, and Company, 1995), 198.

16. Keegan, *The Iraq War*, 78.

17. Kenneth Pollack, "How Saddam Misread the United States," in *The Iraq War Reader: History, Documents, Opinions*, eds. Micah L. Sifry and Christopher Cerf (New York: Touchstone, 2003), 84.

18. Pollack, "How Saddam," 81-85; Keegan, *The Iraq War*, 77-83. As it turns out, the Republican Guard had three of its eight divisions destroyed and a fourth lost about

half its strength. The exits from Kuwait were also not cut off, as at least two Republican Guard divisions escaped and an infantry division, an armored division, and the remnants of a Republican Guard division moved to defend al-Basrah: Pollack, "How Saddam," 84.

19. The Gallup poll questions were as follows: (1) In your opinion, what, if anything, should the United States do concerning the current situation involving Iraq and Kuwait? (August 3-4 poll) and (2) Do you approve or disapprove of the United States' decision to send U.S. troops to Saudi Arabia as a defense against Iraq? (August 9-12 poll). Notably, those opposed to sending U.S. troops were 14 percent (August 3-4 poll) and 17 percent (August 9-12 poll).

20. Pollack, "How Saddam," 81.

21. Smith, *George Bush's War*, 172, 198, 205.

22. Smith, *George Bush's War*, 109.

23. Smith, *George Bush's War*, 221.

24. Elizabeth Drew, "Washington Prepares for War," in Sifry and Cerf, eds., *The Gulf War Reader*, 191-92.

25. Gordon and Trainor, *The Generals' War*, 205; Smith, *George Bush's War*, 249. The vote in the House was 250 to 183 and the vote in the Senate was 52 to 47: Gordon and Trainor, *The Generals' War*, 205; Hallion, *Storm Over Iraq*, 160.

26. George H.W. Bush and Brent Scowcroft, *A World Transformed* (New York: Alfred A. Knopf, 1998), 418.

27. Smith, *George Bush's War*, 237.

28. Sifry and Cerf, eds., *The Iraq War Reader*, 45.

29. Henry Kissinger, "A False Dream," in Sifry and Cerf, eds., *The Gulf War Reader*, 463.

30. Sifry and Cerf, eds., *The Iraq War Reader*, 69.

31. Daniel Yergin, "Oil: The Strategic Prize," in Sifry and Cerf, eds., *The Gulf War Reader*, 24; Thomas L. Friedman, "Washington's 'Vital Interests'," in Sifry and Cerf, eds., *The Gulf War Reader*, 203-5; Gordon and Trainor, *The Generals' War*, 32; Freedman and Karsh, *The Gulf Conflict*, 438.

32. Pollack, "How Saddam," 76; Freedman and Karsh, *The Gulf Conflict*, 180.

33. Drew, "Washington Prepares," 183; Freedman and Karsh, *The Gulf Conflict*, 439.

34. Smith, *George Bush's War*, 79; Gordon and Trainor, *The Generals' War*, 48-49.

35. Freedman and Karsh, *The Gulf Conflict*, 92.

36. Bush and Scowcroft, *A World Transformed*, 321.

37. Bush and Scowcroft, *A World Transformed*, 322.

38. Hallion, *Storm Over Iraq*, 156-58. To give an idea of the level of combat participation of the non-U.S. countries, the UK, France, and Saudi Arabia flew about 8 percent of the air campaign's first 24 hours: Hallion, *Storm Over Iraq*, 166.

39. Harry G. Summers, Jr., *Persian Gulf War Almanac* (New York: Facts on File, 1995), 46-47, 53-54, 65, 76, 89, 131, 202-3, 241; Michael T. Klare, "The Pentagon's New Paradigm," in Sifry and Cerf, eds., *The Gulf War Reader*, 470; Hallion, *Storm Over Iraq*, 158.

40. The coalition countries included Afghanistan, Argentina, Australia, Bahrain, Bangladesh, Belgium, Canada, Czechoslovakia, Denmark, Egypt, France, Germany,

Greece, Honduras, Hungary, Italy, Japan, Kuwait, Morocco, the Netherlands, New Zealand, Niger, Norway, Oman, Pakistan, Poland, Portugal, Romania, Qatar, Saudi Arabia, Senegal, Sierra Leone, South Korea, Spain, Sweden, Syria, Turkey, the UAE, and the UK.

41. Keegan, *The Iraq War*, 77-78, 81.

42. Freedman and Karsh, *The Gulf Conflict*, 120, 123.

43. Summers, *Persian Gulf War*, 52-53, 63-64, 99-100, 200-201; Hallion, *Storm Over Iraq*, 158.

44. Keegan, *The Iraq War*, 75; Klare, "The Pentagon's New Paradigm," 470; Gordon and Trainor, *The Generals' War*, 10.

45. Hallion, *Storm Over Iraq*, 146.

46. Pollack, "How Saddam," 80.

47. A 1989 Pentagon report listed Iraq's military assets as 17 bombers, 280 fighters/bombers, 350 attack helicopters, 1.2 million troops in 45 brigades, and 9 missile boats: Gordon and Trainor, *The Generals' War*, 11.

48. Summers, *Persian Gulf War*, 51-52, 64, 66-67, 202; Keegan, *The Iraq War*, 75; Klare, "The Pentagon's New Paradigm," 470; Freedman and Karsh, *The Gulf Conflict*, 389, 392; Hallion, *Storm Over Iraq*, 128, 146-47.

49. Freedman and Karsh, *The Gulf Conflict*, 63.

50. Gordon and Trainor, *The Generals' War*, 29; Freedman and Karsh, *The Gulf Conflict*, 435.

51. Hallion, *Storm Over Iraq*, 133.

52. Hallion, *Storm Over Iraq*, 156-57.

53. Freedman and Karsh, *The Gulf Conflict*, 110.

54. See Andrew Bennett, Joseph Lepgold, and Danny Unger, "Burden-Sharing in the Persian Gulf War," *International Organization* 48, no. 1 (Winter 1994): 39-75.

55. Freedman and Karsh, *The Gulf Conflict*, 112.

56. Freedman and Karsh, *The Gulf Conflict*, 120.

57. Smith, *George Bush's War*, 129, 132, 147, 211.

58. Smith, *George Bush's War*, 134, 137.

59. Freedman and Karsh, *The Gulf Conflict*, 112.

60. Freedman and Karsh, *The Gulf Conflict*, 112, 347, 358.

61. See Christine Chinkin, "The State That Acts Alone: Bully, Good Samaritan or Iconoclast?," *European Journal of International Law* 11, no. 1 (2000): 31-41; Charles Krauthammer, "The Unipolar Moment," *Foreign Affairs* 70, no. 1 (1990-1991): 23-33; Samuel P. Huntington, "The Clash of Civilizations?," *Foreign Affairs* 72, no. 3 (Summer 1993): 22-49.

62. Gordon and Trainor, *The Generals' War*, 18-19; Freedman and Karsh, *The Gulf Conflict*, 51.

63. Gordon and Trainor, *The Generals' War*, 35-36; Smith, *George Bush's War*, 18-19; Freedman and Karsh, *The Gulf Conflict*, 73.

64. Smith, *George Bush's War*, 17.

65. Bush and Scowcroft, *A World Transformed*, 315; Smith, *George Bush's War*, 17, 64. Bush and Scowcroft make it clear that the initial NSC meeting and Bush's public statements give the wrong impression of their intentions. Bush stated he had kept an

"open mind" but he was determined to have "Kuwait's sovereignty restored": Bush and Scowcroft, *A World Transformed*, 315. Scowcroft was "appalled" by the NSC discussion and didn't believe it reflected Bush's thinking or plans: Bush and Scowcroft, *A World Transformed*, 317.

66. Smith, *George Bush's War*, 63, 66; Freedman and Karsh, *The Gulf Conflict*, 75.

67. Smith, *George Bush's War*, 66.

68. Smith, *George Bush's War*, 67.

69. Bush and Scowcroft, *A World Transformed*, 320; Smith, *George Bush's War*, 68; Freedman and Karsh, *The Gulf Conflict*, 75.

70. Gordon and Trainor, *The Generals' War*, 37; Freedman and Karsh, *The Gulf Conflict*, 76.

71. Gordon and Trainor, *The Generals' War*, 47.

72. Gordon and Trainor, *The Generals' War*, 49.

73. Smith, *George Bush's War*, 88.

74. Summers, *Persian Gulf War*, 91; Gordon and Trainor, *The Generals' War*, 47; Smith, *George Bush's War*, 90; Freedman and Karsh, *The Gulf Conflict*, 94; Sifry and Cerf, eds., *The Gulf War Reader*, 197.Technically, the Air Force was the first to defend Saudi Arabia. A C-141 and 24 F-15 fighters arrived on August 7th. The 82nd deployed on the 7th but didn't arrive in Saudi Arabia until the 8th: Gordon and Trainor, *The Generals' War*, 54-55.

75. Drew, "Washington Prepares," 180; Christopher Hitchens, "Realpolitik in the Gulf: A Game Gone Tilt," in Sifry and Cerf, eds., *The Gulf War Reader*, 107-9.

76. Christopher Cerf and Victor Navasky, "The Experts Speak on the Coming Gulf War," in Sifry and Cerf, eds., *The Iraq War Reader*, 47-49; Drew, "Washington Prepares," 186.

77. Gordon and Trainor, *The Generals' War*, 47; Smith, *George Bush's War*, 77.

78. Gordon and Trainor, *The Generals' War*, 86-98; Hallion, *Storm Over Iraq*, 150-56. Schwarzkopf approved the air campaign plan on September 3rd: Gordon and Trainor, *The Generals' War*, 98.

79. Freedman and Karsh, *The Gulf Conflict*, 204-6.

80. Gordon and Trainor, *The Generals' War*, 140-41.

81. Gordon and Trainor, *The Generals' War*, 158.

82. Smith, *George Bush's War*, 191; Freedman and Karsh, *The Gulf Conflict*, 285.

83. Gordon and Trainor, *The Generals' War*, 164.

84. Smith, *George Bush's War*, 224.

85. Hallion, *Storm Over Iraq*, 2; Freedman and Karsh, *The Gulf Conflict*, 286, 391, 468.

86. Sifry and Cerf, eds., *The Gulf War Reader*, 316; Sifry and Cerf, eds., *The Iraq War Reader*, 64; Hallion, *Storm Over Iraq*, 133.

87. Cerf and Navasky, "The Experts Speak," 74. The fear of casualties would prove unfounded, as the U.S. launched its current RMA. But before the invasion, few were confident the U.S. would launch a new revolution in warfare: Hallion, *Storm Over Iraq*, 1. As noted in the "Current RMA" subsection of Chapter 3, the 1991 Gulf War was the first war in which the U.S. used a disengaged combat strategy. Its forces were able to destroy Iraqi forces from a safe distance. Its forces used

high-precision weapons for the first time, using on-board computers and laser-guided bombs to destroy Iraqi forces with a high rate of accuracy (with a margin of error measured in inches): Keegan, *The Iraq War*, 79.

88. Bush and Scowcroft, *A World Transformed*, 394.

89. Bush and Scowcroft, *A World Transformed*, 395.

90. Gordon and Trainor, *The Generals' War*, 153-55; Smith, *George Bush's War*, 201-3, 224.

91. Bush and Scowcroft, *A World Transformed*, 395.

92. Hallion, *Storm Over Iraq*, 157; Gordon and Trainor, *The Generals' War*, 209; Smith, *George Bush's War*, 237.

93. See Lucien S. Vandenbroucke, "Anatomy of a Failure: The Decision to Land at the Bay of Pigs," *Political Science Quarterly* 99, no. 3 (Autumn 1984): 471-91. Information on the Bay of Pigs operation can be found on the John F. Kennedy Presidential Library and Museum website at http://www.jfklibrary.org/Historical+Resources/JFK+in+History/JFK+and+the+Bay+of+Pigs.htm.

94. Arthur M. Schlesinger, Jr., *A Thousand Days: John F. Kennedy in the White House* (Boston: Houghton Mifflin Company, 1965), 233. The plan to use the CIA to train Cuban exiles for use against Castro was agreed to on March 17, 1960, by President Eisenhower. President Eisenhower, on the whole, seemed uninterested in invading Cuba. He even testified a "program" was in place to train Cuban exiles, but that he knew of no "plan" to attack Cuba: Peter Wyden, *Bay of Pigs: The Untold Story* (New York: Simon & Schuster, 1979), 24-25; Schlesinger, *A Thousand Days*, 222.

95. Wyden, *Bay of Pigs*, 30, 235-37, 278; Peter Kornbluh, *Bay of Pigs Declassified: The Secret CIA Report on the Invasion of Cuba* (New York: The New Press, 1998), 307, 317.

96. Wyden, *Bay of Pigs*, 193, 198-200; Schlesinger, *A Thousand Days*, 270-73; Kornbluh, *Bay of Pigs*, 3; Michael R. Beschloss, *The Crisis Years: Kennedy and Khrushchev: 1960-1963* (New York: HarperCollins, 1991), 116.

97. In total, 1,511 men comprised the Brigade but the number is reduced by about 150 men due to men not participating: Wyden, *Bay of Pigs*, 303; Kornbluh, *Bay of Pigs*, 38.

98. Wyden, *Bay of Pigs*, 210-16; Kornbluh, *Bay of Pigs*, 38. Notably, CIA agent Gray Lynch led one of the invasion parties. Lynch later testified that he did not have Attorney General Robert Kennedy's permission to land with the invasion force: Wyden, *Bay of Pigs*, 217-19.

99. Wyden, *Bay of Pigs*, 205-6; Schlesinger, *A Thousand Days*, 273. Brigade B-26s did fly during the beach landings, but they were badly outmatched by the T-33s and Sea Furies. The CIA and Kennedy reinstated an earlier cancellation of a Brigade bombing run to destroy Cuban airfields during the night of April 17-18, but the three B-26s launched failed to find their target (San Antonio de los Baos): Kornbluh, *Bay of Pigs*, 314.

100. Wyden, *Bay of Pigs*, 231.

101. Kornbluh, *Bay of Pigs*, 312-13.

102. Bissell authorized American pilots to fly combat missions beginning at 2 pm on April 18th. By the end of the operation, four U.S. pilots died at the Bay of Pigs but

President Kennedy insisted he did not know of active U.S. participation: Wyden, *Bay of Pigs*, 278; Kornbluh, *Bay of Pigs*, 317.

103. Wyden, *Bay of Pigs*, 136, 272; Schlesinger, *A Thousand Days*, 278; Kornbluh, *Bay of Pigs*, 318.

104. Max Frankel, *High Noon in the Cold War: Kennedy, Khrushchev, and the Cuban Missile Crisis* (New York: Ballantine Books, 2004), 69.

105. Thomas G. Paterson, "John F. Kennedy and the World," in *John F. Kennedy: Person, Policy, Presidency*, ed. J. Richard Snyder (Wilmington, Del.: Scholarly Resources, 1988), 137-38; Arthur M. Schlesinger, Jr., "Interview with Arthur M. Schlesinger, Jr," in Snyder, ed., *John F. Kennedy*, 3-4.

106. Wyden, *Bay of Pigs*, 120, 165.

107. Theodore H. White, *The Making of the President 1960* (Cutchogue, N.Y.: Buccaneer Books, 1961), 326.

108. Wyden, *Bay of Pigs*, 95.

109. Wyden, *Bay of Pigs*, 78-79, 86, 152, 187, 190-91; Robert B. Zoellick, "Congress and the Making of US Foreign Policy," *Survival* 41, no. 4 (January 1999): 32.

110. The Gallup poll question was as follows: What do you think should be done in the present situation in Cuba? (July 16-21 poll). The public seemed indifferent as only 2 percent opposed sending troops.

111. Wyden, *Bay of Pigs*, 154-55; Frankel, *High Noon*, 108. The *New York Times* reported on the training of the exiles in Guatemala, the intention of removing Castro from power, and of the plans to have Cuban exiles invade the island: Wyden, *Bay of Pigs*, 46, 67, 153-55.

112. Schlesinger, *A Thousand Days*, 251.

113. Frankel, *High Noon*, 11; Larman C. Wilson, "The Monroe Doctrine, Cold War Anachronism: Cuba and the Dominican Republic," *Journal of Politics* 28, no. 2 (May 1966): 322.

114. Schlesinger, "Interview," 5; Beschloss, *The Crisis Years*, 64, 106.

115. Beschloss, *The Crisis Years*, 87. Kennedy informed Soviet Ambassador Andrei Gromyko, during a March 27, 1961, visit to the White House that he would not allow Communists to take Laos (or Southeast Asia) and Cuba: Beschloss, *The Crisis Years*, 87.

116. Wyden, *Bay of Pigs*, 25.

117. Wyden, *Bay of Pigs*, 20-21.

118. Beschloss, *The Crisis Years*, 122.

119. Paterson, "John F. Kennedy," 135-36; Wyden, *Bay of Pigs*, 65.

120. Beschloss, *The Crisis Years*, 59-60, 78.

121. Beschloss, *The Crisis Years*, 62-63.

122. Beschloss, *The Crisis Years*, 79.

123. Beschloss, *The Crisis Years*, 105.

124. Wyden, *Bay of Pigs*, 292; Beschloss, *The Crisis Years*, 121.

125. Wyden, *Bay of Pigs*, 209.

126. Beschloss, *The Crisis Years*, 88, 109, 117.

127. Schlesinger, "Interview," 5; Beschloss, *The Crisis Years*, 131.

128. Beschloss, *The Crisis Years*, 145.

129. Wyden, *Bay of Pigs*, 294.

130. Wyden, *Bay of Pigs*, 295.

131. Frankel, *High Noon*, 68-70; Paterson, "John F. Kennedy," 136; Beschloss, *The Crisis Years*, 125. In fact, Beschloss suggests that Kennedy may have believed that Castro's assassination would have been coordinated with the invasion: Beschloss, *The Crisis Years*, 139.

132. Beschloss, *The Crisis Years*, 105.

133. In the ICB data set, the U.S. and Cuba are listed in the crisis dyad.

134. Kornbluh, *Bay of Pigs*, 11.

135. Three of the commercial freighters were loaded with supplies and did not participate in the assault phase: Kornbluh, *Bay of Pigs*, 38.

136. Kornbluh, *Bay of Pigs*, 38-39.

137. Theodore C. Sorensen, *The Kennedy Legacy* (New York: Macmillan, 1969), 183.

138. Wyden, *Bay of Pigs*, 308.

139. Schlesinger, *A Thousand Days*, 293; Beschloss, *The Crisis Years*, 104. Ironically, after the Bay of Pigs operation, Robert Kennedy remarked that his brother would never have approved the operation, if he had known that the Cuban "forces were as good as they were and would fight": Beschloss, *The Crisis Years*, 133.

140. Beschloss, *The Crisis Years*, 104.

141. Kornbluh, *Bay of Pigs*, 113.

142. Kornbluh, *Bay of Pigs*, 169.

143. Kornbluh, *Bay of Pigs*, 168.

144. Kornbluh, *Bay of Pigs*, 52.

145. Schlesinger, "Interview," 6-7; Paterson, "John F. Kennedy," 128.

146. Beschloss, *The Crisis Years*, 114.

147. Schlesinger, *A Thousand Days*, 256-57; Beschloss, *The Crisis Years*, 107, 114.

148. Wyden, *Bay of Pigs*, 316.

149. Schlesinger, *A Thousand Days*, 287; Beschloss, *The Crisis Years*, 105, 150.

150. Schlesinger, *A Thousand Days*, 262.

151. Kornbluh, *Bay of Pigs*, 73.

152. Wyden, *Bay of Pigs*, 225.

153. Wyden, *Bay of Pigs*, 185.

154. Schlesinger, *A Thousand Days*, 249; Beschloss, *The Crisis Years*, 106.

155. Schlesinger, *A Thousand Days*, 256-57; Beschloss, *The Crisis Years*, 107, 114.

156. Schlesinger, *A Thousand Days*, 233, 259; Wyden, *Bay of Pigs*, 159.

157. Wyden, *Bay of Pigs*, 308.

158. Schlesinger, *A Thousand Days*, 267-68.

159. Kornbluh, *Bay of Pigs*, 303.

160. Wyden, *Bay of Pigs*, 264.

161. Wyden, *Bay of Pigs*, 264-65.

162. Wyden, *Bay of Pigs*, 266-67.

163. Wyden, *Bay of Pigs*, 268.

164. Wyden, *Bay of Pigs*, 270.

165. Schlesinger would join the group around 1 am: Wyden, *Bay of Pigs*, 271.

166. Wyden, *Bay of Pigs*, 270; Beschloss, *The Crisis Years*, 122.

167. Wyden, *Bay of Pigs*, 271.

168. Schlesinger, *A Thousand Days*, 278; Wyden, *Bay of Pigs*, 235-43; Kornbluh, *Bay of Pigs*, 318; Beschloss, *The Crisis Years*, 123. The jets from the *Essex* did not take off until an hour after they were supposed to rendezvous.

169. Richard M. Koster and Guillermo Sanchez, *In the Time of the Tyrants, Panama: 1968-1990* (New York: W.W. Norton and Company, 1990), 274-75, 355, 359; John Dinges, *Our Man in Panama: The Shrewd Rise and Brutal Fall of Manuel Noriega* (New York: Times Books, 1991), 51, 295.

170. Thomas Donnelly, Margaret Roth, and Caleb Baker, *Operation Just Cause: The Storming of Panama* (New York: Lexington Books, 1991), 43; Koster and Sanchez, *In the Time of the Tyrants*, 359.

171. Koster and Sanchez, *In the Time of the Tyrants*, 366; Dinges, *Our Man in Panama*, 305.

172. Hallion, *Storm Over Iraq*, 113-14; Koster and Sanchez, *In the Time of the Tyrants*, 371-72; Dinges, *Our Man in Panama*, 307.

173. Koster and Sanchez, *In the Time of the Tyrants*, 375, 377; Dinges, *Our Man in Panama*, 308, 312; Kevin Buckley, *Panama: The Whole Story* (New York: Simon & Schuster, 1991), 238-40; Donnelly, Roth, and Baker, *Operation Just Cause*, 77, 114, 126, 135, 189, 203, 236-37; Malcolm McConnell, *Just Cause: The Real Story of America's High-Tech Invasion of Panama* (New York: St. Martin's Press, 1991), 38, 47, 74, 80, 99, 130, 132-33, 145-49, 219, 224, 233, 267-68.

174. Hallion, *Storm Over Iraq*, 113.

175. Hallion, *Storm Over Iraq*, 114-15; Dinges, *Our Man in Panama*, 312.

176. The Gallup poll questions were as follows: (1) Do you favor or oppose the following options for U.S. policy toward Panama now? (May 11-12 poll) and (2) Do you favor or oppose the following options for U.S. policy toward Panama at this time? (October 5-6 poll). The amount opposed to sending troops increased from 36 percent (May 11-12 poll) to 74 percent (October 5-6 poll).

177. Donnelly, Roth, and Baker, *Operation Just Cause*, 47, 51, 54.

178. Buckley, *Panama*, 212; Donnelly, Roth, and Baker, *Operation Just Cause*, 78.

179. Buckley, *Panama*, 232.

180. Bush and Scowcroft, *A World Transformed*, 23; Dinges, *Our Man in Panama*, 308.

181. Moments before the invasion, Guillermo Endara was sworn in as president: Dinges, *Our Man in Panama*, 308; McConnell, *Just Cause*, 92-93.

182. Bush and Scowcroft, *A World Transformed*, 61-62.

183. Barbara Ehrenreich, "Who Wants Another Panama?," in Sifry and Cerf, eds., *The Gulf War Reader*, 299; Dinges, *Our Man in Panama*, 313-14.

184. Dinges, *Our Man in Panama*, 313.

185. Bush and Scowcroft, *A World Transformed*, 324. If one reads through Bush and Scowcroft's *A World Transformed*, one will see that Bush dedicates about half of a page to explaining the Panama invasion (as opposed to over 175 pages for the Persian Gulf War). This is probably due to the fact that it became an afterthought (even the invasion date is wrongly listed as December 26th in *A World Transformed*), given the ease and success of the operation: Bush and Scowcroft, *A World Transformed*, 166.

186. Dinges, *Our Man in Panama*, 308; Klare, "The Pentagon's New Paradigm," 470.

187. Donnelly, Roth, and Baker, *Operation Just Cause*, 113.

188. Klare, "The Pentagon's New Paradigm," 470.

189. Koster and Sanchez, *In the Time of the Tyrants*, 362.

190. Koster and Sanchez, *In the Time of the Tyrants*, 372-73, 379; Buckley, *Panama*, 224.

191. Buckley, *Panama*, 229.

192. Dinges, *Our Man in Panama*, 316.

193. Koster and Sanchez, *In the Time of the Tyrants*, 367-68.

194. Buckley, *Panama*, 186-87, 191; Donnelly, Roth, and Baker, *Operation Just Cause*, 63-64.

195. Dinges, *Our Man in Panama*, 318-19.

196. Donnelly, Roth, and Baker, *Operation Just Cause*, 64.

197. Buckley, *Panama*, 183.

198. Noriega, in a televised address, compared the American involvement in the Giroldi coup to the American involvement in the Bay of Pigs operation: Buckley, *Panama*, 209.

199. Buckley, *Panama*, 200; Donnelly, Roth, and Baker, *Operation Just Cause*, 69. Powell did authorize U.S. troops to go to the Comandancia to seize Noriega, but Bush wanted the action to be covert and non-confrontational. The U.S. also set up a couple of roadblocks. But, the U.S. actions were all too late and all for naught. Noriega's Mountain Men and Battalion 2000 arrived unimpeded to rescue Noriega at the Comandancia: Buckley, *Panama*, 206-7; McConnell, *Just Cause*, 10-11.

200. Donnelly, Roth, and Baker, *Operation Just Cause*, 68-69.

201. Dinges, *Our Man in Panama*, 305-6; Buckley, *Panama*, 197-206.

202. In late October, Bush authorized a 3 million dollar CIA plan, called Panama 5, which was designed to remove Noriega from power (either through capturing or killing him). By mid-November, the press revealed the plan, and the plans gave way to a massive military invasion: Buckley, *Panama*, 220-23.

203. Dinges, *Our Man in Panama*, 306.

204. Donnelly, Roth, and Baker, *Operation Just Cause*, 18-19.

205. McConnell, *Just Cause*, 19.

206. Koster and Sanchez, *In the Time of the Tyrants*, 372; Dinges, *Our Man in Panama*, 308; Buckley, *Panama*, 225-27.

207. The advisers included Quayle, Baker, Cheney, Powell, Scowcroft, Scowcroft's deputy Robert Gates, Chief of Staff John Sununu, Joint Chiefs of Staff Director of Operations Lt. General Thomas Kelly, and Press Secretary Marlin Fitzwater.

208. Buckley, *Panama*, 230; Donnelly, Roth, and Baker, *Operation Just Cause*, 98.

209. Buckley, *Panama*, 230-31.

210. Buckley, *Panama*, 231; Donnelly, Roth, and Baker, *Operation Just Cause*, 97-99.

6
Conclusion

Introduction

I BEGAN THIS BOOK WITH A QUESTION, "Why do presidents make such an "unwise" decision as using unilateral force in the first place?" Scholars, policy makers, and even presidents, themselves, believe that unilateralism is the "wrong" choice, but regardless, presidents have acted and continue to act unilaterally a majority of the time. Organizing the research question into international and domestic approaches, I find that presidents act unilaterally based on hegemonic power. I have used statistics, an experiment, and case studies to argue that presidents decide to act unilaterally based on a sequential model determined by international-based factors—military power, the location of the crisis, and the nature of the crisis.

In this chapter, I explain the implications from the statistical, experimental, and case study analyses. In particular, I focus on how well the unilateral use-of-force decision-making theory fares with each of the methods. I then offer directions for future research, which includes expanding the data set and constructing more robust operationalizations of the dependent variables. I finish with some concluding thoughts about why presidents are deciding to act alone.

Implications from the Statistical Analysis

As explained in Chapter 2 and as designed and tested in Chapter 3, I find that presidents, as consistent with the unilateral use-of-force decision-making theory, act unilaterally given the power disparity between the U.S. and a crisis opponent. The statistical analysis conducted in this book serves to answer two of the proposed questions in the introductory chapter: (1) Why does a president make a unilateral use-of-force decision? and (2) Should a president's unilateral decision be viewed as a separate and distinct decision from his use-of-force decision? The statistical test answers these questions in a generalizable and parsimonious fashion, and it allows me to establish a causal relationship from the onset of a crisis to a president's unilateral decision over a long time period (1937 to 1995).

In order to conduct the statistical test, I needed to overcome the shortcomings of unilateral research and devise a new operational definition and coding rules for unilateralism, establish a new sequential model of a president's crisis decisions, and use a new score of military power. Using these new data and methodological techniques, I conduct the empirical tests and find evidence of a realist-based explanation for U.S. crisis behavior.

Data and Methodological Contributions: Coding Rules, a Sequential Model, and the CIMR Score

Traditional studies of conflict behavior include a *use-of-force* dependent variable but not a *type-of-force used* dependent variable. Also, as argued, policy experts, legal scholars, and academics offer widely varying definitions of multilateralism and almost entirely ignore the study of unilateralism. This is a serious shortcoming in conflict and decision making research, and in order to fill this gap, I offer a definition of unilateral use of force—the U.S. acting alone without any military ally or international political support. Next, I construct a *force* variable using the Fordham and Sarver and COW MID data sets, and then using the coding rules derived from the operational definition of unilateralism, I construct a *unilateral use-of-force* dependent variable.

Related to the lack of research on unilateralism is the failure to model a president's crisis decisions as a sequential process consistent with the "series of steps" findings that traces crisis escalation rising from security issues all the way to the outbreak of war.[1] I test the decisions with separate probit models and find that the assumption of two unrelated processes is theoretically incorrect. To fill this research void, I theorize the use-of-force decision as a two-step process, and while controlling for the first decision, I use a heckman probit model to test the second decision.

Finally, I test and conclude that the traditional measure of military power, the CINC score, does not necessarily correlate with a unilateral-multilateral action. In its place, I offer a CIMR score, based on scores of preponderance, technology, and force employment.[2] This alternative measure fares reasonably well when tested on the crisis dyads. The significance of the situational factors in the models reinforces the Meernik and Waterman finding that the "peculiarities" of the crisis are important, and thus deserves a more prominent place in realist doctrine.[3]

Empirical Findings

Using the heckman probit model, I first find that the unilateral decision is strongly associated with the use-of-force decisions for the years 1937 to 1995 and for the years 1950 to 1995. The results of the explanatory factors then suggest an international- and power-based explanation for a president's unilateral use-of-force decision.

CIMR

The *force employment* variable attains statistical significance, is in the expected direction for both data models, and has a significant impact on a president's unilateral use-of-force decision (1937 to 1995, 1950 to 1995). The *technology gap* variable attains statistical significance, is in the expected direction for both data models, and has a significant impact on a president's unilateral use-of-force decision. The *preponderance gap* variable attains statistical significance for the 1950 to 1995 model, is in the expected direction, but it has minimal impact on a president's decision. Its significance justifies its inclusion as a CIMR score, but future researchers may want to further examine it.

Americas Region

The *americas region* variable for the 1937 to 1995 model attains statistical significance, is in the expected direction, and has a significant impact on a president's unilateral use-of-force decision. The variable for the 1950 to 1995 model fails to attain statistical significance, but it is in the expected direction and has some impact on a president's unilateral decision. This result and the evidence from the case studies demonstrate empirical evidence for enforcing the Monroe Doctrine unilaterally.

Crisis Trigger

The *national security crisis* variable attains statistical significance, is in the expected direction, and has a significant impact on a president's unilateral use-of-force decision (1937 to 1995, 1950 to 1995). The *humanitarian crisis* fails to attain statistical significance, is in the wrong direction for the 1937 to

1995 model, and it predicts failure perfectly for the 1950 to 1995 model. It is a variable that needs further testing (these tests were conducted in the experiment and case studies chapters).

Implications from the Experimental Analysis

The experiment conducted in this book serves to answer two of the proposed questions in the introductory chapter: (1) Why does a president make a unilateral use-of-force decision? and (2) Do international factors, such as U.S. military power vis-à-vis an adversary, offer the greatest explanatory power for a unilateral decision? It answers these questions and allows me to determine whether my theoretical model has been correctly specified. Though, perhaps most importantly, I am better able to test the crisis trigger than I was able to in the statistics chapter. Selecting extreme values of domestic- and international-based variables, I am able to look inside the black box of realism and see why the crisis situation matters to a president.

The experiment sheds light on the expected utility calculation the president makes for each type of crisis. For national security threats, the president will act unilaterally, regardless of the size of the relative military gap. For humanitarian and regime change crises, the president will act unilaterally *if* the perceived costs are low.

National Security Threats

The results are consistent with the hypothesis proposed in Chapter 3: a national security threat is positively correlated with unilateralism. But, the experiment reveals two interesting findings. First, presidents will act unilaterally, given a national security threat, even when facing a low probability of unilateral military success. Second, a public clamoring for unilateralism and a high probability of unilateral military support creates a "perfect storm"—presidents, with rare exception, will act unilaterally.

Humanitarian and Regime Change Crises

When facing a humanitarian crisis, a president is likely to choose a multilateral path if either there is low probability of unilateral military success or low public support for unilateralism. Given the majority of the public favors multilateralism in humanitarian situations, it is not difficult to see why a president tends to act multilaterally. The regime change crisis results are consistent with the humanitarian results, but military power played a more significant role in the decision process. Presidents, rarely, will choose to act unilaterally, if there is a low military gap between the U.S. and the target of the regime change.

Implications from the Case Study Analysis

The case studies examined in this book serve to answer two of the proposed questions in the introductory chapter: (1) Should a president's unilateral decision be viewed as a separate and distinct decision from his use-of-force decision? and (2) Do international factors offer the greatest explanatory power for a unilateral decision? It answers these questions, and it allows me to determine the accuracy of my theoretical model. I am better able to delve into the particulars of the statistical data set in offering a detailed explanation of a president's unilateral decision. An explanation that moves beyond the CIMR scores and the coding rules of the crisis situation and into the Oval Office as the president makes the crucial decisions.

Selecting extreme values of the dependent variable, I use a process tracing-method to find that the theory of unilateral use-of-force decision making fares well. For the 1991 Gulf War case, President Bush made a decision to use force and then made a multilateral decision, given the estimate of high casualties and the necessity of increasing military power to overwhelming strength. For the 1961 Bay of Pigs operation, President Kennedy made a decision to use force without overt U.S. involvement, but then made a decision to use the U.S. military when facing defeat by a less powerful adversary. For the 1989 Panama invasion, President Bush made the second decision to act unilaterally after being reassured of quick military victory and low casualties.

1991 Gulf War

President Bush's October 30th decision to double the number of U.S. and coalition forces is consistent with the proposed theory that a president will act multilaterally to increase the military gap between the U.S. and an opponent. While the national security threat and correlation with unilateralism did not happen, Bush acted consistent with how a hegemon should act. Iraq represented a threat to U.S. oil interests and a threat to Middle East stability; so, Bush acted to reverse Iraq's illicit invasion of Kuwait. Fear of a strong Iraqi military and potentially high casualties led Bush to decide to increase military strength with a coalition that eventually accounted for nearly a third of the fighting force.

1961 Bay of Pigs

The Bay of Pigs case represents the necessity of including case studies to complement statistical studies. For coding purposes, the Bay of Pigs was full unilateralism, and Kennedy did act consistent with the hypotheses—a wide military gap and an adversary in the Western hemisphere is positively correlated with unilateralism. But, Kennedy's calculation of potential Soviet involvement led him to try to present the invasion as a multilateral effort. It was only upon facing defeat that Kennedy decided to drastically increase military power by ordering air cover from U.S. aircraft carriers.

1989 Panama Invasion

The Panama invasion represents the ideal unilateralism case. Bush seems to have made the decision to use force and then the decision to use unilateral force in rapid succession and with little hesitation. Like Cuba with the Bay of Pigs invasion, Panama was located in the Western hemisphere and the U.S. had overwhelming military strength vis-à-vis Panama. With no strategic threat (i.e., the Soviets), Bush made his unilateral decision without consulting with Congress, without waiting for public opinion polls, and after being assured of success with minimal casualties. Bush almost entirely disregarded the OAS, and the OAS, itself, proved ineffective at diplomacy. The minimization of domestic influences, the ineffectiveness of a multilateral organization, and a Western hemisphere adversary with a weak military all offer strong evidence in support of the unilateral use-of-force decision making theory.

Directions for Future Research

This book contributes to the work on hegemonic theory, unilateralism, and military revolutions with its examination of crisis actions: using force or not using force and using unilateral force or using multilateral force. Its results highlight areas for future research.

Expanding the Data Set

In terms of generalizability, the first area would be to extend the data set ideally back to the British hegemony and see if the theory holds. The lack of data (e.g., pre-1950 for GDP data and pre-1937 for Gallup poll data) precludes testing from before 1937 and the Fordham and Sarver data set ending at 1995 precludes testing after 1995. In terms of robustness, it would be ideal to test other data sets as well. I applied the coding rules to the ICB data set for a frequency count of full unilateralism, operational multilateralism, and procedural multilateralism (see Chapter 1), but a lack of sufficient observations precluded a statistical test. The Tago USUFAD data set could be tested as well. Also, the crises have been exemplified as three triggers, but future research can better define these crises and specify other crises as well.

Future research may also expand the data set to include the opponent leader's decision making from crisis onset to type of force used against the U.S. Are crisis opponents seeking to lower the costs and adding coalitional partners in the same manner as U.S. presidents? A more detailed operationalization, to include a *type of force used* variable, would answer this question and allow for more robust and generalizable results.

More Robust Operationalizations of the Dependent Variables

A new area may be to better dissect the *no force used* variable to see if a president's political or economic advantage was correlated with outcome success. After all, a president may not need to resort to force, but can simply threaten political or economic sanctions imposed unilaterally or multilaterally. Expanding the operationalization of the dependent variables could also include the decision to initiate a crisis or not initiate a crisis. This would reflect the possibility that presidents may choose not to "select themselves" into a crisis in the first place, if they perceive the potential military operation as too difficult.

A second area would be a more precise, reliable, and accurate reflection of full unilateralism, procedural multilateralism, and operational multilateralism. The coding rules for this book are designed to operationalize full unilateralism at the strategic and tactical levels, but the coding rules do not specify how effective and strong a coalitional military is. While I do include coalitional strength, in terms of the CINC and CIMR score in the case study chapter, future research may want to measure and account for whether presidents add coalitional strength to truly increase military power or whether it is designed to appease domestic and international political audiences.

A Different Methodological Approach

In this book, I have simply added the "next" step to existing research on use-of-force decisions. An alternative methodological approach would be to run the model in reverse.[4] Perhaps, a president first decides to use unilateral or multilateral force, and then he decides to use force if and only if the first decision has been satisfied. For example, a president, facing a humanitarian crisis requiring military intervention, may only want to act multilaterally to lower the costs. If he can assemble a coalition, he may then decide to use force. If he can't assemble a coalition, he may decide to use a non-force alternative (e.g., economic sanctions).

Conclusion

This book is a scientific study of U.S. unilateral uses of force, a study that is badly needed given the lack of testing, the abundance of unsubstantiated statements, and the fact that presidents are making the "wrong" choice to act unilaterally a majority of the time. I have found that presidents act unilaterally, as is consistent with a power-based realist theory. With overwhelming military strength, the necessity of protecting U.S. interests (and the stability of the international system), and the problems of acting multilaterally, it becomes clear that presidents act unilaterally when facing a weak military opponent, when facing a threat in the Western hemisphere, and when facing a national security threat.

This book is also a test of realism. This book organizes the literature along traditional lines—international and domestic explanations—in testing the theory of unilateral use-of-force decision making. Recent studies tend to favor a domestic approach to explaining uses of force decision, but as demonstrated, researchers seem to be missing the crucial type of force decision, and when it is taken into account, one can see that presidents are realists.

So, the answer to the question of "why do presidents act unilaterally?" can be answered with a simple refrain: Because the U.S. is a hegemonic power. The U.S., as other hegemons before it, is acting unilaterally to serve its interests, global interests . . . and because it has the power to do so. While this may be an unpopular answer, it is an answer grounded in scientific fact and an answer that can serve as the foundation for future testing of unilateralism. It is also an answer that gives understanding to presidential decisions and to why the U.S. is "acting alone."

Notes

1. John A. Vasquez, *The War Puzzle* (Cambridge: Cambridge University Press, 1993); John A. Vasquez, "Reexamining the Steps to War: New Evidence and Theoretical Insights," in *Handbook of War Studies II*, ed. Manus I. Midlarsky (Ann Arbor: The University of Michigan Press, 2000); John A. Vasquez, "The Probability of War, 1816-1992: Presidential Address to the International Studies Association, March 25, 2002, New Orleans," *International Studies Quarterly* 48, no. 1 (March 2004): 1-28; J. David Singer, *The Correlates of War II* (New York: Free Press, 1980); William Reed, "A

Unified Model of Conflict Onset and Escalation: Capabilities, Democracy, and Status Quo Evaluations," *American Journal of Political Science* 44, no. 1 (January 2000): 84-93; John G. Ruggie, "Multilateralism: The Anatomy of an Institution," *International Organization* 46, no. 3 (Summer 1992): 561-98.

2. Stephen Biddle, *Military Power: Explaining Victory and Defeat in Modern Battle* (Princeton, N.J.: Princeton University Press, 2004).

3. James Meernik and Peter Waterman, "The Myth of the Diversionary Use of Force by American Presidents," *Political Research Quarterly* 49, no. 3 (September 1996): 573-90.

4. I did some preliminary analysis on running the model in reverse in Chapter 3, and the results demonstrated that a unilateral and use-of-force decision are interdependent but negatively correlated decisions. Unfortunately, the instability of the models prevented more rigorous analysis.

Appendix A
Coding of Crisis Dyads

Actor	*Date*	*Crisis*	*PM*[a]	*OM*[b]	*U*[c]
China	Dec 1937	Japanese Invasion of China. 12/37 Japanese attack U.S. oil tanker convoy being escorted by USS *Panay*. *Panay* was sunk and Japanese fired on survivors. FS			X
UK	Sep 1940	Destroyers-for-Bases Agreement with UK. 9/2/40 FDR signs executive order trading destroyers for 99-year leases of UK bases. FS			X
Denmark	Apr 1941	Occupation of Greenland. 4/19/41 agreement with Denmark to protect Greenland. Grimmett			X
Iceland	Jul 1941	Occupation of Iceland. 7/7/41 agreement for U.S. troops to relieve UK and occupy Iceland. Grimmett			X
Germany	Jul 1941	German Submarines. 3/27/41 U.S., UK, and Canada staff discussions end with agreement for U.S. Atlantic ships. 7/1/41 naval Coastal Frontiers are established. Commanders are tasked with local patrol, convoy escorts, and antisubmarine operations. Grimmett	X	X	
Netherlands	Nov 1941	Occupation of Dutch Guiana. 11/23/41 U.S. occupies Dutch Guiana by agreement with Dutch government to protect bauxite mines. Grimmett			X
China	Oct 1945	Disarming Japanese. 10/45 50,000 U.S. Marines sent to North China to assist Nationalists in disarming and repatriating Japanese in China and in controlling ports, railroads, and airfields. Grimmett		X	
China	Apr 1946	China Civil War. 4/46 truce between Communists and Nationalists breaks down. U.S. transports Nationalists troops within China. Siegel			X
Yugoslavia	Jul 1946	Security of Trieste. U.S. and UK protest Yugoslavian obstruction of Allied Military Government in Trieste. Late June, as many as 10 U.S. and UK ships lay off the coast. In July, USN cruiser *Fargo* makes a port call. Siegel		X	
Chile	Nov 1946	Chilean Inauguration. After Leftist victory in September and tensions over the following month, U.S. announces a 5-ship squadron would visit Chile for the inauguration. Siegel			X

			PM[a]	OM[b]	U[c]
Yugoslavia	Nov 1946	Shooting Down of U.S. Aircraft. 11/46 U.S. army transport plane shot down by Yugoslavia. U.S. troops along zonal occupation line and air forces in northern Italy reinforced as a result. FS; Grimmett			X
Uruguay	Feb 1947	Uruguayan Inauguration. 2/23/47 U.S. Navy and Army Air contingents sent to Uruguay for 3/1/47 inauguration to emphasize support for new government. Siegel			X
Yugoslavia	Aug 1947	Security of Trieste. 8/47 questions about division of Trieste remain. 9/3/47 withdrawal accord was signed; 5,000 U.S. troops remain with equal contingents of UK and Yugoslav troops. 9/16/47 12 U.S. troops blocked 2,000 Yugoslavian troops from western zone of city. Throughout, combatant from Sixth Fleet stationed off Trieste. Siegel	X	X	
Russia	Jan 1948	Security of Berlin. 1/20/48 U.S. and UK propose to merge their economic zones at Allied Control Council. Soviets walk out of meeting. 1/48 USSR begins to interfere with trains to Berlin. http://www.cia.gov/csi/books/17240/art-4.html		X	
Russia	Apr 1948	Security of Berlin. 4/1/48 USSR temporarily restricted access to Berlin, termed a "baby blockade." IDV		X	
Russia	Jun 1948	Security of Berlin. 6/24/48 USSR imposes land blockade on U.S., UK, and French sectors of Berlin. 6/26/48 Allies airlift supplies until after blockade is lifted in 5/49. U.S. bombers sent to bases in UK. Grimmett; Siegel		X	
China	Nov 1949	Evacuation of Shanghai. 11-12/49 Marines sent to Shanghai to aid in evacuation of Americans. 12/8/49 Nationalist forces withdraw to Taiwan. FS; Siegel; Grimmett			X
Russia	Jul 1950	Korean War: Security of Europe. Heightened concern about Soviet action in Europe. Over two years, U.S. forces were built up in Europe. Mid-July, Sixth Fleet was augmented with one carrier (*Midway*) and one destroyer division. Marine force was reinforced. Mid-August, two destroyers visited Iceland to deter "large" Soviet fishing boats. Major U.S. Army divisions were reintroduced into Europe in this period. FS; Siegel			X

[a] PM = Procedural Multilateralism; [b] OM = Operational Multilateralism; [c] U = Full Unilateralism

(*continued*)

Actor	*Date*	*Crisis*	*PM*[a]	*OM*[b]	*U*[c]
Lebanon	Aug 1950	Political Developments in Lebanon. 8/50 U.S. legation was bombed and Lebanese Prime Minister assassinated. Lebanese government requested USS *Midway, Leyte, Salem,* Columbus, and destroyers visit Beirut and give aircraft carrier demonstration. Demonstrates U.S. commitment to region, despite presence in Korean War. FS; Siegel			X
Yugoslavia	Mar 1951	Security of Yugoslavia. 3/51 Tito announces that Soviet forces were massing along Yugoslav border. Mid-March reinforced Marine battalion arrives in area and Mediterranean relief force arrives ahead of schedule to cover "politically critical spring period." Troops may have been involved in a search for plane shot down by Soviets. Siegel; FS; IDV			X
China	Jul 1953	Korean War: Nuclear Threat. U.S. nuclear threat against China as part of efforts to force an agreement. 7/27/53 Armistice Agreement signed. U.S. and South Korea sign Mutual Defense Treaty in 1954. FS; IDV			X
N. Korea	Aug 1953	Security of South Korea. Series of disputes repatriating Korean War prisoners between 8/6-9/6/53. 7/27/53 Armistice established Military Armistice Committee to supervise DMZ and troop withdrawals. FS; IDV	X	X	
N. Vietnam	Mar 1954	French-Viet Minh War: Dien Bien Phu. 3/13/54 Battle for Dien Bien Phu begins. 3/19/54 U.S. naval forces in region put on alert, including carriers *Wasp* and *Essex*. Eisenhower speculated to press about possibility of U.S. airstrikes. 4/18/54 Marine pilots flew 25 aircraft to French airfield in Indochina. 4/29/54 Eisenhower announces non-intervention decision. 5/7/54 Dien Bien Phu fell. 4/21-6/10/54 U.S. Air Force transports flew French paratroopers to Indochina. Siegel; IDV; FS			X
Guatemala	May 1954	Guatemala Accepts USSR Aid. 1/54 leftist government in Guatemala requests Soviet bloc aid. 5/20/54 Soviet aid from Poland arrives and on same day, Caribbean Sea Frontier established air-sea patrols to protect Honduras from invasion and to control arms shipments to Guatemala. 5/21/54 U.S. signs bilateral defense agreement with Honduras. 6/3/54 U.S. airlifts arms to Honduras. Three B-36 bombers sent to Nicaragua. 6/7/54 Carrier and Marines sent to area for evacuation. 6/18/54 Complete arms		X	

		embargo against Guatemala announced. 6/29/54 Coup leads to anti-communist government in Guatemala. FS; Siegel			
China	Jul 1954	PRC Shootdown of UK Airliner. 7/23/54 PRC aircraft shot down UK Cathay Pacific airliner, killing 10 people (including 6 Americans). U.S. Navy aircraft from carriers, Philippine Sea and Hornet, provided air cover for rescue operations. 7/26/54 U.S. aircraft shot down two PRC fighters that fired on them. Siegel; FS			X
N. Vietnam	Jul 1954	French-Viet Minh War: Dien Bien Phu. Mid-July, possibility of U.S. intervention grew and 3rd Marine Division was put on alert to deploy to Indochina from 7/12-17/54. Geneva armistice agreement on 7/17/54 ended crisis. Siegel; IDV; FS		X	
China	Aug 1954	China-Taiwan: Tachen Islands. 9/8/54 SEATO formed. 12/2/54 U.S.-Taiwan Defense Pact signed. 9/3/54 PRC bombarded Quemoy and Matsu. Taiwan responded on 9/7/54 with air strikes against China mainland. U.S. sent Seventh Fleet to region. After U.S.-Taiwan Defense Pact, PRC bombarded Tachen Islands on 1/10/55. Taiwan responded and staged battles on Tachen, Quemoy, and Matsu. 3/25/55 Taiwan fortified Quemoy with U.S. help. U.S. and PRC ended crisis by talking on 4/23/55. IDV			X
Italy	Oct 1954	Accord on Trieste: Withdrawal of Troops. 10/5/54 settlement reached on Trieste. Sixth Fleet moves into Adriatic as 3,000 U.S. Army occupation troops were withdrawn. Withdrawal completed on 10/26/54. Siegel; FS			X
Austria	Aug 1955	Austrian State Treaty: Withdrawal of Troops. 5/15/55 U.S., UK, France, and USSR restore Austria's independence and neutrality. U.S. troops in Austria sent to Camp Darby, Italy, as provision of treaty. FS; http://www.setaf.army.mil/historyen.html			X
Jordan	Apr 1956	Jordan: UK General Glubb Ousted. King Hussein was alarmed with leftist parliament's dismissal of UK General Glubb as commander of Jordanian Arab Legion. U.S. responds by sending two carriers (*Coral Sea* and *Randolph*) and amphibious force to Eastern Mediterranean. Formation of new cabinet ends crisis. Can; IDV; FS			X

[a] PM = Procedural Multilateralism; [b] OM = Operational Multilateralism; [c] U = Full Unilateralism

(*continued*)

Actor	*Date*	*Crisis*	*PM*[a]	*OM*[b]	*U*[c]
Egypt	Jul 1956	Egypt Nationalizes Suez Canal. 7/26/56 Egypt nationalizes Suez Canal. France and UK begin preparations for military operation. U.S. sends two carriers, *Coral Sea* and *Randolph,* and amphibious force to Eastern Mediterranean. Siegel; FS; IDV			X
Egypt	Nov 1956	Suez Crisis. 10/29/56 Israel, in agreement with UK and France, invades Sinai. 10/31/56 UK and French paratroopers land in Sinai. Egypt responds with appeal for assistance from Soviets. U.S. opposes invasion and sends Sixth Fleet to Eastern Mediterranean. 11/1-2/56 Marines evacuate 2,000 Western nationals from Haifa and Alexandria. U.S. Air Force transports fly Western nationals out of Amman and Damascus. 11/6/56 U.S. makes nuclear threat in response to Soviet intervention threat. U.S. states it will not allow Soviets to attack its UK and French allies. UN sends emergency policy force and NATO issues makes a strong counterthreat to Soviets on 11/13/56. Siegel; IDV; FS			X
Indonesia	Feb 1957	Indonesia Political-Military Crisis. 2/14/57 3rd Marine division prepared for deployment to Sumatra following revolt. U.S. involved in covert effort to overthrow Indonesia government at the time. U.S. is upset with Sukarno's neutrality and his allowance of Communist Party. CIA conducted paramilitary operations with rebels on islands. FS; IDV			X
Jordan	Apr 1957	Jordan Political-Military Unrest. 4/10/57 King Hussein dismissed leftist cabinet, which led to urban demonstrations from 4/22-24/57. 4/25/57 martial law declared and Sixth Fleet deployed to Eastern Mediterranean to demonstrate U.S. support for Hussein. Marines were readied for deployment as well. Siegel; FS; IDV			X
China	Jul 1957	China-Taiwan Tension. 6/57 buildup of PRC forces across from Taiwan. 7/57 four carriers sent following the shelling of Kinmen island. FS	X		
Syria	Aug 1957	Political Developments in Syria. 8/18/57 appointment of high ranking pro-Soviet military official led to fears in Turkey of invasion. 8/21/57 Turkey reinforces its border. 9/8/57 U.S. expresses support for Turkey as part of Eisenhower doctrine, Deploys Sixth Fleet to Eastern Mediterranean and aircraft sent to Ankara, Turkey. 10/7/57 Turkish troops partake in NATO exercises. Siegel; IDV; FS			X

Indonesia	Dec 1957	Indonesia-Netherlands Crisis. 12/3/57 Labor groups begin seizing Dutch businesses in Indonesia. 46,000 Dutch nationals were repatriated. FS; IDV			X
Indonesia	Feb 1958	Indonesia Political-Military Crisis. Revolts against authority of Sukarno regime from 12/57-6/58. 3/58 U.S. Navy and Marines, as part of South China Sea Force, operated north of Sumatra over concern of evacuating U.S. nationals and their property. Siegel; FS			X
Lebanon	May 1958	Lebanon Political Crisis. 5/8/58 rioting occurs after pro-communist editor is killed. 5/12/58 Lebanese army takes over security. 5/15/58 Lebanese President Chamoun believes Syrian partisans had entered country and may need U.S. assistance. Three aircraft carriers and contingent of marines deployed off coast. U.S. and UK had developed contingency plans, beginning in 11/57, for military intervention in Lebanon and Jordan in event of actual or imminent coup d'etat in either country. BK; Siegel; IDV; FS		X	
Lebanon	Jul 1958	Lebanon Political Crisis. 7/14/58 Lebanese President Chamoun requests U.S. assistance following rioting. Coup in Iraq on same day overthrows pro-Western government. 5,790 Marines deployed to Lebanon. U.S. Army troops arrive on 7/19/58. More than 60 navy vessels supported the operation, including three carriers. U.S. troops departed by 10/25/58. U.S. and UK had developed contingency plans, beginning in 11/57, for military intervention in Lebanon and Jordan in event of coup d'etat in either country. Siegel; FS; IDV; BK		X	
Jordan	Jul 1958	Jordan Political Crisis. 7/17/58 Following coup in Iraq against pro-Western government, Jordan's King Hussein requests and receives UK paratrooper contingent. U.S. surface vessels redeployed in concert with UK operation. U.S. and UK had developed contingency plans, beginning in 11/57, for military intervention in Lebanon and Jordan in event of actual or imminent coup d'etat in either country. IDV; Siegel; FS; BK		X	

[a] PM = Procedural Multilateralism; [b] OM = Operational Multilateralism; [c] U = Full Unilateralism

(*continued*)

Actor	*Date*	*Crisis*	*PM*[a]	*OM*[b]	*U*[c]
China	Jul 1958	China-Taiwan: Quemoy Islands. 9/8/54 SEATO formed. 12/2/54 U.S.-Taiwan Defense Pact signed. 7/17/58 PRC masses troops on mainland. 8/23/58 PRC bombards Quemoy and Matsu. Taiwan responds with fire. U.S. sends Marines and Seventh Fleet on 8/27/58. U.S. suggests it would intervene if Quemoy was invaded. Crisis ends with 9/14/58 PRC-U.S. talks. 10/6/58 Ceasefire announced. Siegel; IDV; FS	X	X	
Russia	Feb 1959	Security of Berlin. 11/10/58 Moscow announces its intention to turn over Berlin and access routes to East Germany. Sets 5/27/59 deadline. 12/31/59 NATO rejects Moscow demand for a "free city" and control to East Germany. 2/16/59 NATO suggests foreign ministers meeting to deal with crisis. 3/30/59 Moscow agrees to May conference. U.S. continued to reinforce its combat forces in Europe and put nuclear weapons on its aircraft. IDV, Siegel; FS	X	X	
Russia	May 1959	Security of Berlin. 4-9/59 Soviets interfered with supply trains to Berlin. U.S. Navy put on advanced state of alert; Second Fleet conducted exercised in the Western Atlantic to display U.S. resolve. Marines put on alert for deployment. 9/30/59 Soviet harassment ends and ends crisis. FS; Siegel	X	X	
China	Jul 1959	China-Taiwan Conflict. In relation to growing China-Taiwan tension, two carrier battle groups (*Ranger* and *Lexington*) conduct operations in vicinity of Taiwan. Siegel; FS	X		
Laos	Aug 1959	Civil War in Laos. 1950 agreement to supply military and economic aid to Laos. CIA Civil Air Team began operations on 7/1/57. Special Forces inserted in summer of 1959. Civil War breaks out and U.S. works with Hmong ethnic group. 1/23/73 Paris Agreement on Vietnam. 6/3/74 end of operations. Leary			X
Cuba	Nov 1959	Political Developments: Cuba. 11/59 Soviet trade delegation visits Cuba and Eisenhower decides to work with anti-Castro forces inside of Cuba. Cuba charges that U.S. bombed Havana. FS; http://www.pbs.org/wgbh/amex/castro/timeline/index.html			X
Cuba	Nov 1960	Cuba Supports Insurgents. 11/9/60 Cuba-supported rebels invaded Nicaragua. 11/13/60 dissident Guatemalan army units captured a port. Both Nicaragua and Guatemala appeal to U.S. for support. 11/17/61 Eisenhower responds that U.S. Navy will deploy to region. IDV; FS			X

Laos	Feb 1961	Civil War in Laos. 1950 agreement to supply military and economic aid to Laos. CIA Civil Air Team began ops on 7/1/57. Special Forces inserted in summer 1959. Civil War breaks out; U.S. works with Hmong ethnic group. 1/23/73 Paris Agreement on Vietnam. 6/3/74 end of operations. Leary		X	
Dom. Rep.	Jun 1961	Trujillo Assassinated in Dominican Republic. 5/31/61 General Trujillo was assassinated. Balaguer takes power and JFK pressures him to hold elections. U.S. troops and ships deployed off coast 5/2-11/25/61. U.S. was prepared to deploy Marines in 11/61 to support Balaguer regime against Trujillo's brothers. IDV; FS			X
Russia	Jun 1961	Security of Berlin. 6/61 20,000 East German refugees to West. 7/61 30,000 refugees. 6/3-4/61 Vienna Summit between JFK and Khrushchev made no progress on Berlin. USSR threatened to sign separate treaty with East Germany, which would restrict access to Berlin. Three powers objected. On returning to Moscow after the summit, Khrushchev repeated his ultimatum, while Kennedy announced to the American people that the U.S. would fight to defend its rights in Berlin and the freedom of West Berliners. He also called up military reserve units. 7/25-10/28/61 Mobilization involving several European countries. FS; IDV; Siegel	X	X	
Kuwait	Jul 1961	Security of Kuwait. 6/19/61 mutual defense treaty with UK. Iraq threatens Kuwait and UK send troops to protect Kuwait on 7/1/61. Pan-Arab force organized to defend Kuwait. U.S. was not involved in crisis. IDV			X
Laos	May 1962	Civil War in Laos. Protection of Thai border. 5/16/62 SEATO agreement to send member state forces to Thailand. IDV	X	X	
Cuba	Oct 1962	Cuban Missile Crisis. OAS resolution 10/23/62 authorized member states use of force. IDV	X	X	
Yemen	Feb 1963	Civil War in Yemen. 9/62 following outbreak of civil war in Yemen, number of U.S. destroyers assigned to Middle East force increased from three to four. Patrol established in Red Sea to protect U.S. interests and nationals. Patrols lasted until 3/63. Siegel; FS			X

[a] PM = Procedural Multilateralism; [b] OM = Operational Multilateralism; [c] U = Full Unilateralism

(*continued*)

Actor	*Date*	*Crisis*	*PM*[a]	*OM*[b]	*U*[c]
Turkey	Apr 1963	Withdraw Missiles from Turkey. 4/25/63 McNamara informs JFK that last of Jupiter missiles in Turkey will be dismantled as part of Cuban Missile Crisis agreement. IDV; FS; http://andromeda.rutgers.edu/~hbf/missile.htm			X
Jordan	Apr 1963	Political Crisis in Jordan. Jordan feared Israeli control of West Bank. 4/20-26/63 Pro-Egypt demonstrations break out in West Bank. Army put down riot and killed 13 demonstrators; curfew was lifted on 4/26. U.S. worked to convince Jordan that a pro-Egypt proxy in West Bank would bring Israeli intervention. U.S. wanted stability. U.S. and UK worked together during crisis, shared intelligence and coordinated moves. http://muse.jhu.edu/journals/israel_studies/v007/7.1shemesh.html		X	
Laos	Apr 1963	Civil War in Laos. 1950 agreement to supply military and economic aid to Laos. CIA Civil Air Team began operations on 7/1/57. Special Forces inserted in summer of 1959. Civil War breaks out; U.S. works with Hmong ethnic group. 1/23/73 Paris Agreement on Vietnam. 6/3/74 end of operations. Leary		X	
S. Vietnam	Jun 1963	Buddhist Crisis in South Vietnam. Diem forces crackdown against monks. U.S. grows frustrated with Diem. http://www.historyplace.com/unitedstates/vietnam/index-1961 .html; FS			X
S. Vietnam	Nov 1963	Assassination of Diem. 8/25/63 U.S. naval forces stationed off South Vietnam in preparation to evacuate Americans. 9/11/63 Navy returns to normal ops. 11/1/63 Military coup d'eteat. U.S. approves it but is surprised Diem is killed. Creates a power vacuum. Viet Cong use vacuum to increase power over rural population to 40 percent. Aircraft carriers, *Hancock* and *Oriskany*, and amphibious force operated off coast 11/7/63 returned to normal ops. http://www.historyplace.com/unitedstates/vietnam/index-1961.html; FS			X
Panama	Jan 1964	Security of Panama Canal. 1/9/64 U.S. student raise U.S. flag at Balboa High School. Massive rioting follows. U.S. troops fire on demonstrators and kill 26. 1/9/64 Panama broke diplomatic relations with U.S. Amphibious force kept in region until week after 4/3/64 U.S.-Panamanian agreement restored diplomatic relations. IDV; Siegel			X

Cyprus	Jan 1964	Cyprus-Greece-Turkey Crisis. 1/21/64 Conflict between Greek and Turkish forces on Cyprus. Sixth Fleet deploys to vicinity of Cyprus. Aircraft carriers deployed off Cyprus for most of March, early June, and from 8/8/64-9/2/64. U.S., UK, UN, and NATO acted as mediators during crisis. Siegel; FS; IDV			X
S. Vietnam	Jan 1964	Coup in South Vietnam. 11/2/63 Diem is assassinated. Creates a power vacuum. Viet Cong use vacuum to increase power over rural population to 40 percent. 1/30/64 General Minh ousted from power in a bloodless coup by General Nguyen Khanh. http://www.historyplace.com/unitedstates/vietnam/index-1961.html; FS			X
Laos	May 1964	Civil War in Laos. 1950 agreement to supply military and economic aid to Laos. CIA Civil Air Team began operations on 7/1/57. Special Forces inserted in summer of 1959. Civil War breaks out and U.S. works with Hmong ethnic group. 1/23/73 Paris Agreement on Vietnam. 6/3/74 end of operations. Leary		X	
Cyprus	Aug 1964	Cyprus-Greece-Turkey Crisis. 1/21/64 conflict between Greek and Turkish forces on Cyprus. Sixth Fleet deploys to vicinity of Cyprus. Aircraft carriers deployed off Cyprus for most of March, early June, and from 8/8/64-9/2/64. U.S., UK, UN, and NATO acted as mediators during crisis. Siegel; FS; IDV			X
N. Vietnam	Aug 1964	Tonkin Gulf Incident. 7/31-8/3/64 South Vietnamese commandos in speed boats harass North Vietnamese defense. 8/2/64 North Vietnam attack on *Maddox*. 8/4/64 Attack on two destroyers. IDV	X		
N. Vietnam	Nov 1964	Viet Cong Attack Bien Hoa Barracks. 11/1/64 5 U.S., 2 RVN killed. 4/29/52 ANZUS treaty. 6/65 Australian combat troops arrive. 5/65 New Zealand agrees to send combat troops. 9/8/54 SEATO Treaty. 8/1/62 Foreign Assistance Act. Historyplace .com	X	X	
N. Vietnam	Feb 1965	Viet Cong Attack Pleiku. 2/6/65 Eight U.S. killed in attack on U.S. military compound. Respond with Flaming Dart I. 4/29/52 ANZUS treaty. 8/1/62 Foreign Assistance Act. Historyplace.com	X		

[a] PM = Procedural Multilateralism; [b] OM = Operational Multilateralism; [c] U = Full Unilateralism

(*continued*)

Actor	*Date*	*Crisis*	*PM*[a]	*OM*[b]	*U*[c]
N. Vietnam	Feb 1965	Viet Cong Attack Qui Nhon. 2/10/65. 23 U.S. killed in bombing of enlisted barracks. U.S. responds with Flaming Dart II. Historyplace.com	X		
Dom. Rep.	Apr 1965	Civil War in Dominican Republic (Evacuation). 4/24/65 Civil war breaks out and American embassy cables Americans may be in danger. 4/27-30/65 2,400 evacuees removed by amphibious forces. 4/28 Marines arrive. 4/30 Army troops arrive by air. By 5/17 over 22,000 U.S. troops on island. Siegel; FS			X
Cyprus	Jul 1965	Political Developments in Cyprus. 8/3/65 growing tension in Cyprus centered on electoral system, carrier and Marines operated off the island. Siegel; FS			X
N. Vietnam	Jul 1965	Vietnam War: Withdraw Troops from Europe. 7/65 Major European allies opposed U.S. escalation of the war in Vietnam, and the economic strains imposed by the war and a growing balance-of-payments problem caused demands in Congress to remove large numbers of U.S. troops from Europe. LexisNexis http://www.lexisnexis.com/academic/guides/area_studies/nsf/nsflbj.asp			X
Dom. Rep.	Sep 1965	Civil War in Dominican Republic (OAS force). 5/14/65 OAS troops arrive, eventually includes contingents from Brazil, Honduras, Paraguay, Panama, Costa Rica, and El Salvador. 5/26 U.S. Marines begin to withdraw from country. 8/31/65 OAS resolution reached, called "Act of Dominican Reconciliation." U.S. Army troops withdrawn on 9/21/66. Siegel; FS	X	X	
Israel	Jun 1967	Arab-Israel: Six Day War. 6/5/67 Israel launches preemptive strike on Egypt. 6/6/67 Soviets signal intervention. 6/10/67 LBJ orders 6th Fleet to move 50 miles off Syrian coast to signal that U.S. was prepared to resist Soviet intervention. IDV			X
N. Korea	Jan 1968	USS *Pueblo* Incident. 1/22/68 DPRK seizes ship. LBJ calls up reserves and orders ships to the region. IDV			X
Russia	Sep 1968	Invasion of Czechoslovakia. 8/20/68 Warsaw Pact invades Czechoslovakia. 10/18/68 Moscow Protocol signed, which legalized USSR troops in Czechoslovakia. 10/8/68 NATO held discussions but reached no decisions. LBJ cancelled future SALT I talks. IDV	X	X	

N. Korea	Apr 1969	North Korea: Shooting Down of EC-121. 4/15/69 DPRK shoots down EC-121. Nixon orders ships to Sea of Japan along with armed escorts for flights. IDV			X
Jordan	Sep 1970	Civil War in Jordan. 9/19/70 Syria invades Jordan. 9/21/70 U.S. and Israel work out joint military plan to prevent Palestinian victory in Jordan. U.S. airborne forces in Germany placed on alert and Sixth Fleet moves toward Lebanon. IDV		X	
N. Korea	Feb 1971	Withdraw Troops from South Korea. 7/8/70 The U.S. State Department announces that it has officially informed the South Korean government of the U.S. plan to gradually withdraw U.S. troops starting in July 1971. The decision to slowly decrease U.S. troops in South Korea is part of the Nixon Doctrine to reduce American presence overseas. NYT (7/8/70); http://memory.loc.gov/cgi-bin/query/r?frd/cstdy:@field(DOCID+kp0117)			X
N. Vietnam	May 1972	North Vietnamese Offensive in South Vietnam. 3/30/72 North Vietnam launches spring offensive. South Vietnam resorts to ground fighting and U.S. resumes B-52 bombings. 4/24/72 New attack by North Vietnam forces South Vietnamese troops to withdraw from Central Highlands. 5/8/72 Nixon orders mining of North Vietnamese ports. IDV	X	X	
N. Vietnam	Dec 1972	Breakdown of Peace Talks: North Vietnam. 12/14/72 Nixon orders bombings of North Vietnam to bring them back to peace table. IDV			X
Laos	Feb 1973	Civil War in Laos. 1/23/73 Paris Agreement on Vietnam effectively ends support for anti-communist forces. Leary; FS			X
Cambodia	Feb 1973	Civil War in Cambodia. 1/23/73 Paris Agreement on Vietnam effectively ends support for anti-communist forces. Leary; FS		X	
Egypt	Oct 1973	Arab-Israel: Yom Kippur War. 10/26/73 UN Security Council cease-fire resolution. U.S. mediates during crisis. U.S. fears Soviet involvement, which had placed seven airborne divisions on alert. U.S. places nuclear forces on alert. IDV	X	X	
Cyprus	Jul 1974	Cyprus-Greece-Turkey Crisis. 7/15/74 coup in Cyprus by Athens. UN Security Council passes cease-fire resolutions and UN force supervised cease-fire on 8/16/74. U.S. naval forces evacuated Americans from Cyprus during crisis. IDV; Grimmett			X

[a] PM = Procedural Multilateralism; [b] OM = Operational Multilateralism; [c] U = Full Unilateralism

(*continued*)

Actor	Date	Crisis	PM[a]	OM[b]	U[c]
N. Vietnam	Apr 1975	Collapse of Regime in South Vietnam. 1/23/73 Paris Agreement on Vietnam effectively ends support for South Vietnam. IDV; Leary; FS		X	
N. Korea	May 1975	Security of South Korea. 5/18/75 U.S. announces it would "strike back harder than it did in Vietnam" if North Korea attacked South Korea. U.S. states it will use nuclear weapons or increase its ground troop strength. U.S. relocates nuclear weapons from 9/75 2 NK infiltrators were intercepted; two ROK troops were killed in the exchange. DMZ to rear areas. Vanderbilt television archives; Zelikow	X	X	
Cambodia	May 1975	USS *Mayaguez* Incident. 5/14/75 Ford orders force to be used after Cambodia seizes cargo ship. IDV			X
Lebanon	Mar 1976	Civil War in Lebanon. 3/76 additional U.S. carrier sent to Lebanon during civil war. Zelikow			X
N. Korea	Aug 1976	Korea Tree-Cutting Incident. 8/19/76 U.S. and ROK troops enter DMZ to cut down tree after 8/17/76 incident. IDV	X	X	
Uganda	Feb 1977	Safety of Americans in Uganda. 2/23/77 U.S. aircraft carrier task force sent off coast of Kenya because Americans were not allowed to leave Uganda. 3/2/77 Amin lifts ban on American departures from Uganda. Zelikow			X
Zaire	May 1978	Invasion of Shaba Province, Zaire. 5/16/78 U.S. decides to airlift French and Belgian troops to Zaire. IDV; Zelikow		X	
Cuba	Oct 1979	Soviet Troops in Cuba. U.S. is only listed actor. U.S. did not want Soviets to escalate its troop presence in Cuba. Marines conducted maneuvers and fired artillery in Guantanamo. Zelikow; NYT			X
S. Korea	Oct 1979	Park Chung Hee Assassinated. 10/29/79 U.S. deploys carrier and planes to deter action by NK. NYT; Zelikow	X	X	
Iran	Nov 1979	Hostage Crisis. 11/4/79 U.S. embassy in Tehran stormed. IDV			X

Russia	Jan 1980	Soviet Invasion of Afghanistan. 12/24/79 Invasion. U.S. takes diplomatic measures. IDV			X
Syria	May 1981	Syrian Missiles to Lebanon. U.S. mediates and sends ships to the region. No apparent connection between diplomatic and military moves. IDV; Zelikow	X		
Libya	Aug 1981	Gulf of Sidra Dispute. 8/12/81 Sixth Fleet holds maneuvers in the Gulf of Sidra. 8/19/81 shoots down two Libyan fighters. IDV; Zelikow			X
Nicaragua	Oct 1981	Security of Central America. Border violations and U.S. Navy maneuvers in Caribbean. 11/16/81 Reagan proposes Contra funding. HF, Siegel; Zelikow			X
Sudan	Oct 1981	Sadat Assassinated/Security of Sudan. 10/11/81 U.S. efforts to protect Sudan from Libyan threats and fear of Libyan involvement in assassination. Siegel; Zelikow			X
Egypt	Nov 1981	Security of Middle East and Persian Gulf. 10/10/81 Bright Star war games with Egypt, Somalia, Sudan, and Oman. Zelikow; NYT		X	
Egypt	Mar 1982	Sinai Peacekeeping Force. 8/3/81 Treaty of Peace establishes multinational force and observers. 670 U.S. soldiers arrive in Sinai. Multinational Force and Observer Website; Zelikow	X	X	
Israel	Jun 1982	Israeli Invasion of Lebanon. 6/9/82 invasion of Lebanon. U.S. mediated to prevent escalation of Israel-Syria crisis and sends ships if evacuation is needed. IDV; NYT; Zelikow			X
Lebanon	Aug 1982	Cease-fire in Lebanon: Peacekeeping Force. 8/21-26/82 Arrival of multinational force of France, U.S., and Italy. IDV; Zelikow	X	X	
Lebanon	Sep 1982	Palestinians Massacred: Peacekeeping Force. 9/29/82 Arrival of new multinational force of France, U.S., and Italy. IDV; Zelikow	X	X	
Morocco	Nov 1982	Improved Relations with Morocco. Increased cooperative military ties. U.S. use of military facilities in Morocco. Japan Diplomatic Bluebook; Zelikow			X

[a] PM = Procedural Multilateralism; [b] OM = Operational Multilateralism; [c] U = Full Unilateralism

(continued)

Actor	*Date*	*Crisis*	*PM*[a]	*OM*[b]	*U*[c]
Oman	Nov 1982	Relations with Oman. 12/6/82 Jade Tiger exercises. 2,500 U.S. troops hold exercises in Oman. NYT; Zelikow			X
Cuba	Apr 1983	Security of Caribbean Area. U.S. Navy in Caribbean as signal to Cuba not to interfere with U.S. interests in Caribbean Sea. Zelikow			X
Nicaragua	Jul 1983	Security of Central America. 1982 bilateral agreement that extends 5/21/54 agreement. Agreement allows U.S. to station troops in Honduras. Mid-1983 U.S. and Honduras sign new training agreement and build Regional Center for Military Training that trains Salvadoran and Honduran troops. 7/83 U.S. troops and ships sent for Honduran exercises. 8/83-2/84 U.S.-Honduran Big Pine II exercises. 5,000 troops and two carrier task forces involved. Zelikow	X	X	
Syria	Sep 1983	Civil War in Lebanon. Frequent gun battles and attacks on Marines in Lebanon. 8/28/83 Marines retaliate. 8/29/83 Carrier *Eisenhower* ordered to return to Eastern Mediterranean. 9/8/83 *Bowen* provides naval gunfire support. 9/25/83 *New Jersey* provides naval gunfire support. 10/23/83 Suicide bomber strikes marine barracks in Beirut. Siegel; Zelikow		X	
Grenada	Oct 1983	Invasion of Grenada. 10/21/83 OECS request to "take appropriate action." IDV	X	X	
Iran	Oct 1983	Security of Persian Gulf. Iranian threats to block oil exports from the Persian Gulf. U.S. sends ARG Alpha to Indian Ocean on 10/8/83 and carrier *Ranger* to northern Arabian Sea on 10/10/83. Siegel; Zelikow			X
Russia	Nov 1983	Security of Western Europe. Deployment of Pershing missiles. NATO requested U.S. to deploy Intermediate range missiles in 1978. 11/23/83 Federal Republic of Germany Bundestag votes to deploy Pershing II missiles. Zelikow	X	X	
Lebanon	Dec 1983	Attacks on U.S Forces in Lebanon. 12/3/83 Two F-14s fired on by anti-aircraft artillery. 12/4/83 U.S. aircraft from carriers launched to strike anti-aircraft positions. Two U.S. Navy planes were shot down and a U.S. airman was taken prisoner by Syrian forces. Siegel; Zelikow			X

Nicaragua	Jan 1984	Security of Central America. U.S. plans and conducts military exercises in Honduras from 1-6/84 to deter Nicaragua. NYT; Zelikow		X	
Nicaragua	Feb 1984	Nicaraguan Insurgency Support in El Salvador. U.S. reconnaissance flights from Honduras to observe arms flows into El Salvador. Zelikow			X
El Salvador	Mar 1984	Elections in El Salvador. 3/13/84 Carrier *America* left for operations off the east coast of Central America to coincide with 3/25/84 Salvadoran elections. Siegel; Zelikow			X
Nicaragua	Apr 1984	Security of Caribbean Sea. U.S. Navy maneuvers in Caribbean. Zelikow; NYT			X
Nicaragua	Jun 1984	Cut in U.S. Aid to Nicaraguan Insurgents. Congress votes to cut off funding for Contras. 5/84 Congress finds out Boland Amendment was ignored. Passed second Boland Amendment in 10/84. NYT; WP; Heritage Foundation; Zelikow			X
Lebanon	Sep 1984	Bomb Attack on U.S. Embassy in Lebanon. 9/20/84 Bomb attack on U.S. embassy kills 23 people. U.S. sends three ships off Lebanon to provide contingency response capability. Siegel; Zelikow			X
Nicaragua	Nov 1984	Security of Central America. 11/84 U.S. conducts military exercises in Honduras to deter Nicaragua. NYT; Zelikow		X	
Nicaragua	Feb 1985	Honduras: Military Presence and Exercises. 2/11-5/3/85 U.S.-Honduran Big Pine III and Universal Trek exercises. 7,000 U.S. troops and 5,000 Honduran troops. Exercise involved massive amphibious landing. FS; country-data.com			X
Nicaragua	Jun 1985	Honduras: Military Exercises and Construction. U.S. military states it is prepared for Nicaragua. Continues exercises with Honduras and construction. NYT (6/4/85); FS			X
Lebanon	Jun 1985	TWA Hijacking: Naval Presence near Lebanon. 6/14/85 TWA Flight 847 was hijacked. Carrier *Nimitz* and 1,800 Marines sent to Eastern Mediterranean. Siegel			X

[a] PM = Procedural Multilateralism; [b] OM = Operational Multilateralism; [c] U = Full Unilateralism

(*continued*)

Actor	*Date*	*Crisis*	*PM*[a]	*OM*[b]	*U*[c]
Nicaragua	Jan 1986	Honduras: Military Exercises and Construction. 6/86 Congress approves Contra aid. The Defense Department has used a variety of methods to establish a small American military presence in Honduras without obtaining explicit approval from Congress, according to Congressional sources and the General Accounting Office. The methods include military exercises during which airstrips, roads, barracks, radar stations and the like have been built. Helicopters, weapons and other equipment, brought in during the maneuvers, have been left behind in American hands. NYT (7/14/86)			X
Libya	Jan 1986	Gulf of Syrte Operations. 1/23-30 and 2/11-14/86 naval exercises in Gulf of Syrte. 3/20 U.S. planes destroyed threatening Libyan ships, planes, and missiles sites. IDV; FS			X
N. Korea	Jan 1986	Military Exercises with South Korea. 1/86 North Korea suspends talks with South Korea after annual "Team Spirit" U.S.-South Korea military exercise. FS		X	
Libya	Apr 1986	Airstrikes on Libya. 4/15/86 Air raids on Tripoli and Benghazi after 4/5 discotheque bombing. IDV			X
Japan	Oct 1986	Military Exercises in Japan. 10/86 Keen Edge 87-1 U.S.-Japan joint military exercise. FS			X
Nicaragua	Dec 1986	Helicopters Transport Honduran Troops. 12/7-8/86 U.S. helicopter ferry Honduran troops during clash with Nicaragua. Series of military exercises begin 12/29 and last until 5/87. FS	X	X	
Nicaragua	Jan 1987	Military Exercises with Honduras. 12/29/86-5/87 Involves up to 50,000 U.S. troops. FS			X
Iran	Jan 1987	Naval Presence Near Iran. 1-2/87 hostages taken in Lebanon. Three carrier groups and Marines head toward Lebanon and Iran. Siegel; FS			X
Lebanon	Jan 1987	Hostages in Lebanon. 1-2/87 hostages taken in Lebanon. Three carrier groups and Marines head toward Lebanon and Iran. Siegel; FS			X
Iran	Jun 1987	Protection of Persian Gulf Shipping. 6/30/87 battleship and two carrier groups in Persian Gulf to protect shipping. UK, France, Italy, Belgium, Netherlands sent minesweepers after Panamian tanker struck in 8/87. Remain there through end of Iran-Iraq War on 8/20/88. Grimmett; FS			X

Egypt	Aug 1987	Military Exercises in Egypt and Somalia. 8/15-20/87 Bright Star 87 military exercises, a JCS-directed, USCENTCOM-held in Egypt and Somalia. FS		X	
Nicaragua	Mar 1988	Troop Deployment and Exercises in Honduras. 3/16/88 3,200 troops sent to Honduras after Nicaraguan offensive against Contra camps in Honduras. IDV			X
Panama	Mar 1988	Troop Deployment to Panama. 3/14-4/8/88 Marine and Army forces, as well as a carrier group sent to Panama. Siegel; FS			X
Panama	May 1989	Brigade-Sized Troop Deployment to Panama. 5/11/89 More Army and Marine forces sent to Panama. Conduct exercises. Occurs after violent election campaign and annulment of election by Noriega. Siegel; FS			X
Iran	Aug 1989	Hostages in Lebanon. 8/1/89 Col. William Higgins is killed in Lebanon. Navy ships, *America, Coral Sea, Iowa,* and *Belknap* head towards Lebanon and Iran. Siegel; FS			X
Panama	Oct 1989	Military Alert in Panama. Unsuccessful coup attempt on Noriega. 12,000 troops put on alert. FS			X
Panama	Dec 1989	Invasion of Panama. 12/20/89 27,684 U.S. troops, over 300 aircraft invade Panama to remove Noriega from power. IDV			X
Iraq	Aug 1990	Persian Gulf War. 8/2/90 Iraqi forces invaded Kuwait. UN Security adopted Resolution 660. 8/7/90 U.S. announces it will deploy troops to Saudi Arabia. 11/29/90 UN Security Council adopts Resolution 678 authorizing force. 1/17/91 Air campaign begins. 2/24/91 Land campaign begins. 4/12/91 End of crisis. IDV	X	X	
Iraq	Apr 1991	U.S. Troops in Northern Iraq. 4/91 Up to 10,000 U.S. troops enter Northern Iraq, withdrawn by 7/15/91. 4/5/91 UN Resolution 688 calls on states to assist Kurds. 4/7/91 U.S., UK, and France conduct Provide Comfort operation. 4/10/91 U.S., UK, and France establish "no-fly" zone. 4/17/91 U.S. forces enter northern Iraq. FS; globalsecurity.org	X	X	

[a] PM = Procedural Multilateralism; [b] OM = Operational Multilateralisn; [c] U = Full Unilateralism

(*continued*)

Actor	*Date*	*Crisis*	*PM*[a]	*OM*[b]	*U*[c]
N. Korea	Nov 1991	Troop Withdrawal from South Korea Canceled. 11/21/91 Planned withdrawal of 6,000 U.S. troops canceled in response to North Korean nuclear weapons development. In order to maintain pressure on North Korea, however, Secretary of Defense Dick Cheney took other steps to ensure a strong military posture in the South, including delaying the planned withdrawal of 6,000 U.S. troops from the peninsula and enlarging other military exercises. NYT; FS; http://www.brookings.edu/press/books/chapter_1/goingcritical.pdf			X
Iraq	Jul 1992	Military Exercises in Kuwait and Persian Gulf. 8/3/92 U.S. holds military exercises in Kuwait, following Iraqi refusal to recognize new UN border and refusal to cooperate with UN inspection teams. Grimmett; FS			X
Iraq	Aug 1992	Enforcement of "No-Fly Zone." 8/18/92 U.S., UK, and France announce "air exclusion zone" over Iraq. UK sent six Tornadoes, France 10 Mirages, and U.S. had 200 planes to enforce the ban. 8/26/92 Southern no fly zone ban announced by U.S., UK, France, and Russia. IDV; FS; Grimmett	X	X	
Somalia	Dec 1992	Famine Relief in Somalia. 12/10/92 30,000 U.S. troops and carrier group sent to Somalia for famine relief in response to UN Security Council resolution. UN approved of deployment. Called operation Restore Hope, part of U.S.-led United Nations Unified Task Force (UNITAF). 5/93 U.S. force replaced by UN force with U.S. participation as part of United Nations Operation in Somalia (UNOSOM II). Grimmett; FS	X	X	
Iraq	Jan 1993	Attack on Iraqi Installations. 1/21/93 U.S. planes fired at targets in Iraq after pilots sensed Iraqi radar or anti-aircraft fire directed at them. U.S. aircraft fired a missile and dropped cluster bombs on an Iraqi ground radar in the northern no-fly zone when the radar beam search was directed at them while they were escorting a French reconnaissance airplane. 1/22/93 A U.S. F-4G fired two missiles at an air defense battery in the northern no-fly zone after the battery's radar actively tracked U.S. aircraft patrolling the zone. Iraq denied it had tracked the aircraft and claimed there were no air defense batteries at that location. A U.S. A-6 Intruder aircraft fired a	X	X	

		laser-guided bomb at an Iraqi anti-aircraft position in the southern no-fly zone after the pilot thought he saw anti-aircraft fire directed at his and other U.S. aircraft patrolling that zone. Iraq denied firing on any U.S. aircraft. U.S. Defense Department officials subsequently said that the U.S. aircraft were not being tracked by Iraqi radar and that they were trying to establish whether or not Iraq had fired on the U.S. planes. Grimmett; FS; http://www.globalsecurity.org/wmd/library/report/crs/94-049.htm			
Somalia	Oct 1993	Additional Troops Deployed to Somalia. 10/8/93 5,300 additional U.S. troops and aircraft carrier deployed to Somalia after U.S. soldiers killed in 10/3-4/93 Battle of Mogadishu. Grimmett; FS			X
Rwanda	Apr 1994	Refugee Relief in Zaire and Rwanda. 4/12/94 Clinton announces U.S. forces deployed to Burundi to conduct evacuation operations (Operation Distant Runner) of U.S. citizens and foreign nationals from Rwanda. Grimmett; FS			X
Haiti	Jul 1994	Military Simulation of Haiti Invasion. 7/7/94 Military exercises in Caribbean simulate an invasion of Haiti. 2,000 Marines and four ships stationed off of Haiti. 7/15/94 U.S. Army paratrooper step up night exercises. 7/31/94 UN Security Council Resolution 940 authorizes force to be used to depose military leadership. IDV; FS; NYT			X
Haiti	Sep 1994	Intervention in Haiti. 7/31/94 UN Security Council Resolution 940 authorizes force to be used to depose military leadership. 9/18/94 Military junta agrees to leave Haiti. 9/21/94 1,500 U.S. troops deployed (and later increased to 20,000) to enforce the agreement. Aristide returned to power on 10/15/94. IDV; Grimmett; FS	X	X	
Iraq	Oct 1994	Iraqi Threat to Kuwait. 10/7/94 Iraqi deployed troops near Kuwaiti border. Clinton sent aircraft carrier *Eisenhower* and 4,000 troops to Kuwait. 10/9/94 36,000 more troops sent. 10/10/94 UK, France, Russia, Egypt, and Turkey agreed to defend Kuwait. 10/10/94 UN Security Council Resolution condemns Iraq's deployment. 10/12/94 Gulf States, UK, and France sent forces to defend Kuwait. IDV; FS	X	X	

[a] PM = Procedural Multilateralism; [b] OM = Operational Multilateralism; [c] U = Full Unilateralism

(*continued*)

Actor	*Date*	*Crisis*	*PM*[a]	*OM*[b]	*U*[c]
Somalia	Jan 1995	Withdrawal from Somalia. 2/27/95 Clinton reported that 1,800 U.S. troops deployed to Mogadishu to assist in withdrawal of UN forces assigned there as part of UN Operation in Somalia (UNOSOM II). Mission completed by 3/1/95. Grimmett; FS	X	X	
Bosnia	May 1995	Hostage Crisis in Bosnia. 2/92-1/96 UN Protection Force (UNPROFOR); 5/29-30/95 Hundreds of UN observes taken hostage by Serbs in Bosnia. Carrier task force, Marine contingent, and attack submarine moved into Adriatic. 5/26/95, UN twice bombed a Bosnian Serb ammunitions dump after the Serbs ignored UN ultimatums to abandon certain heavy weapons in the Sarajevo exclusion zone. The Serbs retaliated by taking hostage hundreds of poorly armed UN peacekeepers, some of whom were then chained to key military targets as human shields against further air strikes. The Serbs made clear that they no longer viewed the UN forces as impartial peacekeepers and accused UNPROFOR of "flagrant interference in the conflict" and "siding with one party"; they also declared all UN and NATO resolutions null and void. The UN, for its part, accused the Serbs of "terrorist" acts and barely bothered to feign impartiality. FS; NYT; http://www.cato.org/pubs/fpbriefs/fpb-034.html	X	X	
Iraq	Aug 1995	Troops, Ships Deployed to Persian Gulf. 7/95 Iraq threatens to end cooperation with UNSCOM and IAEA, if sanctions are not lifted. 8/95 U.S. troops, ships deployed to Persian Gulf in response to Iraqi threats. 8/17/95 Two carriers sent as part of Operation Vigilant Sentinel. FS			X

Bosnia	Dec 1995	Troop Deployment to Bosnia. 12/95 8,000 U.S. troops sent to Bosnia as part of Dayton Agreement. Implementation Force (IFOR), authorized by UN, under the command of NATO, monitored compliance with the agreement. Following the Dayton Peace Agreement, the U.S. took a greater stand trying to maintain peace and stability in the Balkans. In December 1995 the transfer of authority from the United Nations to NATO has begun. The UN Security Council voted unanimously to authorize NATO to send 60,000 troops to relieve 20,000 UN solders in Bosnia, therefore shutting down a UN mission that failed to restore peace in the war-torn Balkans. The U.S. sent some 20,000 troops as part of NATO forces, in order to maintain stability. FS; Grimmett; http://www.earlham.edu/~pols/globalprobs/bosnia/role.html	X	X

Sources: BK = Blechman and Kaplan (1978); FS = Fordham and Sarver Descriptive List of U.S. Uses of Force, 1870-1995; Grimmett = Grimmett (2004); IDV = ICB Data Viewer (http://www.cidcm.umd.edu/icb/dataviewer/); Leary = Leary (1999-2000); NYT = New York Times; Siegel = Siegel (1991); Zelikow = Zelikow (1987); as well as cited websites.

[a] PM = Procedural Multilateralism; [b] OM = Operational Multilateralisn; [c] U = Full Unilateralism

Appendix B

Experiment Instructions and Crisis Scenarios

Instructions

Foreign Policy Decision Making

In this study, I am interested in learning about decision making in various U.S. foreign policy events. Specifically, I am interested in your ability to comprehend and advocate a decision at the national level. Comprehension of national level decisions is based on the quality of the decision you make in the context of a simulated international crisis.

In the next pages, you'll face a hypothetical international crisis. The case will contain a brief background on the crisis, and the information available to a president as he prepares to make a decision. Read the information carefully, and then respond to the situation, *assuming the president will be influenced based on the option you advise.*

Following the case is a questionnaire in which you'll record your decision. Please respond to all the questions.

Thank you for your cooperation, Brad Podliska

The Juneria Humanitarian Crisis

During the past several months, the civil war in Juneria has crippled that country's infrastructure and destroyed its food supply. Warlords have confiscated crops and food supplies and use it as payment in exchange for military service in their private armies. The result is widespread famine with innocent women and children starving to death. The famine in Juneria becomes a fixture on the nightly news.

The U.S. President has expressed his concerns for the innocent victims of Juneria's civil war, and he wants to do something. After exhausting all non-force alternatives, the president has decided to get rid of the warlords with military force. The president has to make a decision to act unilaterally with only a U.S. military force *or* to partner with other nations and form a multinational military force. The American people understand the costs and benefits of acting unilaterally or multilaterally, and the following polls numbers reflect their support of the president in his decision to act unilaterally.

[Over 70 percent of the public supports the president in his decision to act alone and use unilateral force.]

[Less than 30 percent of the public supports the president in his decision to act alone and use unilateral force.]

The Combatant Commander for the region advises the President that in the mission to separate the warlords,

[the U.S. military, acting alone is facing a poorly trained, poorly equipped, and fragmented militia enemy, which is plagued by low morale.]

[the U.S. military, acting alone is facing a well-trained, well-equipped, and tenacious enemy, which is considered to be the most powerful in its region.]

The President has to make a decision, and you are his close confidant and adviser. He must decide from one of the following two alternatives: act unilaterally with only a U.S. military force or partner with other nations and form a multinational military force.

Please go to the next page to answer several questions.

Please do not go back to read the scenario.
The choice I think the U.S. President should make is: (**mark only one choice**)

1. Act unilaterally with only a U.S. military force to get rid of the warlords: ____. (If you select this option, answer question #3 and skip question #4.)

Or

2. Partner with other nations and form a multinational military force to get rid of the warlords: ____. (If you select this option, answer question #4 and skip question #3.)
3. How much do you support using ***unilateral*** force: (circle a number on the scale)

   Not at all 0 1 2 3 4 5 6 7 8 9 10 A great deal
4. How much do you support using ***multilateral*** force: (circle a number on the scale)

   Not at all 0 1 2 3 4 5 6 7 8 9 10 A great deal

Answer all of these remaining questions:
How dangerous is the military mission: (circle a number on the scale)

Not at all 0 1 2 3 4 5 6 7 8 9 10 Very dangerous

How many casualties may the U.S. receive in this operation: (circle a number on the scale)

None 0 10 20 30 40 50 60 70 80 90 100 A high amount

How supportive is the American public for unilateral operations: (circle a number on the scale)

Not supportive 0 1 2 3 4 5 6 7 8 9 10 Very supportive

The main reason for this military operation is: (circle a number on the scale)

a. U.S. national security

   Not at all the reason 0 1 2 3 4 5 6 7 8 9 10 Very much the reason

b. Regime change in Juneria

   Not at all the reason 0 1 2 3 4 5 6 7 8 9 10 Very much the reason

c. Humanitarian hardship in Juneria

   Not at all the reason 0 1 2 3 4 5 6 7 8 9 10 Very much the reason

Regime Change in Evilaen

During the past year, the Evilaenese dictator, a bitter enemy of the U.S., has continued to violate international law and defy the civilized world with his actions. The dictator has brutalized his own people, committing atrocities against minority populations. In his latest action, the dictator is working to destabilize the newly emerging democracies of his neighboring countries, Katiana and Cona Mai.

The U.S. President has expressed his concerns in the past for the Evilaenese dictator's actions and tried unsuccessfully to remove the dictator from power with such non-force actions as economic and diplomatic sanctions. The president has decided the only remaining option is to invade Evilaen and remove the dictator from power. The president has to make a decision to act unilaterally with only a U.S. military force *or* to partner with other nations and form a multinational military force for the invasion. The American people understand the costs and benefits of acting unilaterally or multilaterally, and the following polls numbers reflect their support of the president in his decision to act unilaterally.

[Over 70 percent of the public supports the president in his decision to act alone and use unilateral force.]

[Less than 30 percent of the public supports the president in his decision to act alone and use unilateral force.]

The Combatant Commander for the region advises the President that in the regime change mission,

[the U.S. military, acting alone is facing a poorly trained, poorly equipped, and fragmented militia enemy, which is plagued by low morale.]

[the U.S. military, acting alone is facing a well-trained, well-equipped, and tenacious enemy, which is considered to be the most powerful in its region.]

The President has to make a decision, and you are his close confidant and adviser. He must decide from one of the following two alternatives: act unilaterally with only a U.S. military force or partner with other nations and form a multinational military force.

Please go to the next page to answer several questions.

Please do not go back to read the scenario.
The choice I think the U.S. President should make is: (**mark only one choice**)

1. Act unilaterally with only a U.S. military force to remove the Evilaenese dictator from power: ____. (If you select this option, answer question #3 and skip question #4.)

Or

2. Partner with other nations and form a multinational military force to remove the Evilaenese dictator from power: ____. (If you select this option, answer question #4 and skip question #3.)
3. How much do you support using ***unilateral*** force: (circle a number on the scale)

   Not at all 0 1 2 3 4 5 6 7 8 9 10 A great deal
4. How much do you support using ***multilateral*** force: (circle a number on the scale)

   Not at all 0 1 2 3 4 5 6 7 8 9 10 A great deal

Answer all of these remaining questions:
How dangerous is the military mission: (circle a number on the scale)

Not at all 0 1 2 3 4 5 6 7 8 9 10 Very dangerous

How many casualties may the U.S. receive in this operation: (circle a number on the scale)

None 0 100 200 300 400 500 600 700 800 900 1000 A high amount

How supportive is the American public for unilateral operations: (circle a number on the scale)

Not supportive 0 1 2 3 4 5 6 7 8 9 10 Very supportive

The main reason for this military operation is: (circle a number on the scale)

a. U.S. national security

   Not at all the reason 0 1 2 3 4 5 6 7 8 9 10 Very much the reason

b. Regime change in Evilaen

   Not at all the reason 0 1 2 3 4 5 6 7 8 9 10 Very much the reason

c. Humanitarian hardship in Evilaen

   Not at all the reason 0 1 2 3 4 5 6 7 8 9 10 Very much the reason

The Sugabaneria National Security Threat

For the past several months, a narco-terrorist group, Sugabaneria, has been waging an unconventional war on the U.S. Sugabaneria, which is located in several countries unfriendly to the U.S., supports its terrorist campaign against the U.S. by growing and selling cocaine, a significant amount of which is sold in America. In the past month, Sugabaneria organized a truck bomb to explode outside a U.S. embassy, killing 100 Americans. Sugabaneria has also purchased high-technology military weapons that give them the capability to threaten U.S. interests in the region.

The U.S. President has labeled Sugabaneria's actions as a threat to national security, and he tried unsuccessfully to stop Sugabaneria's actions with such non-force measures as threats and highly publicized arrests. However, these measures have not worked and Sugabaneria's power continues to grow as its war on America continues. The president has decided the only remaining option is to attack Sugabaneria group members in the countries where they reside. The president has to make a decision to act unilaterally with only a U.S. military force *or* to partner with other nations and form a multinational military force. The American people understand the costs and benefits of acting unilaterally or multilaterally, and the following polls numbers reflect their support of the president in his decision to act unilaterally.

[Over 70 percent of the public supports the president in his decision to act alone and use unilateral force.]

[Less than 30 percent of the public supports the president in his decision to act alone and use unilateral force.]

The Combatant Commander for the region advises the President that in the mission to wipe out Sugabaneria,

[the U.S. military, acting alone is facing a poorly trained, poorly equipped, and fragmented militia enemy, which is plagued by low morale.]

[the U.S. military, acting alone is facing a well-trained, well-equipped, and tenacious enemy, which is considered to be the most powerful in its region.]

The President has to make a decision, and you are his close confidant and adviser. He must decide from one of the following two alternatives: act unilaterally with only a U.S. military force or partner with other nations and form a multinational military force.

Please go to the next page to answer several questions.

Please do not go back to read the scenario.
The choice I think the U.S. President should make is: (**mark only one choice**)

1. Act unilaterally with only a U.S. military force to wipe out Sugabaneria: ____. (If you select this option, answer question #3 and skip question #4.)

Or

2. Partner with other nations and form a multinational military force to wipe out Sugabaneria: ____. (If you select this option, answer question #4 and skip question #3.)
3. How much do you support using ***unilateral*** force: (circle a number on the scale)

   Not at all 0 1 2 3 4 5 6 7 8 9 10 A great deal
4. How much do you support using ***multilateral*** force: (circle a number on the scale)

   Not at all 0 1 2 3 4 5 6 7 8 9 10 A great deal

Answer all of these remaining questions:
How dangerous is the military mission: (circle a number on the scale)

Not at all 0 1 2 3 4 5 6 7 8 9 10 Very dangerous

How many casualties may the U.S. receive in this operation: (circle a number on the scale)

None 0 100 200 300 400 500 600 700 800 900 1000 A high amount

How supportive is the American public for unilateral operations: (circle a number on the scale)

Not supportive 0 1 2 3 4 5 6 7 8 9 10 Very supportive

The main reason for this military operation is: (circle a number on the scale)

a. U.S. national security

   Not at all the reason 0 1 2 3 4 5 6 7 8 9 10 Very much the reason

b. Regime change in the countries where Sugabaneria is located

   Not at all the reason 0 1 2 3 4 5 6 7 8 9 10 Very much the reason

c. Humanitarian hardship brought on by Sugabaneria

   Not at all the reason 0 1 2 3 4 5 6 7 8 9 10 Very much the reason

Bibliography

Achen, Christopher H., and Duncan Snidal. "Rational Deterrence Theory and Comparative Case Studies." *World Politics* 41, no. 2 (January 1989): 143-69.

Allison, Graham T. "Military Capabilities and American Foreign Policy." *Annals of the American Academy of Political and Social Science* 406 (1973): 17-37.

Alvarez, Jose E. "Multilateralism and Its Discontents." *European Journal of International Law* 11, no. 2 (2000): 393-411.

Ashby, Christopher. "Multilateralism vs. Unilateralism: Principle or Policy?" In *Multilateralism v Unilateralism: Policy Choices in a Global Society*, edited by John B. Attanasio and Joseph J. Norton. London: The British Institute of International and Comparative Law, 2004.

Attanasio, John B. "Introduction: Multilateralism, Unilateralism, and Leadership." In *Multilateralism v Unilateralism: Policy Choices in a Global Society*, edited by John B. Attanasio and Joseph J. Norton. London: The British Institute of International and Comparative Law, 2004.

Bajpai, Kanti. "U.S. Nonproliferation Policy After the Cold War." In *Unilateralism and U.S. Foreign Policy: International Perspectives*, edited by David M. Malone and Yuen Foong Khong. Boulder, Colo.: Lynne Rienner, 2003.

Beinart, Peter. *The Good Fight: Why Liberals–and Only Liberals–Can Win the War on Terror and Make America Great Again.* New York: HarperCollins, 2006.

Bennett, Andrew, Joseph Lepgold, and Danny Unger. "Burden-Sharing in the Persian Gulf War." *International Organization* 48, no. 1 (Winter 1994): 39-75.

Bennett, D. Scott, and Allan C. Stam, III. "The Declining Advantages of Democracy: A Combined Model of War Outcome and Duration." *Journal of Conflict Resolution* 42, no. 3 (June 1998): 344-66.

Bennett, D. Scott, and Allan C. Stam, III. "*EUGene*: A Conceptual Manual." *International Interactions* 26, no. 2 (2000): 179-204.

Beschloss, Michael R. *The Crisis Years: Kennedy and Khrushchev: 1960-1963*. New York: HarperCollins, 1991.

Betts, Richard K. "Why Surprise Succeeds, II: The Fog of Peace." In *Surprise Attack: Lessons for Defense Planning*, edited by Richard Betts. Washington, D.C.: The Brookings Institution, 1982.

Biddle, Stephen. *Military Power: Explaining Victory and Defeat in Modern Battle*. Princeton, N.J.: Princeton University Press, 2004.

———. "The Past as Prologue: Assessing Theories of Future Warfare." *Security Studies* 8, no. 1 (Autumn 1998): 1-74.

———. "Victory Misunderstood: What the Gulf War Tells Us about the Future of Conflict." *International Security* 21, no. 2 (Autumn 1996): 139-79.

Binder, Sarah A. "The Dynamics of Legislative Gridlock, 1947-96." *American Political Science Review* 93, no. 3 (September 1999): 519-33.

Blechman, Barry M., and Stephen S. Kaplan. *Force Without War: U.S. Armed Forces as a Political Instrument*. Washington, D.C.: The Brookings Institution, 1978.

Bodansky, Daniel. "What's So Bad about Unilateral Action to Protect the Environment?" *European Journal of International Law* 11, no. 2 (2000): 339-47.

Bolton, John R. "Unilateralism Is Not Isolationism." In *Understanding Unilateralism in American Foreign Relations*, edited by Gwyn Prins. London: Royal Institute of International Affairs, 2000.

Boot, Max. "Doctrine of the 'Big Enchilada'." *Washington Post*, 14 October 2002.

Brecher, Michael, and Jonathan Wilkenfeld. *A Study of Crisis*. Ann Arbor: University of Michigan Press, 2000.

Bremer, Stuart A. "Dangerous Dyads: Conditions Affecting the Likelihood of Interstate War, 1816-1965." *Journal of Conflict Resolution* 36, no. 2 (June 1992): 309-41.

Brenfors, Martha, and Malene Maxe Petersen. "The Legality of Unilateral Humanitarian Intervention–A Defence." *Nordic Journal of International Law* 69, no. 4 (2000): 449-99.

Brooks, Stephen G., and William C. Wohlforth. "International Relations Theory and the Case against Unilateralism." *Perspectives on Politics* 3, no. 3 (September 2005): 509-24.

Brown, Bernard E. "The Case Method in Comparative Politics." In *Cases in Comparative Politics*, edited by Bernard E. Brown and James B. Christoph. Boston: Little, Brown, 1976.

Brule, David, and Alex Mintz. "Blank Checks or Marching Order? Public Opinion and Presidential Use of Force in the United States." In *Crossing Boundaries*, edited by Harvey Starr. New York: Palgrave Macmillan, 2006.

Buckley, Kevin. *Panama: The Whole Story*. New York: Simon & Schuster, 1991.

Bueno de Mesquita, Bruce. "The Contribution of Expected Utility Theory to the Study of International Conflict." In *Handbook of War Studies*, edited by Manus I. Midlarsky. Boston: Unwin Hyman, 1989.

———. *The War Trap*. New Haven, Conn.: Yale University Press, 1981.

Bueno de Mesquita, Bruce, and David Lalman. *War and Reason*. New Haven, Conn.: Yale University Press, 1992.

Bueno de Mesquita, Bruce, and Randolph M. Siverson. "War and the Survival of Political Leaders: A Comparative Study of Regime Types and Political Accountability." *American Political Science Review* 89, no. 4 (December 1995): 841-55.

Bueno de Mesquita, Bruce, James D. Morrow, and Ethan Zorick. "Capabilities, Perception, and Escalation." *American Political Science Review* 91, no. 1 (March 1997): 15-27.

Bueno de Mesquita, Bruce, James D. Morrow, Randolph M. Siverson, and Alastair Smith. "An Institutional Explanation of the Democratic Peace." *American Political Science Review* 93, no. 4 (December 1999): 791-807.

Bueno de Mesquita, Bruce, James D. Morrow, Randolph M. Siverson, and Alastair Smith. "Policy Failure and Political Survival: The Contribution of Political Institutions." *Journal of Conflict Resolution* 43, no. 2 (April 1999): 147-61.

Bueno de Mesquita, Bruce, James D. Morrow, Randolph M. Siverson, and Alastair Smith. "Testing Novel Implications from the Selectorate Theory of War." *World Politics* 56, no. 3 (April 2004): 363-88.

Burke, John P., and Fred I. Greenstein. *How Presidents Test Reality: Decisions on Vietnam, 1954 and 1965.* New York: Russell Sage Foundation, 1989.

Burley, Anne-Marie. "Regulating the World: Multilateralism, International Law, and the Projection of the New Deal Regulatory State." In *Multilateralism Matters: The Theory and Praxis of an Institutional Form*, edited by John Gerard Ruggie. New York: Columbia University Press, 1993.

Bush, George H.W., and Brent Scowcroft. *A World Transformed.* New York: Alfred A. Knopf, 1998.

Cameron, Charles M. *Veto Bargaining: Presidents and the Politics of Negative Power.* Cambridge: Cambridge University Press, 2000.

Campbell, Donald T., and Julian C. Stanley. *Experimental and Quasi-Experimental Designs for Research.* Chicago: Rand McNally, 1966.

Caporaso, James A. "International Relations Theory and Multilateralism: The Search for Foundations." *International Organization* 46, no. 3 (Summer 1992): 599-632.

Cerf, Christopher, and Victor Navasky. "The Experts Speak on the Coming Gulf War." In *The Iraq War Reader: History, Documents, Opinions*, edited by Micah L. Sifry and Christopher Cerf. New York: Touchstone, 2003.

Chinkin, Christine. "The State That Acts Alone: Bully, Good Samaritan or Iconoclast?" *European Journal of International Law* 11, no. 1 (2000): 31-41.

Chiozza, Giacomo, and H.E. Goemans. "International Conflict and the Tenure of Leaders: Is War Still 'Ex Post' Inefficient." *American Journal of Political Science* 48, no. 3 (July 2004): 604-19.

Claude, Jr., Inis L. *Swords into Plowshares: The Problems and Progress of International Organization.* 4th ed. New York: Random House, 1971.

Clement, Sophia. "The United States and NATO: A Selective Approach to Multilateralism." In *Unilateralism and U.S. Foreign Policy: International Perspectives*, edited by David M. Malone and Yuen Foong Khong. Boulder, Colo.: Lynne Rienner, 2003.

Cockayne, James, and David Malone. "Creeping Unilateralism: How Operation Provide Comfort and the No-Fly Zones in 1991 and 1992 Paved the Way for the Iraq Crisis of 2003." *Security Dialogue* 37, no. 1 (March 2006): 123-41.

Colaresi, Michael. "When Doves Cry: International Rivalry, Unreciprocated Cooperation, and Leadership Turnover." *American Journal of Political Science* 48, no. 3 (July 2004): 555-70.

Colaresi, Michael, and William R. Thompson. "Hot Spots or Hot Hands? Serial Crisis Behavior, Escalating Risks, and Rivalry." *Journal of Politics* 64, no. 4 (November 2002): 1175-98.

Collier, David. "New Perspectives on the Comparative Method." In *Comparative Political Dynamics*, edited by Dankart A. Rustow and Kenneth P. Erikson. New York: HarperCollins, 1991.

Conley, Richard S. *The Presidency, Congress and Divided Government.* College Station: Texas A&M University Press, 2003.

Coppedge, Michael. "Thickening Thin Concepts and Theories: Combining Large N and Small in Comparative Politics." *Comparative Politics* 31, no. 4 (July 1999): 465-76.

Corbetta, Renato, and William J. Dixon. "Danger beyond Dyads: Third-Party Participants in Militarized Interstate Disputes." *Conflict Management and Peace Science* 22, no. 1 (March 2005): 39-61.

Corbetta, Renato, and William J. Dixon. "Multilateralism, Major Powers, and Militarized Disputes." *Political Research Quarterly* 57, no. 1 (March 2004): 5-14.

Cowhey, Peter F. "Elect Locally—Order Globally: Domestic Politics and Multilateral Cooperation." In *Multilateralism Matters: The Theory and Praxis of an Institutional Form*, edited by John Gerard Ruggie. New York: Columbia University Press, 1993.

Cox, Robert W. *Production, Power, and World Order.* New York: Columbia University Press, 1987.

Cupitt, Richard T., Rodney L. Whitlock, and Lynn Williams Whitlock. "British Hegemony and Militarized Interstate Disputes, 1815-1939." *Conflict Management and Peace Science* 12, no. 2 (Spring 1993): 41-64.

Dahl, Robert A. *Who Governs? Democracy and Power in an American City.* New Haven, Conn.: Yale University Press, 1961.

DeRouen, Jr., Karl R. "The Decision Not to Use Force at Dien Bien Phu: A Poliheuristic Perspective." In *Integrating Cognitive and Rational Theories of Foreign Policy Decision Making*, edited by Alex Mintz. New York: Palgrave Macmillan, 2003.

———. "The Indirect Link: Politics, the Economy, and the Use of Force." *Journal of Conflict Resolution* 39, no. 4 (December 1995): 671-95.

———. "Presidents and the Diversionary Use of Force: A Research Note." *International Studies Quarterly* 44, no. 2 (June 2000): 317-28.

de Waal, Alex, and Rakiya Omaar. "Can Military Intervention Be 'Humanitarian?'." *Middle East Report* 187/188 (March–June 1994): 2-8.

Diehl, Paul F., and Jean Kingston. "Messenger or Message?: Military Buildups and the Initiation of Conflict." *Journal of Politics* 49, no. 3 (August 1987): 801-13.

Dinges, John. *Our Man in Panama: The Shrewd Rise and Brutal Fall of Manuel Noriega.* New York: Times Books, 1991.

Dolzer, Rudolf. "Unilateralism and Current Transatlantic Relations." In *Multilateralism v Unilateralism: Policy Choices in a Global Society*, edited by John B. Attanasio and Joseph J. Norton. London: The British Institute of International and Comparative Law, 2004.

Dombrowski, Peter, and Rodger A. Payne. "Global Debate and the Limits of the Bush Doctrine." *International Studies Perspective* 4, no. 4 (November 2003): 395-408.

Donnelly, Thomas, Margaret Roth, and Caleb Baker. *Operation Just Cause: The Storming of Panama.* New York: Lexington Books, 1991.

Downs, Anthony. *An Economic Theory of Democracy.* New York: Harper and Brothers, 1957.

Downs, George W., and Michael Jones. "Reputation, Compliance, and International Law." *Journal of Legal Studies* 31, no. S1 (January 2002): S95-S114.

Drew, Elizabeth. "Washington Prepares for War." In *The Gulf War Reader: History, Documents, Opinions,* edited by Micah L. Sifry and Chistopher Cerf. New York: Times Books, 1991.

Duffield, Mark, and Joe Stork. "Bosnia Is the Classic Case of Using Humanitarian Aid as a Smokescreen to Hide Political Failure." *Middle East Report* 187/188 (March–June 1994): 18-23.

Duffield, Mark, and John Prendergast. "Sovereignty and Intervention after the Cold War: Lessons from the Emergency Relief Desk." *Middle East Report* 187/188 (March–June 1994): 9-15.

Dupuy, Pierre-Marie. "The Place and Role of Unilateralism in Contemporary International Law." *European Journal of International Law* 11, no. 1 (2000): 19-29.

Ebbinghaus, Bernhard. "When Less Is More: Selection Problems in Large-N and Small-N Cross-National Comparisons." *International Sociology* 20, no. 2 (June 2005): 133-52.

Eckstein, Harry. "Case Study and Theory in Political Science." In *The Handbook of Political Science, Vol. 7: Strategies of Inquiry,* edited by Fred Greenstein and Nelson Polsby. Menlo Park, Calif.: Addison-Wesley, 1975.

Edwards, III, George C. "Aligning Tests with Theory: Presidential Approval as a Source of Influence in Congress." *Congress and the Presidency* 24, no. 2 (Autumn 1997): 113-30.

———. *At the Margins: Presidential Leadership of Congress.* New Haven, Conn.: Yale University Press, 1989.

Ehrenreich, Barbara. "Who Wants Another Panama?." In *The Gulf War Reader: History, Documents, Opinions,* edited by Micah L. Sifry and Christopher Cerf. New York: Times Books, 1991.

Ellsworth, Harry Alanson. *One Hundred Eighty Landings of United States Marines, 1800-1934.* Washington, D.C.: History and Museums Division, Headquarters, United States Marine Corps, 1934. Reprint, Washington, D.C.: History and Museums Division, Headquarters, United States Marine Corps, 1974.

Farr, Warner D. "The Third Temple's Holy of Holies: Israel's Nuclear Weapons." *Counterproliferation Papers Series* 2 (September 1999).

Fearon, James D. "Domestic Political Audiences and the Escalation of International Disputes." *American Political Science Review* 88, no. 3 (September 1994): 577-92.

———. "Signaling Versus the Balance of Power and Interests: An Empirical Test of a Crisis Bargaining Model." *Journal of Conflict Resolution* 38, no. 2 (June 1994): 232-69.

Finnemore, Martha. "Military Intervention and the Organization of International Politics." In *Collective Conflict Management and Changing World Politics*, edited by Joseph Lepgold and Thomas G. Weiss. Albany: State University of New York Press, 1998.

Fisher, Louis. *Constitutional Conflicts between Congress and the President*. 3rd ed. Lawrence: University Press of Kansas, 1991.

———. "War Powers: The Need for Collective Judgment." In *Divided Democracy: Cooperation and Conflict between the President and Congress*, edited by James A. Thurber. Washington, D.C.: CQ Press, 1991.

Fonseca, Jr., Gelson. "The United States and Latin America: Multilateralism and International Legitimacy." In *Unilateralism and U.S. Foreign Policy: International Perspectives*, edited by David M. Malone and Yuen Foong Khong. Boulder, Colo.: Lynne Rienner, 2003.

Forde, Steven. "International Realism and the Science of Politics: Thucydides, Machiavelli, and Neorealism." *International Studies Quarterly* 39, no. 2 (June 1995): 141-60.

Fordham, Benjamin O. "Partisanship, Macroeconomic Policy, and U.S. Uses of Force, 1949-1994." *Journal of Conflict Resolution* 42, no. 4 (August 1998): 418-39.

———. "The Politics of Threat Perception and the Use of Force: A Political Economy Model of U.S. Uses of Force, 1949-1994." *International Studies Quarterly* 42, no. 3 (September 1998): 567-90.

———. "U.S. Uses of Force, 1870-1995." Benjamin Fordham Homepage. 2001. <http://bingweb.binghamton.edu/~bfordham/list.pdf> (August 8, 2009).

———. "A Very Sharp Sword: The Influence of Military Capabilities on American Decisions to Use Force." *Journal of Conflict Resolution* 48, no. 5 (October 2004): 632-56.

Fordham, Benjamin O., and Christopher C. Sarver. "Militarized Interstate Disputes and United States Uses of Force." *International Studies Quarterly* 45, no. 2 (September 2001): 455-66.

Foster, Dennis M., and Glenn Palmer. "Presidents, Public Opinion, and Diversionary Behavior: The Role of Partisan Support Reconsidered." *Foreign Policy Analysis* 2, no. 3 (July 2006): 269-88.

Foyle, Douglas. *Counting the Public In: Presidents, Public Opinion, and Foreign Policy*. New York: Columbia University Press, 1999.

Franck, Thomas M., and Nigel S. Rodley. "After Bangladesh: The Law of Humanitarian Intervention by Military Force." *American Journal of International Law* 67, no. 2 (April 1973): 275-305.

Frankel, Max. *High Noon in the Cold War: Kennedy, Khrushchev, and the Cuban Missile Crisis*. New York: Ballantine Books, 2004.

Freedman, Lawrence. "Arms Race: Nuclear Arms Race." In *The Oxford Companion to American Military History*, edited by John Whiteclay Chambers, II. New York: Oxford University Press, 1999.

Freedman, Lawrence, and Efraim Karsh. *The Gulf Conflict, 1990-1991: Diplomacy and War in the New World Order.* Princeton, N.J.: Princeton University Press, 1993.

Frendreis, John P. "Explanation of Variation and Detection of Covariation: The Purpose and Logic of Comparative Analysis." *Comparative Political Studies* 16, no. 2 (July 1983): 255-72.

Freudenschuss, Helmut. "Between Unilateralism and Collective Security: Authorizations of the Use of Force by the UN Security Council." *European Journal of International Law* 5, no. 1 (1994): 492-531.

Friedman, Thomas L. "Washington's 'Vital Interests'." In *The Gulf War Reader: History, Documents, Opinions*, edited by Micah L. Sifry and Chistopher Cerf. New York: Times Books, 1991.

Gartner, Scott Sigmund, and Gary M. Segura. "War, Casualties, and Public Opinion." *Journal of Conflict Resolution* 42, no. 3 (June 1998): 278-300.

Gartzke, Erik, and Michael W. Simon. "'Hot Hand': A Critical Analysis of Enduring Rivalries." *Journal of Politics* 61, no. 3 (August 1999): 777-98.

Geddes, Barbara. "How the Cases You Choose Affect the Answers You Get: Selection Bias in Political Science." *Political Analysis* 2, no. 1 (1990): 131-50.

Gerring, John. "What Is a Case Study and What Is It Good For?." *American Political Science Review* 98, no. 2 (May 2004): 341-54.

Gibson, Carlos, and Celso Pastor. "American Regionalism and the United Nations." *Annals of the American Academy of Political and Social Science* 360 (July 1965): 120-24.

Gilpin, Robert. "The Theory of Hegemonic War." *Journal of Interdisciplinary History* 18, no. 4 (Spring 1988): 591-613.

———. *War and Change in World Politics.* New York: Cambridge University Press, 1981.

Gleditsch, Nils P., and H. Hegre. "Peace and Democracy–Three Levels of Analysis." *Journal of Conflict Resolution* 41, no. 2 (April 1997): 283-310.

Gochman, Charles S., and Zeev Maoz. "Militarized Interstate Disputes, 1816-1976." *Journal of Conflict Resolution* 28, no. 4 (December 1984): 585-616.

Goemans, H.E. "Fighting for Survival: The Fate of Leaders and the Duration of War." *Journal of Conflict Resolution* 44, no. 5 (October 2000): 555-79.

Goertz, Gary, and Paul F. Diehl. "Enduring Rivalries: Theoretical Constructs and Empirical Patterns." *International Studies Quarterly* 37, no. 2 (June 1993): 147-71.

Goertz, Gary, and Paul F. Diehl. "(Enduring) Rivalries." In *Handbook of War Studies II*, edited by Manus I. Midlarsky. Ann Arbor: The University of Michigan Press, 2000.

Goldstein, Joshua S. *Long Cycles: Prosperity and War in the Modern Age.* New Haven, Conn.: Yale University Press, 1988.

Gordon, Michael R., and Bernard E. Trainor. *The Generals' War: The Inside Story of the Conflict in the Gulf.* Boston: Little, Brown, and Company, 1995.

Gordon, Philip H., and Jeremy Shapiro. *Allies at War: America, Europe, and the Crisis Over Iraq.* New York: McGraw-Hill, 2004.

Grieco, Joseph M. *Cooperation among Nations: Europe, America, and Non-Tariff Barriers to Trade.* Ithaca, N.Y.: Cornell University Press, 1990.

Grimmett, Richard. *Instances of Use of United States Armed Forces Abroad, 1798-2004.* Washington, D.C.: Congressional Research Service, 2004.

Gujarati, Damodar N. *Basic Econometrics.* 4th ed. Boston: McGraw-Hill, 2003.

Haass, Richard N. "Military Force: A User's Guide." *Foreign Policy* 96 (Autumn 1994): 21-37.

Hallion, Richard P. *Storm Over Iraq: Air Power and the Gulf War.* Washington, D.C.: Smithsonian Institution Press, 1992.

Hashim, Ahmed S. "The Revolution in Military Affairs Outside the West." *Journal of International Affairs* 51, no. 2 (Spring 1998): 431-45.

Heckman, James. "Sample Selection Bias as a Specification Error." *Econometrica* 47, no. 1 (January 1979): 153-62.

Helton, A. "Reaction and Inattention Within the U.S. Government." In *Multilateralism v Unilateralism: Policy Choices in a Global Society*, edited by John B. Attanasio and Joseph J. Norton. London: The British Institute of International and Comparative Law, 2004.

Hendrickson, David C. "Preemption, Unilateralism, and Hegemony: The American Tradition?" *Orbis* 50, no. 2 (Spring 2006): 273-87.

Hickey, Jr., James E. "Challenges to Security Council Monopoly Power Over the Use of Force in Enforcement Actions: The Case for Regional Organizations." *IUS GENTIUM* 10 (Fall 2004): 69-121.

Hitchens, Chrisopher. "Realpolitik in the Gulf: A Game Gone Tilt." In *The Gulf War Reader: History, Documents, Opinions*, edited by Micah L. Sifry and Chistopher Cerf. New York: Times Books, 1991.

Holloway, Steven. "U.S. Unilateralism at the UN: Why Great Powers Do Not Make Great Multilateralists." *Global Governance* 6, no. 3 (July–September 2000): 361-81.

Holsti, Ole R. "Public Opinion and U.S. Foreign Policy after the Cold War." In *After the End: Making U.S. Foreign Policy in the Post-Cold War World*, edited by James M. Scott. Durham, N.C.: Duke University Press, 1998.

Hugill, Peter J. "The American Challenge to British Hegemony, 1861-1947." *Geographical Review* 99, no. 3 (July 2009): 403-25.

Hundley, Richard O. *Past Revolutions, Future Transformations: What can the history of revolutions in military affairs tell us about transforming the U.S. military?*. Santa Monica, Calif.: Rand, 1999.

Huntington, Samuel P. "The Clash of Civilizations?" *Foreign Affairs* 72, no. 3 (Summer 1993): 22-49.

Huth, Paul, D. Scott Bennett, and Christopher Gelpi. "System Uncertainty, Risk Propensity, and International Conflict among the Great Powers." *Journal of Conflict Resolution* 36, no. 3 (September 1992): 478-517.

Ikenberry, G. John. *After Victory: Institutions, Strategic Restraint, and the Rebuilding of Order after Major Wars.* Princeton, N.J.: Princeton University Press, 2001.

———. "Is American Multilateralism in Decline?." *Perspectives on Politics* 1, no. 3 (September 2003): 533-50.

———. "Multilateralism and U.S. Grand Strategy." In *Multilateralism and US Foreign Policy: Ambivalent Engagement*, edited by Stewart Patrick and Shepard Forman. Boulder, Colo.: Lynne Rienner, 2002.

Jacobson, Gary C. "Partisan Polarization in Presidential Support: The Electoral Connection." *Congress and the Presidency* 30, no. 1 (Spring 2003): 1-36.

———. "The Bush Presidency and the American Electorate." *Presidential Studies Quarterly* 33 no. 4 (December 2003): 701-29.

Jakobsen, Peter Viggo. "National Interest, Humanitarianism or CNN: What Triggers UN Peace Enforcement after the Cold War?." *Journal of Peace Research* 33, no. 2 (May 1996): 205-15.

James, Patrick, and John R. Oneal. "The Influence of Domestic and International Politics on the President's Use of Force." *Journal of Conflict Resolution* 35, no. 2 (June 1991): 307-32.

Jentleson, Bruce W. "The Pretty Prudent Public: Post Post-Vietnam American Opinion on the Use of Military Force." *International Studies Quarterly* 36, no. 1 (March 1992): 49-73.

Jentleson, Bruce W., and Rebecca L. Britton. "Still Pretty Prudent: Post-Cold War American Public Opinion on the Use of Military Force." *Journal of Conflict Resolution* 42, no. 4 (August 1998): 395-417.

Jervis, Robert. "Cooperation under the Security Dilemma." *World Politics* 30, no. 2 (January 1978): 167-214.

Jia, Qingguo. "In Search of Absolute Security: U.S. Nuclear Policy." In *Unilateralism and U.S. Foreign Policy: International Perspectives*, edited by David M. Malone and Yuen Foong Khong. Boulder, Colo.: Lynne Rienner, 2003.

Jones, Daniel M., Stuart A. Bremer, and J. David Singer. "Militarized Interstate Disputes, 1816-1992: Rationale, Coding Rules, and Empirical Patterns." *Conflict Management and Peace Science* 15, no. 2 (Fall 1996): 163-213.

Kadera, Kelly M. *The Power-Conflict Story: A Dynamic Model of Interstate Rivalry*. Ann Arbor: The University of Michigan Press, 2001.

Kagan, Robert. "Power and Weakness." *Policy Review* 113 (June 2002): 3-28.

Kahler, Miles. "Multilateralism with Small and Large Numbers." *International Organization* 46, no. 3 (Summer 1992): 681-708.

Kamienski, Lukasz. "The RMA and War Powers." *Strategic Insight* (September 2003): 1-5.

Kaplan, Stephen S., and Barry M. Blechman. *Political Uses of the United States Armed Forces, 1946-1976* [Computer File]. Ann Arbor, Mich.: Inter-university Consortium for Political and Social Research, 1978.

Kawashima, Yutaka. "Multilateralism versus U.S. Unilateralism: The Role of the UN Security Council as the Authorizing Body for the United States' Use of Force." In *Multilateralism v Unilateralism: Policy Choices in a Global Society*, edited by John B. Attanasio and Joseph J. Norton. London: The British Institute of International and Comparative Law, 2004.

Keaney, Thomas A. "The Linkage of Air and Ground Power in the Future of Conflict." *International Security* 22, no. 2 (Autumn 1997): 147-50.

Keegan, John. *The Iraq War*. New York: Alfred A. Knopf, 2004.

Kennedy, John F. *Profiles in Courage*. New York: HarperCollins, 1956.

Keohane, Robert O. "Multilateralism: An Agenda for Research." *International Journal* 45 (Autumn 1990): 731-64.

———. "Reciprocity in International Relations." *International Organization* 40, no. 1 (Winter 1986): 1-27.

Kim, Woosang, and James D. Morrow. "When Do Power Shifts Lead to War?" *American Journal of Political Science* 36, no. 4 (November 1992): 896-922.

King, Gary, Robert O. Keohane, and Sidney Verba. *Designing Social Inquiry: Scientific Inference in Qualitative Research.* Princeton, N.J.: Princeton University Press, 1994.

Kissinger, Henry. *Does America Need a Foreign Policy? Toward a Diplomacy for the 21st Century.* New York: Simon & Schuster, 2001.

———. "A False Dream." In *The Gulf War Reader: History, Documents, Opinions,* edited by Micah L. Sifry and Chistopher Cerf. New York: Times Books, 1991.

Klare, Michael T. "The Pentagon's New Paradigm." In *The Gulf War Reader: History, Documents, Opinions,* edited by Micah L. Sifry and Chistopher Cerf. New York: Times Books, 1991.

Klein, James, Gary Goertz, and Paul Diehl. "The New Rivalry Data Set: Procedures and Patterns." Paper presented at the Annual Meeting of the Peace Science Society, Houston, November 2004.

Konovalov, Alexander. "Multilateralism and Unilateralism in a New Security Environment." In *Multilateralism v Unilateralism: Policy Choices in a Global Society,* edited by John B. Attanasio and Joseph J. Norton. London: The British Institute of International and Comparative Law, 2004.

Kornbluh, Peter. *Bay of Pigs Declassified: The Secret CIA Report on the Invasion of Cuba.* New York: The New Press, 1998.

Koster, Richard M., and Guillermo Sanchez. *In the Time of the Tyrants, Panama: 1968-1990.* New York: W.W. Norton and Company, 1990.

Krauthammer, Charles. "The Unipolar Moment." *Foreign Affairs* 70, no. 1 (1990-1991): 23-33.

Krepinevich, Andrew F. "Cavalry to Computer: The Pattern of Military Revolutions." *National Interest* 37 (Fall 1994): 30-42.

Krisch, Nico. "Unilateral Enforcement of the Collective Will: Kosovo, Iraq, and the Security Council." *Max Planck Yearbook of United Nations Law* 3 (1999): 59-103.

Kugler, Jacek, and Douglas Lemke. "The Power Transition Research Program: Assessing Theoretical and Empirical Advances." In *Handbook of War Studies II,* edited by Manus I. Midlarsky. Ann Arbor: University of Michigan Press, 2000.

Kugler, Jacek, and Douglas Lemke, eds. *Parity and War: Evaluations and Extensions of "The War Ledger."* Ann Arbor: University of Michigan Press, 1996.

Kuhn, Thomas S. *The Structure of Scientific Revolutions.* 2nd ed. Chicago: The University of Chicago Press, 1970.

Kull, Steven. "The FP Interview: Vox Americani." *Foreign Policy* 126 (September–October 2001): 28-38.

———. "Public Attitudes Toward Multilateralism." In *Multilateralism and US Foreign Policy: Ambivalent Engagement,* edited by Stewart Patrick and Shepard Forman. Boulder, Colo.: Lynne Rienner, 2002.

———. "What the Public Knows that Washington Doesn't." *Foreign Policy* 101 (Winter 1995-1996): 102-15.

Laird, Melvin R. "Iraq: Learning the Lessons of Vietnam." *Foreign Affairs* 84, no. 6 (November–December 2005): 22-43.

Lake, David A. "Powerful Pacifists: Democratic States and War." *American Political Science Review* 86, no. 1 (March 1992): 24-37.

Lalman, David. "Conflict Resolution and Peace." *American Journal of Political Science* 32, no. 3 (August 1988): 590-615.

Layne, Christopher. "Kant or Cant: The Myth of the Democratic Peace." *International Security* 19, no. 2 (Autumn 1994): 5-49.

Leary, William. "CIA Air Operations in Laos, 1955-1974." *Studies in Intelligence* (Winter 1999-2000): 71-86.

Lebow, Richard Ned. "The Long Peace, the End of the Cold War, and the Failure of Realism." *International Organization* 48, no. 2 (Spring 1994): 249-77.

Leeds, Brett Ashley, and David R. Davis. "Domestic Political Vulnerability and International Disputes." *Journal of Conflict Resolution* 41, no. 6 (December 1997): 814-34.

Leng, Russell J. "Influence Strategies and Interstate Conflict." In *The Correlates of War II*, edited by J. David Singer. New York: Free Press, 1980.

———. "When Will They Ever Learn? Coercive Bargaining in Recurrent Crises." *Journal of Conflict Resolution* 27, no. 3 (September 1983): 379-419.

Levy, Jack S. "The Diversionary Theory of War: A Critique." In *Handbook of War Studies*, edited by Manus I. Midlarsky. Boston: Unwin Hyman, 1989.

———. "Theories of General War." *World Politics* 37, no. 3 (April 1985): 344-74.

Lian, Bradley, and John R. Oneal. "Presidents, the Use of Military Force, and Public Opinion." *Journal of Conflict Resolution* 37, no. 2 (June 1993): 277-300.

Lieber, Keir A. *War and the Engineers: The Primacy of Politics over Technology*. Ithaca, N.Y.: Cornell University Press, 2005.

Lijphart, Arend. "The Comparable-Case Strategy in Comparative Research." *Comparative Political Studies* 8, no. 2 (July 1975): 158-77.

Lindsay, James M. "Congress and the Use of Force in the Post-Cold War Era." In *The United States and the Use of Force in the Post-Cold War Era*. Washington, D.C.: The Aspen Institute, 1995.

Lobel, Jules, and Michael Ratner. "Bypassing the Security Council: Ambiguous Authorizations to Use Force, Cease-Fires and the Iraqi Inspection Regime." *American Journal of International Law* 93, no. 1 (January 1999): 124-54.

Luck, Edward. "The United States, International Organization, and the Quest for Legitimacy." In *Multilateralism and US Foreign Policy: Ambivalent Engagement*, edited by Stewart Patrick and Shepard Forman. Boulder, Colo.: Lynne Rienner, 2002.

Luttwak, Edward N. "Toward a Post-Heroic Warfare." *Foreign Affairs* 74, no. 3 (May–June 1995): 109-22.

Lyman, Princeton N. "The Growing Influence of Domestic Factors." In *Multilateralism and US Foreign Policy: Ambivalent Engagement*, edited by Stewart Patrick and Shepard Forman. Boulder, Colo.: Lynne Rienner, 2002.

Mack, Andrew. "The United States and the Asia-Pacific Bilateralism Plus 'Multilateralism a' la Carte." In *Unilateralism and U.S. Foreign Policy: International Perspectives*, edited by David M. Malone and Yuen Foong Khong. Boulder, Colo.: Lynne Rienner, 2003.

Maddison, Angus. *Monitoring the World Economy 1820 - 1992.* Paris: OECD, 1995.

———. *The World Economy: Historical Statistics.* Paris: OECD Development Centre, 2003.

———. *The World Economy: A Millennial Perspective.* Paris: OECD Development Centre, 2001.

Mahbubani, Kishore. "The United Nations and the United States: An Indispensable Partnership." In *Unilateralism and U.S. Foreign Policy: International Perspectives,* edited by David M. Malone and Yuen Foong Khong. Boulder, Colo.: Lynne Rienner, 2003.

Mahoney, James. "Strategies of Causal Inference in Small-N Analysis." *Sociological Methods and Research* 28, no. 4 (May 2000): 387-424.

Malone, David M. "A Decade of U.S. Unilateralism?" In *Unilateralism and U.S. Foreign Policy: International Perspectives,* edited by David M. Malone and Yuen Foong Khong. Boulder, Colo.: Lynne Rienner, 2003.

Malone, David M., and Yuen Foong Khong. "Resisting the Unilateral Impulse: Multilateral Engagement and the Future of U.S. Leadership." In *Unilateralism and U.S. Foreign Policy: International Perspectives,* edited by David M. Malone and Yuen Foong Khong. Boulder, Colo.: Lynne Rienner, 2003.

Malone, David M., and Yuen Foong Khong. "Unilateralism and U.S. Foreign Policy: International Perspectives." In *Unilateralism and U.S. Foreign Policy: International Perspectives,* edited by David M. Malone and Yuen Foong Khong. Boulder, Colo.: Lynne Rienner, 2003.

Malone, David M., and Yuen Foong Khong, eds. *Unilateralism and U.S. Foreign Policy: International Perspectives.* Boulder, Colo.: Lynne Rienner, 2003.

Maoz, Zeev. "Resolve, Capabilities, and the Outcomes of Interstate Disputes, 1816-1976." *Journal of Conflict Resolution* 27, no. 2 (June 1983): 195-229.

Maoz, Zeev, and Bruce M. Russett. "Normative and Structural Causes of the Democratic Peace." *American Political Science Review* 87, no. 3 (September 1993): 624-38.

Marshall, Monty G., and Keith Jaggers. *Polity IV Data Set* [Computer file; version p4v2002]. College Park, Md.: Center for International Development and Conflict Management, University of Maryland, 2002.

Martin, Lisa L. "The Rational State Choice of Multilateralism." In *Multilateralism Matters: The Theory and Praxis of an Institutional Form,* edited by John Gerard Ruggie. New York: Columbia University Press, 1993.

Mastanduno, Michael, David A. Lake, and G. John Ikenberry. "Toward a Realist Theory of State Action." *International Studies Quarterly* 33, no. 4 (December 1989): 457-74.

Maynes, Charles William. "Two Blasts Against Unilateralism." In *Understanding Unilateralism in American Foreign Relations,* edited by Gwyn Prins. London: Royal Institute of International Affairs, 2000.

Mazaar, Michael J. *The Revolution in Military Affairs: A Framework for Defense Planning.* Carlisle, Pa.: Strategic Studies Institute, 1994.

McConnell, Malcolm. *Just Cause: The Real Story of America's High-Tech Invasion of Panama.* New York: St. Martin's Press, 1991.

McDermott, Rose. "Experimental Methodology in Political Science." *Political Analysis* 10, no. 4 (Autumn 2002): 325-42.

———. "Experimental Methods in Political Science." *Annual Review in Political Science* 5 (June 2002): 31-61.

McGee, Gale W. "The Monroe Doctrine—A Stopgap Measure." *The Mississippi Valley Historical Review* 38, no. 2 (September 1951): 233-50.

McKeown, Timothy. "Case Studies and the Statistical Worldview." *International Organization* 53, no. 1 (January 1999): 161-90.

McNamara, Robert S., and James G. Blight. *Wilson's Ghost: Reducing the Risk of Conflict, Killing, and Catastrophe in the 21st Century.* New York: PublicAffairs, 2001.

Mearsheimer, John. "The False Promise of International Institutions." *International Security* 19, no. 3 (Winter 1994-1995): 5-49.

Meernik, James, and Peter Waterman. "The Myth of the Diversionary Use of Force by American Presidents." *Political Research Quarterly* 49, no. 3 (September 1996): 573-90.

Meinig, Donald W. *The Shaping of America: A Geographical Perspective on 500 Years of History, Volume 4: Global America, 1915-2000.* New Haven, Conn.: Yale University Press, 2004.

Metz, Steven, and James Kievit. *The Revolution in Military Affairs and Conflict Short of War.* Carlisle, Pa.: Strategic Studies Institute, 1994.

Mintz, Alex. "The Decision to Attack Iraq: A Noncompensatory Theory of Decision Making." *Journal of Conflict Resolution* 37, no. 4 (December 1993): 595-618.

Mintz, Alex, and Nehemia Geva. "The Poliheuristic Theory of Foreign Policy Decision Making." In *Decision Making on War and Peace: The Cognitive-Rational Debate,* edited by Nehemia Geva and Alex Mintz. Boulder, Colo.: Lynne Rienner Publishers, 1997.

Mitchell, Sara McLaughlin, and Will H. Moore. "Presidential Uses of Force During the Cold War: Aggregation, Truncation, and Temporal Dynamics." *American Journal of Political Science* 46, no. 2 (April 2002): 438-52.

Mook, Douglas G. "In Defense of External Invalidity." *American Psychologist* 38, no. 4 (April 1983): 379-87.

Morgenthau, Hans J. *Politics Among Nations: The Struggle for Power and Peace.* 5th ed. New York: Knopf, 1973.

Morrow, James D. "Arms versus Allies: Tradeoffs in the Search for Security." *International Organization* 47, no. 2 (Spring 1993): 207-33.

———. "Capabilities, Uncertainty and Resolve: A Limited Information Model of Crisis Bargaining." *American Journal of Political Science* 33, no. 4 (November 1989): 941-72.

———. "A Rational Choice Approach to International Choice." In *Decision Making on War and Peace: The Cognitive-Rational Debate,* edited by Nehemia Geva and Alex Mintz. Boulder, Colo.: Lynne Rienner Publishers, 1997.

Most, Benjamin A., and Harvey Starr. *Inquiry, Logic and International Politics.* Columbia: University of South Carolina Press, 1989.

Mueller, John E. "A Review: American Public Opinion and the Gulf War: Some Polling Issues." *Public Opinion Quarterly* 57, no. 1 (Spring 1993): 80-91.

———. "Trends in Popular Support for the Wars in Korea and Vietnam." *American Political Science Review* 65, no. 2 (June 1971): 358-75.

———. *War, Presidents and Public Opinion.* New York: John Wiley, 1973.

Munck, Gerardo L. "Canons of Research Design in Qualitative Analysis." *Studies in Comparative International Development* 33, no. 3 (September 1998): 18-45.

Murray, Williamson, and MacGregor Knox. "Thinking about Revolutions in Warfare." In *The Dynamics of Military Revolution: 1300-2050*, edited by MacGregor Knox and Williamson Murray. Cambridge: Cambridge University Press, 2001.

Nanda, Ved P. "The Validity of United States Intervention in Panama under International Law." *American Journal of International Law* 84, no. 2 (April 1990): 494-503.

Neustadt, Richard E. *Presidential Power and the Modern Presidents: The Politics of Leadership from Roosevelt to Reagan.* New York: Free Press, 1990.

North, Douglass C. "Transaction Costs, Institutions, and Economic History." *Journal of Institutional and Theoretical Economics* 140, no. 1 (1984): 7-17.

Nye, Jr., Joseph S. "The Changing Nature of World Power." *Political Science Quarterly* 105, no. 2 (Summer 1990): 177-92.

———. "Redefining the National Interest." *Foreign Affairs* 78, no. 4 (July–August 1999): 22-35.

———. *Understanding International Conflict: An Introduction to Theory and History.* 4th ed. New York: Longman, 2003.

Obama, Barack. "Defense Guiding Principles." 2009. <http://www.whitehouse.gov/issues/defense/> (8 August 2009).

O'Brien, Patrick Karl, and Armand Clesse. *Two Hegemonies: Britain 1846-1914 and the United States 1941-2001.* Aldershot, UK: Ashgate, 2002.

Offutt, Milton. *The Protection of Citizens Abroad by the Armed Forces of the United States.* Baltimore: Johns Hopkins University Press, 1928.

Olson, Mancur. *The Logic of Collective Action.* New York: Schocken, 1968.

Oneal, John R., Brad Lian, and James H. Joyner, Jr. "Are the American People 'Pretty Prudent'? Public Responses to U.S. Uses of Force, 1950-1988." *International Studies Quarterly* 40, no. 2 (June 1996): 261-79.

Organski, A.F.K.. *World Politics.* New York: Knopf, 1958.

Organski, A.F.K., and Jacek Kugler. *The War Ledger.* Chicago: University of Chicago Press, 1980.

Ostrom, Jr., Charles W., and Brian L. Job. "The President and the Political Use of Force." *American Political Science Review* 80, no. 2 (June 1986): 541-66.

Pape, Robert A. *Bombing to Win: Air Power and Coercion in War.* Ithaca, N.Y.: Cornell University Press, 1996.

Parker, Geoffrey. *The Military Revolution: Military Innovation and the Rise of the West, 1500-1800.* Cambridge: Cambridge University Press, 1996.

Paterson, Thomas G. "John F. Kennedy and the World." In *John F. Kennedy: Person, Policy, Presidency,* edited by J. Richard Snyder. Wilmington, Del.: Scholarly Resources, 1988.

Patrick, Stewart. "Multilateralism and Its Discontents: The Causes and Consequences of U.S. Ambivalence." In *Multilateralism and US Foreign Policy: Ambivalent Engagement*, edited by Stewart Patrick and Shepard Forman. Boulder, Colo.: Lynne Rienner, 2002.

Pellet, Alan. "Brief Remarks on the Unilateral Use of Force." *European Journal of International Law* 11, no. 2 (2000): 385-92.

Pollack, Kenneth. "How Saddam Misread the United States." In *The Iraq War Reader: History, Documents, Opinions*, edited by Micah L. Sifry and Christopher Cerf. New York: Touchstone, 2003.

Press, Daryl G. "Lessons from Ground Combat in the Gulf: The Impact of Training and Technology." *International Security* 22, no. 2 (Autumn 1997): 137-46.

———. "The Myth of Air Power in the Persian Gulf War and the Future of Warfare." *International Security* 26, no. 2 (Fall 2001): 5-44.

Prestowitz, Clyde. *Rogue Nation: American Unilateralism and the Failure of Good Intentions.* New York: Basic Books, 2003.

Prins, Gwyn. "US Unilateralism and European Initiatives on Defence and Security." In *Understanding Unilateralism in American Foreign Relations*, edited by Gwyn Prins. London: Royal Institute of International Affairs, 2000.

Przeworski, Adam, and Henry Teune. *The Logic of Comparative Social Inquiry.* New York: Krieger Publishing Company, 1970.

Rabkin, Jeremy. "When Can America Be Bound by International Law?." In *Understanding Unilateralism in American Foreign Relations*, edited by Gwyn Prins. London: Royal Institute of International Affairs, 2000.

Ragin, Charles C. "The Distinctiveness of Comparative Social Science." In *The Comparative Method: Moving Beyond Qualitative and Quantitative Strategies*, edited by Charles Ragin. Berkeley: University of California Press, 1987.

Raknerud, Arvid, and Havard Hegre. "The Hazard of War: Reassessing the Evidence for the Democratic Peace." *Journal of Peace Research* 34, no. 4 (November 1997): 385-404.

Reed, William. "A Unified Model of Conflict Onset and Escalation: Capabilities, Democracy, and Status Quo Evaluations." *American Journal of Political Science* 44, no. 1 (January 2000): 84-93.

Reisman, W. Michael. "Unilateral Action and the Transformations of the World Constitutive Process: The Special Problem of Humanitarian Intervention." *European Journal of International Law* 11, no. 1 (2000): 3-18.

Reisman, W. Michael, and Scott Shuchart. "Unilateral Action in an Imperfect World Order." In *Multilateralism v Unilateralism: Policy Choices in a Global Society*, edited by John B. Attanasio and Joseph J. Norton. London: The British Institute of International and Comparative Law, 2004.

Reiter, Dan, and Curtis Meek. "Determinants of Military Strategy, 1903-1994: A Quantitative Empirical Test." *International Studies Quarterly* 43, no. 2 (June 1999): 363-87.

Reiter, Dan, and Erik R. Tillman. "Public, Legislative, and Executive Constraints on the Democratic Initiation of Conflict." *Journal of Politics* 64, no. 3 (August 2002): 810-26.

RFD. "Unilateral and Multilateral Options in the Execution of Foreign Policy." *International Organization* 23, no. 3 (Summer 1969): 641-754.

Richardson, James D. *Compilation of the Messages and Papers of the Presidents*, Volume 2. New York: Bureau of National Literature, 1907.

Richman, Alvin. "Poll Trends: American Support for International Involvement." *Public Opinion Quarterly* 57, no. 2 (Summer 1993): 264-76.

———. "Trends: American Support for International Involvement: General and Specific Components of Post-Cold War Changes." *Public Opinion Quarterly* 60, no. 2 (Summer 1996): 305-21.

Rivkin, Jr., David B., and Lee A. Casey. "Enfeebling the Presidency: The Executive Branch Is a Co-equal Branch, or so the Framers Said." *National Review* 58, no. 11 (June 2006): 32-38.

Rockman, Bert A. "Reinventing What for Whom?: President and Congress in the Making of Foreign Policy." *Presidential Studies Quarterly* 30, no. 1 (March 2000): 133-54.

Rosen, Steven. "War, Power and the Willingness to Suffer." In *Peace, War, and Numbers*, edited by Bruce Russett. Beverly Hills, Calif.: Sage, 1972.

Rousseau, David L., Christopher Gelpi, Dan Reiter, and Paul K. Huth. "Assessing the Dyadic Nature of the Democratic Peace, 1918-88." *American Political Science Review* 90, no. 3 (September 1996): 512-33.

Ruggie, John G. "Multilateralism: The Anatomy of an Institution." *International Organization* 46, no. 3 (Summer 1992): 561-98.

———. *Winning the Peace*. New York: Columbia University Press, 1996.

Russett, Bruce M., and Harvey Starr. "From Democratic Peace to Kantian Peace: Democracy and Conflict in the International System." In *Handbook of War Studies II*, edited by Manus Midlarsky. Ann Arbor: University of Michigan Press, 2000.

Russett, Bruce M., and Miroslav Nincic. "American Opinion on the Use of Military Force Abroad." *Political Science Quarterly* 91, no. 3 (Autumn 1976): 411-31.

Sands, Philippe. "American Unilateralism." *Proceedings of the American Society of International Law Annual Meeting* 96 (2002): 85-94.

Schlesinger, Jr., Arthur M. "Interview with Arthur M. Schlesinger, Jr." In *John F. Kennedy: Person, Policy, Presidency*, edited by J. Richard Snyder. Wilmington, Del.: Scholarly Resources, 1988.

———. *A Thousand Days: John F. Kennedy in the White House*. Boston: Houghton Mifflin Company, 1965.

———. "Unilateralism in Historical Perspective." In *Understanding Unilateralism in American Foreign Relations*, edited by Gwyn Prins. London: Royal Institute of International Affairs, 2000.

Sears, David O. "College Sophomores in the Laboratory: Influences of a Narrow Data Base on Social Psychology's View of Human Nature." *Journal of Personality and Social Psychology* 51, no. 3 (1986): 515-30.

Siegel, Adam B. *The Use of Naval Forces in the Post War Era: U.S. Navy and U.S. Marine Corps Crisis Response Activity, 1946–1990*. Alexandria, Va.: Center for Naval Analyses Research Manual 90-246, 1991.

Sifry, Micah L., and Christopher Cerf, eds.. *The Gulf War Reader: History, Documents, Opinions.* New York: Times Books, 1991.

Sifry, Micah L., and Christopher Cerf, eds. *The Iraq War Reader: History, Documents, Opinions.* New York: Touchstone, 2003.

Singer, J. David. "Confrontational Behavior and Escalation to War 1816-1980: A Research Plan." *Journal of Peace Research* 19, no. 1 (1982): 37-48.

———. *The Correlates of War II.* New York: Free Press, 1980.

———. "Escalation and Control in International Conflict: A Simple Feedback Model." *General Systems Yearbook* 15 (1970): 163-73. Reprint, J. David Singer, ed., *The Correlates of War I.* New York: Free Press, 1979.

———. "Reconstructing the Correlates of War Data Set on Material Capabilities of States, 1816-1985." *International Interactions* 14, no. 2 (May 1987): 115-32.

Siverson, Randolph M., and Harvey Starr. *The Diffusion of War: A Study of Opportunity and Willingness.* Ann Arbor: University of Michigan Press, 1991.

Slechta, J.J. "The Monroe Doctrine and the Foreign Policy of the United States in the Western Hemisphere." *Annals of the American Academy of Political and Social Science* 54, no. 1 (1914): 124-29.

Smith, Alastair. "International Crises and Domestic Politics." *American Political Science Review* 92, no. 3 (September 1998): 623-38.

———. "Testing Theories of Strategic Choice: The Example of Crisis Escalation." *American Journal of Political Science* 43, no. 4 (October 1999): 1254-83.

Smith, Jean Edward. *George Bush's War.* New York: Henry Holt and Company, 1992.

Smith, Wayne S. "The Trend Towards Unilateralism in US Foreign Policy." In *Understanding Unilateralism in American Foreign Relations,* edited by Gwyn Prins. London: Royal Institute of International Affairs, 2000.

Sobel, Richard. *The Impact of Public Opinion on Foreign Policy.* New York: Oxford University Press, 2001.

Sorensen, Theodore C. *The Kennedy Legacy.* New York: Macmillan, 1969.

Spiezio, K. Edward. "British Hegemony and Major Power War, 1815-1939: An Empirical Test of Gilpin's Model of Hegemonic Governance." *International Studies Quarterly* 34, no. 2 (June 1990): 165-81.

Stam, III, Allan C. *Win, Lose, or Draw: Domestic Politics and the Crucible of War.* Ann Arbor: The University of Michigan Press, 1999.

Stein, Janice Gross, and David A. Welch. "Rational and Psychological Approaches to the Study of International Conflict: Comparative Strengths and Weaknesses." In *Decision Making on War and Peace: The Cognitive-Rational Debate,* edited by Nehemia Geva and Alex Mintz. Boulder, Colo.: Lynne Rienner Publishers, 1997.

Stepanova, Ekaterina. "The Unilateral and Multilateral Use of Force by the United States." In *Unilateralism and U.S. Foreign Policy: International Perspectives,* edited by David M. Malone and Yuen Foong Khong. Boulder, Colo.: Lynne Rienner, 2003.

Stoll, Richard J. "Nice States Finish…Pretty Well: Collective Security Behavior in Militarized Interstate Disputes, 1816-1992." *International Interactions* 24, no. 3 (September 1998): 287-313.

Summers, Jr., Harry G. *Persian Gulf War Almanac.* New York: Facts on File, 1995.

Tago, Atsushi. "Determinants of Multilateralism in US Use of Force: State of Economy, Election Cycle, and Divided Government." *Journal of Peace Research* 42, no. 5 (September 2005): 585-604.

Thakur, Ramesh. "UN Peace Operations and U.S. Unilateralism and Multilateralism." In *Unilateralism and U.S. Foreign Policy: International Perspectives*, edited by David M. Malone and Yuen Foong Khong. Boulder, Colo.: Lynne Rienner, 2003.

Thompson, William R. "Systemic Leadership, Evolutionary Processes, and International Relations Theory: The Unipolarity Question." *International Studies Review* 8, no. 1 (March 2006): 1-22.

Tucker, Robert W. "Alone or With Others: The Temptations of Post-Cold War Power." *Foreign Affairs* 78, no. 6 (November–December 1999): 15-20.

Van Creveld, Martin. *Technology and War: From 2000 B.C. to the Present*. New York: The Free Press, 1989.

Vandenbroucke, Lucien S. "Anatomy of a Failure: The Decision to Land at the Bay of Pigs." *Political Science Quarterly* 99, no. 3 (Autumn 1984): 471-91.

Van Evera, Stephen. *Causes of War*. Ithaca, N.Y.: Cornell University Press, 1999.

———. *Guide to Methods to Students of Political Science*. London: Cornell University Press, 1997.

Vasquez, John A. "The Probability of War, 1816-1992: Presidential Address to the International Studies Association, March 25, 2002, New Orleans." *International Studies Quarterly* 48, no. 1 (March 2004): 1-28.

———. "The Realist Paradigm and Degenerative versus Progressive Research Programs: An Appraisal of Neotraditional Research on Waltz's Balancing Proposition." *American Political Science Review* 91, no. 4 (December 1997): 899-912.

———. "Reexamining the Steps to War: New Evidence and Theoretical Insights." In *Handbook of War Studies II*, edited by Manus I. Midlarsky. Ann Arbor: The University of Michigan Press, 2000.

———. "The Steps to War: Toward a Scientific Explanation of Correlates of War Findings." In *The Scientific Study of Peace and War*, edited by John Vasquez and Marie Henehan. New York: Lexington Books, 1992.

———. *The War Puzzle*. Cambridge: Cambridge University Press, 1993.

Voeten, Erik. "Outside Options and the Logic of Security Council Actions." *American Political Science Review* 95, no. 4 (December 2001): 845-58.

Waltz, Kenneth N. *Theory of International Politics*. Boston: McGraw-Hill, 1979.

Wang, Gungwu. "China and the World since 1949." In *The Making of the Twentieth Century*, edited by Christopher Thorne. New York: St. Martin's, 1977.

Wang, Kevin H. "Presidential Responses to Foreign Policy Crises: Rational Choice and Domestic Politics." *Journal of Conflict Resolution* 40, no. 1 (March 1996): 68-97.

Warner, Christopher G. *Implementing Joint Vision 2010: A Revolution in Military Affairs for Strategic Air Campaigns*. Maxwell AFB, Ala.: Air University Press, 1999.

Wayman, Frank W., J. David Singer, and Gary Goertz. "Capabilities, Allocations, and Success in Militarized Disputes and Wars, 1816-1976." *International Studies Quarterly* 27, no. 4 (December 1983): 497-515.

Weber, Steve. "Shaping the Postwar Balance of Power: Multilateralism in NATO." *International Organization* 46, no. 3 (Summer 1992): 633-80.

Wedgwood, Ruth. "NATO's Campaign in Yugoslavia." *American Journal of International Law* 93, no. 4 (October 1999): 828-34.

———. "Unilateral Action in a Multilateral World." In *Multilateralism and US Foreign Policy: Ambivalent Engagement*, edited by Stewart Patrick and Shepard Forman. Boulder, Colo.: Lynne Rienner, 2002.

Weitsman, Patricia. "The High Price of Friendship." *New York Times*, 31 August 2006.

White, Theodore H. *The Making of the President 1960.* Cutchogue, N.Y.: Buccaneer Books, 1961.

Wiarda, Howard J., and Lana L. Wylie. "New Challenges in U.S. Foreign Policy." In *Comparative Foreign Policy: Adaptation Strategies of the Great and Emerging Powers*, edited by Steven W. Hook. Upper Saddle River, N.J.: Prentice-Hall, 2002.

Wilson, Larman C. "The Monroe Doctrine, Cold War Anachronism: Cuba and the Dominican Republic." *Journal of Politics* 28, no. 2 (May 1966): 322-46.

Wyden, Peter. *Bay of Pigs: The Untold Story.* New York: Simon & Schuster, 1979.

Yergin, Daniel. "Oil: The Strategic Prize." In *The Gulf War Reader: History, Documents, Opinions*, edited by Micah L. Sifry and Chistopher Cerf. New York: Times Books, 1991.

Zelikow, Philip. "The U.S. and the Use of Force: A Historical Summary." In *Democracy, Strategy and Vietnam: Implications for American Policymaking*, edited by George K. Osborn, Asa A. Clark, IV, Daniel J. Kaufman, and Douglas E. Lute. Lexington, Mass.: Lexington Books, 1987.

Zoellick, Robert B. "Congress and the Making of US Foreign Policy." *Survival* 41, no. 4 (January 1999): 20-41.

Index

About the Author

Bradley F. Podliska has a B.A. (with honors) in international relations from the University of Wisconsin–Madison, an M.A. in security studies from Georgetown University, and a Ph.D. in political science from Texas A&M University. He is an instructor and analyst with the Department of Defense, for which he has lived and worked overseas. He is also an officer in the U.S. Air Force Reserve and was deployed to Joint Base Balad, Iraq, in support of Operation Iraqi Freedom. He is married and resides in Arlington, Virginia.

www.ingramcontent.com/pod-product-compliance
Lightning Source LLC
LaVergne TN
LVHW092133260926
848997LV00001B/7